Attachment-Informed Grief Therapy

Attachment-Informed Grief Therapy bridges the fields of attachment studies and thanatology, uniting theory, research, and practice to enrich our understanding of how and why people grieve and how we can help the bereaved. In its pages, clinicians and students will gain a new understanding of the etiology of complicated grief and its treatment and will become better equipped to formulate accurate and specific case conceptualization and treatment plans. The authors also illustrate the ways in which the therapeutic relationship is a crucially important—though largely unrecognized—element in grief therapy, and offer guidelines for an attachment informed view of the therapeutic relationship that can serve as the foundation of all grief therapy.

Phyllis Kosminsky is a clinical social worker specializing in work with the bereaved, particularly those who have experienced a traumatic loss. Over the past 20 years Dr. Kosminsky has provided individual counseling to hundreds of bereaved individuals and has conducted trainings for mental health professionals nationally and internationally in the treatment of normal and problematic grief. Her publications include journal articles, book chapters, and the book *Getting Back to Life When Grief Won't Heal*.

John (Jack) Jordan is a psychologist in private practice in Pawtucket, Rhode Island, where he has worked with survivors of traumatic losses for almost 40 years. He is the consultant for the Grief Support Services of Samaritans in Boston, and the professional advisor to the Loss and Healing Council of the American Foundation for Suicide Prevention. Jack provides training in the U.S. and internationally, and he has published over 45 articles, chapters, and full books, including *Grief After Suicide: Understanding the Consequences and Caring for the Survivors*.

The Series in Death, Dying, and Bereavement

Robert A. Neimeyer, Consulting editor

"An excellent discussion of attachment, one of the major mediators of the mourning process. Well written with many clinical examples of how an understanding of attachment theory and its relationship to brain development can assist the clinician in facilitating a person's adaptation to the loss of a loved one."

J. William Worden, PhD, ABPP, clinical psychologist and author of
Grief Counseling & Grief Therapy: A Handbook for the
Mental Health Practitioner

"This book, by two thoughtful and creative clinicians, will educate, engage, and enrich the work of therapists and those working with the bereaved. It is both scholarly and user friendly. Key concepts in attachment, neuroscience, emotion regulation, and trauma are explained in ways that make clinical sense. A rich selection of case material illustrate practical procedures, their rationale, and clinical outcomes. The bottom line for clinicians: this book is highly relevant to your work."

Simon Shimshon Rubin, PhD, director of the International
Center for the Study of Loss, Bereavement, and Human
Resilience at the University of Haifa in Israel

"This is a connected and caring book—a perfect combination when writing about the tender subjects of attachment, loss, and grief. The authors reach out from the pages to connect with readers who are practicing clinicians, students, trainees, or bereaved loved ones with the perfect mix of theory, research, neuroscience, psychotherapy, and lived experience."

Judith Kay Nelson, PhD, dean emerita at the Sanville Institute
for Clinical Social Work and Psychotherapy in Berkeley,
California, and author of *Seeing Through Tears: Crying and Attachment*

"This book is a gold mine of information that will serve the needs of new and seasoned therapists as well as students. It helps us see our clients through the lens of attachment theory and neurobiology, which adds new and powerful dimensions to our work. The real-life examples bring information to life and allow the reader to be transported into the therapeutic setting to see how grieving clients will respond."

Jane Vair Bissler, PhD, LPCC-S, FT, clinical director and
clinical counselor at Counseling for Wellness and Kelly's
Grief Center in Kent, Ohio

"This thoughtful and clearly written volume provides a thorough description and review of attachment theory, including its roots in neurobiology. This review is well-integrated into the authors' conceptualization of grief, based in theory and their extensive clinical expertise. The text is richly illustrated with extended clinical examples that will help therapists implement their approach, making the book a must-read for clinicians who want to integrate a deep understanding of attachment into their work with bereaved clients."

Laurie Anne Pearlman, PhD, coauthor of *Treating*
Traumatic Bereavement: A Practitioner's Guide

"No self-respecting and ethically conscientious grief professional would set about the work of counseling a dying or bereaved person without paying attention to that individual's attachment history, both from developmental years and adult life, for how it shapes and determines the loss experience. Kosminsky and Jordan's impressive volume equips clinicians to make that appraisal accurately, understand it thoroughly, and use it effectively in grief therapy."

Louis A. Gamino, PhD, ABPP, FT, professor of psychiatry and behavioral science at Texas A&M University Health Science Center College of Medicine

"This is an exceptional text! Written by two highly skilled clinicians it presents the state of the art in attachment theory and bereavement in both a highly engaging and practical form. This book effectively bridges both research and practice and attachment and thanatology in a way that no others texts have previously done. Richly illustrated with clinical examples this impressive book will enrich the understanding and skills of both beginning and experienced clinician."

Christopher Hall, MA, BEd, chief executive officer of the Australian Centre for Grief and Bereavement

Rosenblatt—Parent Grief: Narratives of Loss and Relationship

Rosenblatt & Wallace—African-American Grief

Rubin, Malkinson, & Witztum—Working With the Bereaved: Multiple Lenses on Loss and Mourning

Silverman—Widow to Widow, Second Edition

Tedeschi & Calhoun—Helping Bereaved Parents: A Clinician's Guide

Thompson & Neimeyer—Grief and the Expressive Arts: Practices for Creating Meaning

Werth—Contemporary Perspectives on Rational Suicide

Werth & Blevins—Decision Making near the End of Life: Issues, Developments, and Future Directions

Formerly the Series in Death Education, Aging, and Health Care
Hannelore Wass, Consulting editor

Bard—Medical Ethics in Practice

Benoliel—Death Education for the Health Professional

Bertman—Facing Death: Images, Insights, and Interventions

Brammer—How to Cope with Life Transitions: The Challenge of Personal Change

Cleiren—Bereavement and Adaptation: A Comparative Study of the Aftermath of Death

Corless & Pittman-Lindeman—AIDS: Principles, Practices, and Politics, Abridged Edition

Corless & Pittman-Lindeman—AIDS: Principles, Practices, and Politics, Reference Edition

Curran—Adolescent Suicidal Behavior

Davidson—The Hospice: Development and Administration. Second Edition

Davidson & Linnolla—Risk Factors in Youth Suicide

Degner & Beaton—Life-Death Decisions in Health Care

Doka—AIDS, Fear, and Society: Challenging the Dreaded Disease

Doty—Communication and Assertion Skills for Older Persons

Epting & Neimeyer—Personal Meanings of Death: Applications for Personal Construct Theory to Clinical Practice

Haber—Health Care for an Aging Society: Cost-Conscious Community Care and Self-Care Approaches

Hughes—Bereavement and Support: Healing in a Group Environment

Irish, Lundquist, & Nelsen—Ethnic Variations in Dying, Death, and Grief: Diversity in Universality

Klass, Silverman, & Nickman—Continuing Bonds: New Understanding of Grief

Lair—Counseling the Terminally Ill: Sharing the Journey

Leenaars, Maltsberger, & Neimeyer—Treatment of Suicidal People

Leenaars & Wenckstern—Suicide Prevention in Schools

Leng—Psychological Care in Old Age

Leviton—Horrendous Death, Health, and Well-Being

Leviton—Horrendous Death and Health: Toward Action

Lindeman, Corby, Downing, & Sanborn—Alzheimer's Day Care: A Basic Guide

Lund—Older Bereaved Spouses: Research with Practical Applications

Neimeyer—Death Anxiety Handbook: Research, Instrumentation, and Application

Attachment-Informed Grief Therapy

The Clinician's Guide to Foundations and Applications

Phyllis S. Kosminsky and
John R. Jordan

Routledge
Taylor & Francis Group

NEW YORK AND LONDON

First published 2016
by Routledge
711 Third Avenue, New York, NY 10017

and by Routledge
2 Park Square, Milton Park, Abingdon, Oxon, OX14 4RN

Routledge is an imprint of the Taylor & Francis Group, an informa business

Library of Congress Cataloging in Publication Data
Kosminsky, Phyllis.
  Attachment informed grief therapy : the clinician's guide to foundations and applications / by Phyllis S. Kosminsky and John R. Jordan.
    pages cm
  Includes bibliographical references and index.
  1. Grief therapy.   2. Attachment behavior.   I. Jordan, John R.   II. Title.
  RC455.4.L67K67 2016
  155.9'37—dc23   2015025883

ISBN: 978-0-415-85720-8 (hbk)
ISBN: 978-0-415-85721-5 (pbk)
ISBN: 978-0-203-79839-3 (ebk)

Typeset in Minion
by Keystroke, Station Road, Codsall, Wolverhampton

For Lucile Schoenfeld Glick (1928–1961) and Jay Milton Glick (1928–2011)

P.S.K.

For Gladys C. Jordan (1918–2014) and Robert F. Jordan (1915–1974)

J.R.J.

Table of Contents

Foreword

Series Editor's Foreword

The past 20 years have witnessed a dramatic increase in attention to the universal phenomenon of grief and loss, owing more perhaps to factors outside the field of bereavement studies (e.g., the upsurge of terrorism, death by natural or human-made disaster, random acts of violence, the more widespread institutionalization of palliative care) than it has to efforts within the mental health professions, *per se*. Still, both clinical researchers and practicing therapists have responded to this enhanced awareness by developing a growing range of techniques of grief therapy, and, in far more limited number, theories and models of bereavement adaptation that render the dynamics of adjusting to loss more visible. What has been lacking in this effort, however, have been broad and deep *meta-theories* that can both encompass conceptual developments in the field and promote the informed application of relevant methods in actual work with bereaved people.

Until now.

In *Attachment-Informed Grief Therapy*, Phyllis Kosminsky and Jack Jordan offer what many therapists have yearned for, and what all of us need, whether we know it or not: a flexible, over-arching model that helps us appreciate what is universal in bereavement— the often-powerful separation distress and related emotions that are at the heart of loss—and what is highly individual in our reactions to it—particularly how we respond to these same emotions. Given the very definition of bereavement as the loss of a significant other, it is not surprising that the authors turn to the wealth of classical and contemporary scholarship in attachment theory to shape a more nuanced understanding of how individuals strive to manage this turbulent affect and organize the story of what has transpired. What is surprising—and immensely helpful—is the care with which they have integrated the strands of a widely dispersed literature, weaving together findings on secure and insecure attachment patterns in childhood and adult relationships, interpersonal neuroscience, traumatology and suicidology, while also linking them to specific models of bereavement adaptation that are more "experience near" for practicing grief therapists. Thus, clinicians who are familiar with the Dual Process Model of Bereavement, with its dialectical attention to loss and restoration coping, or with the Two-Track Model of Bereavement, with its appreciation of the biopsychosocial challenges of grief and the reworking of the relationship with the deceased, will find that these models take on new relevance when viewed through an attachment lens. Likewise, therapists who find inspiration in meaning reconstruction and narrative models will find these usefully interpreted and extended when augmented by a deeper acquaintance with an attachment perspective. In each of these cases, the discovery of a way forward with a given client will be enhanced by drawing on such theories in an attachment-informed way.

As I savored this book's clear, uncluttered prose and apt clinical illustrations, two overriding "take home messages" continued to consolidate in my mind. The first was a sharper appreciation of the quite distinctive struggles and needs of different mourners with complicated bereavement responses as a function of their attachment histories. Thus, conceptualizing a given client's level of attachment security or insecurity, and in the latter instance, distinguishing between the learned strategies for emotion regulation relied upon by anxious, avoidant, and disorganized mourners, permits the therapist to modulate his or her stance in relation to each and to select approaches and techniques of specific relevance to helping a client tolerably explore grief-related affect and ultimately find new coherence in a changed life story.

Perhaps more fundamentally, by focusing significantly on the person of the therapist rather than only on his or her toolbox of techniques, Kosminsky and Jordan firmly graft grief therapy to its humanistic roots, thereby cultivating an intelligent hybrid of relational responsiveness and compassionate care for another in distress. Viewed in this perspective, the offer of an attuned attachment to an emotionally disregulated client is itself re-regulating, providing the safe container grievers require to begin to mindfully sort through the significance of their loss, more deeply "mentalize" its meaning for their lives, and bravely explore the adaptive changes it will require. Still more important than this general practice of presence is the refinement of this relational offer as a function of the client's predominant attachment style, as well as the intensity of its expression in a given moment of therapeutic encounter. Informed by the clearer reading of the therapy process afforded by an attachment lens, we as therapists are better positioned to modulate our own style in light of our clients' needs and readiness, and more cogently help them regulate and understand their distress and render their lives and losses more meaningful.

In summary, Kosminsky and Jordan set for themselves a tall order: to integrate cutting edge research on the developmental, social and neuropsychology of attachment, and to bring it to bear on the most fundamental challenge to that same attachment, namely the permanent physical separation from a loved one entailed by bereavement. And as readers will agree as they digest chapter after chapter of clinically relevant coverage, the authors succeed at this task admirably. Like me, I trust that you as a clinical colleague will be a better therapist for having studied the volume that follows.

Robert A. Neimeyer, PhD
Series Editor
Memphis, Tennessee
September 2015

Acknowledgments

The field of death and dying attracts some wonderful people, and many of them have had a hand in bringing this book to completion. First on the list is Robert Neimeyer, who suggested that Jack Jordan and I think about writing a book after hearing us give a presentation on attachment and loss at a meeting in 2011. That meeting was the annual conference of the Association for Death Education and Counseling (ADEC), an organization that has been pivotal in my professional development. It was through my membership in ADEC that I met my co-author. Jack is a clinician's clinician, the ideal blend of insight, compassion, and humor. Jack's work with suicide survivors, and his advocacy, writing, and teaching related to suicide postvention, are more than enough to fill anyone's professional plate. I am deeply grateful for his willingness to be my partner in this project, and I hope that its completion will not bring to an end our working lunches at Modern Pizza.

It is impossible to measure the contributions of colleagues with whom I have enjoyed years of conversation on many of the subjects discussed in this book. These include, but are no means limited to, all of my friends in ADEC and in the International Work Group on Death, Dying, and Bereavement, as well as my long time colleagues at the Center for Hope/Family Centers. Special thanks to Christopher Hall, whose invitation to deliver a paper in Australia was a great incentive for me to get my thoughts in order, and to Jane Bissler, who read and commented on early versions of the manuscript. Thanks to Carrie Arnold for her careful review and thoughtful comments on several key chapters. Thanks to all the members of my monthly supervision group in New York for their friendship and unflagging enthusiasm for my work.

The editorial staff at Routledge has been consistently available and helpful with all of our questions and concerns. Special thanks to Anna Moore, Elizabeth Graber, and Zoey Peresman for their diligence and patience throughout the publication process. Many thanks to our reassuringly alert copy editor Sarah Cheeseman and to our production editor Sioned Jones, for keeping us, and the manuscript, on track.

It is traditional for writers to thank family members for their love and support and I have received plenty of both from my husband Jay and my children, Lily and Eli, during the writing of this book. But their contributions go well beyond emotional sustenance. Eli's expert (and kind) advice about all things technology related got me off to a sound start, and his ongoing assistance kept me from melting down on more than one occasion. My husband made thoughtful and substantive contributions to the manuscript, and offered his usual excellent editorial input without regard for his personal safety. My daughter Lily took time that she didn't have as a first year medical student to read and comment on multiple drafts of the manuscript. You guys are my favorite people in the world.

Without my clients I would not have my work and I could not have written this book. Although I have taken pains not to identify them in the text, they know their stories and will no doubt recognize bits of them in these pages. To all of them: thank you for letting me share something of your journey with others. Most of all, thank you for allowing me to journey with you. Stories of loss are also stories of love. Every bereaved person is someone who has taken the risk of opening their heart to another person—of being attached. My clients are some of the most interesting, most courageous, and most alive people I have had the privilege to know.

My father Jay Glick was, and continues to be, a source of strength, comfort, and inspiration for me. Thanks for everything, Dad.

–Phyllis S. Kosminsky

There are always too many people to thank for their impact and influence in bringing a project like this book to fruition. I can only mention a few of them here. First, my co-author, Phyllis Kosminsky, has been a wonderful collaborator on this book. When Phyllis and I discovered that we shared a mutual interest in attachment theory and interpersonal neuroscience, and that our thinking was remarkably in synch about the clinical implications of these important bodies of theory and research for grief therapy, we were off and running. The mutual learning and excitement that our conversations have generated have never faded, and we both hope that the reader will feel some of that energy as they read the book. Phyllis is an empathic soul, a gifted clinician, and an insightful thinker, and it has been my pleasure to share this journey with her.

Bob Neimeyer, the Editor of this series, has been a long time mentor, colleague, role model, and friend of mine. His support of this book, and his general dedication to serving the needs of all people who are bereaved, have been and continue to be an inspiration to me. My many, many colleagues and friends in ADEC, and in the International Work Group on Death, Dying, and Bereavement, have also been instrumental in the development of my thinking about these topics. It is because of the magnificent support and sharing that both of these organizations foster that I became a grief therapist early in my career, and I have never wanted to do anything else with my professional life. Likewise, in addition to my own experiences of loss, my true teachers about bereavement have been my clients. Their courage in facing the reality of their own loss, their openness in sharing their pain with me, and their willingness to allow me to serve as a transitional attachment figure at a very difficult time in their lives, have formed the real foundation for the content of this book.

Finally, I want to thank the people who have served as attachment figures in my own life. My children, Kate and John, are amazing, and are pursuing their own versions of service to others in their chosen paths in life. Their gift to me has been the privilege of being their father, and watching them blossom as they move into the world. My wife, Mary Ruby, has truly served as my secure base and safe haven for nearly 40 years—my gratitude for her patience with me, and my not infrequent bouts of frustration and complaining about the process of writing books, is boundless. And last but not least, the devotion to each other and to their children that my parents showed me growing up has been my template for family life even to this very day. My father's death in 1974 was too early in our relationship, but it was the pivotal loss in my own life that started me down the path of grief counseling. And my mother's ability to overcome the many adversities of her childhood and go on to become a loving wife and mother could not have served as a better model of "earned security"—my understanding of human resilience in the face of loss has its roots in her story. To both of them, I owe so much—including the insights that have allowed me to produce this book with Phyllis.

–John R. Jordan, Ph.D.

Introduction

As psychotherapists, we have devoted a good part of our professional lives to understanding the nature of grief and caring for people who are bereaved. At the same time, we have worked to come to terms with our own personal losses. Experiences and lessons from these two domains, the professional and the personal, have each, in their own way, contributed to the evolution of our thinking about the importance of attachment in life and the emotional and physical impact of loss. The questions that interest us—questions about love, loss, and healing—have occupied many other minds over the centuries, so on the one hand, there may be little that can be said about these subjects that is entirely new. On the other hand, developments in attachment theory, along with the burgeoning field of neuroscience that now underpins it, suggest to us new and compelling ways of thinking about these questions.

In what amounts to a kind of professional awakening for both of us, attachment theory has become integral to our work as grief therapists. We find ourselves incorporating insights from attachment theory and neuroscience into our work regularly, as it informs both our "macro" understanding of how our clients cope with their losses, and our "micro" understanding of what we are doing and why we are doing it in the moment to moment flow of grief therapy. We have written this book so that we can share our sense of excitement and discovery about this incredibly useful model of the nature of human connection, and of the human response to the loss of those connections.

Insights from attachment theory have also helped us understand the meaning of our own losses. We each had a parent die early in our lives—P.S.K. lost her mother at the age of 9, and J.R.J. lost his father at the age of 26—and we each lost our surviving parent in the two years prior to writing this book. Attachment theory has significantly enhanced our understanding of our own reactions to loss, helping us to see the normality and universality of our own lifelong mourning processes. Our interest in writing a book about attachment theory thus arises from a sense that this theoretical model has served us well in both our professional and personal lives.

Other Traditions that Have Influenced Our Approach

In addition to attachment theory, which forms the conceptual heart of this book, we have been influenced by several other intellectual streams. One of these streams is the development of interpersonal neuroscience. The remarkable surge in knowledge about the brain has seen the application of contemporary neuroscience to the understanding of all types of human relations, from romantic attachments to parenting to psychotherapy (Cassidy & Shaver, 2008; A. N. Schore, 2012). Another influence is traumatology, and the clinical advances that have helped us better understand the impact of traumatic events in people's lives, including early relational trauma at the hands of caregivers and traumatic bereavement in the course of adult lives (Allen, 2013; Lanius et al., 2010; M. S. Stroebe et al., 2013). Lastly, we have been influenced by the changes that have emerged in the practice of general psychotherapy. Modern psychodynamic approaches, which have been powerfully influenced by attachment theory, offer a way to understand both the problems that clients bring to treatment and the role of the therapeutic alliance in promoting healing and bringing about change (Costello, 2013; Obegi & Berant, 2010; Wallin, 2007). With a few notable exceptions, developments in these fields of inquiry have not made their way into the literature on grief and mourning, nor have they been incorporated into the practice of grief therapy (Mikulincer & Shaver, 2008b, 2013; Shaver & Fraley, 2008; Shear & Shair, 2005; Zech & Arnold, 2011).

Organization of the Book

Attachment-Informed Grief Therapy is divided into three broad sections. In Part I, we discuss the roots of attachment theory and describe its evolution from a theory of infant development to what Allan Schore has described as a "theory of regulation" (A. N. Schore, 2003a, 2003b). In what was then a radical turn from psychoanalytic theory, John Bowlby introduced the idea of an inborn and biologically based attachment system that directs infants to seek proximity to their caregivers when distressed or hurt (Bowlby, 1982). Bowlby's thinking about attachment has become the basis for a remarkable, and by now, robust tradition of empirical research that continues to this day (Cassidy & Shaver, 2008; Mikulincer & Shaver, 2007). Chapter 1 also reviews the "Strange Situation" studies conducted by Mary Ainsworth, research that substantiated and elaborated Bowlby's hypotheses about the impact of relational security on infant behavior (Ainsworth et al., 1978).

In Chapter 2 we trace the extension of attachment theory into the study of child and then adult development and functioning in close relationships. Mary Main, a researcher in developmental psychology, advanced the field of attachment studies through the creation of the Adult Attachment Interview (AAI), a research method that could be used to identify the attachment orientation of adults (George et al., 1985; Main et al., 1998; Main et al., 2008). At about the same time, Peter Fonagy contributed the concept of mentalization, the ability to think about our own and other people's behavior in terms of inner feelings, needs, and psychological defenses (Fonagy et al., 2000). Mentalization has since come to be seen as a key component of attachment bonds (Allen et al., 2008; Jurist & Meehan, 2009). These theoretical advances and the empirical research that has followed from them have enhanced our understanding of the intergenerational transmission of attachment styles, and have been instrumental in bringing attention to the impact of early relational trauma on attachment across the lifespan. After reviewing the ideas of Main and Fonagy, we direct our attention to the work of attachment researchers and theorists in the social psychology (as opposed to developmental psychology) tradition of attachment studies (Cassidy & Shaver, 2008; Mikulincer & Shaver, 2007).

In Chapter 3 we discuss the work of theorists and researchers in the relatively new field of interpersonal neuroscience, work that has strengthened the scientific foundation of attachment theory (Cozolino, 2014; Montgomery, 2013; A. N. Schore, 2002c, 2009; D. J. Siegel, 2012b). Chapter 3, together with the preceding chapters on the evolution of attachment theory in developmental and social psychology, provides a scientific underpinning for the theoretical and clinical material presented in the rest of the book.

In Part II we set forth our thinking about the integration of attachment theory into the field of thanatology and the practice of grief therapy. In Chapter 4 we review two models of the mourning process that have particular resonance with attachment theory: the Two Track Model of Bereavement (TTM) and the Dual Process Model of Bereavement (DPM) (Rubin et al., 2011, 2012; M. S. Stroebe & Schut, 2010). We discuss theory and research concerning the role of insecure attachment in problematic grief and the implications of variations in attachment orientation for the practice of grief therapy. As we will throughout the rest of the book, we illustrate this with a number of case examples from our own practices.

In Chapter 5 we explore the impact of the relationship with the deceased as a significant factor influencing the trajectory of bereavement. This includes both the kinship relationship (partner loss, child loss, etc.), and the nature of the ongoing internal relationship with the loved one after the death, i.e., their continuing bond with the deceased. We also suggest the need to expand our analysis of the relationship between attachment and loss. Bowlby's ideas were developed on the basis of observations of the reactions of children who have been separated from their attachment figure(s). This model applies to some losses, but not to others. In particular, it does not adequately explain the grief, helplessness, and guilt of parents who lose a child. These responses, we propose, are related to the loss of the parent's role as their child's caregiver.

Chapter 6 looks at the mediating effect of the nature of the death on how people respond to loss. Here we focus on the effects of traumatic bereavement—the death of a loved one in a sudden, unexpected, and often violent fashion—on how the mourner responds, and how they cope. We discuss the nature of trauma in general, including some of the neurobiology of the trauma response. We also discuss traumatic death from an attachment theory perspective by exploring the impact of dysregulation of affect and meaning-making after traumatic deaths. These become major foci of clinical work in attachment-informed grief therapy.

In Part III we bring together all of the aforementioned information about attachment theory, neuroscience, and bereavement in order to illustrate how this material can be of use to clinicians who provide grief therapy. Chapter 7 is a presentation of our own model of attachment-informed grief therapy. This chapter includes a working definition of attachment-informed grief therapy, and a clear explication of our assumptions about attachment, grief, and complicated grief. We then outline what we regard as the key components of attachment-informed grief therapy and their importance in helping bereaved clients to heal. These components include the therapeutic relationship, strengthening emotional self-regulation, restoring or strengthening the capacity for meaning-making, and the integration of new information and skills. These components are discussed in greater depth in Chapters 8–10.

In Chapter 8 we discuss the specific features that make for a strong therapeutic alliance in grief therapy, and also elaborate on what makes this relationship particularly important in work with the bereaved. In this chapter we also identify and describe five core capacities that we believe grief therapists need to have in order to foster an effective working alliance with bereaved clients. Chapter 9 concentrates on strengthening affect regulation in bereavement recovery, and includes case examples and suggestions regarding specific techniques that can be used with clients to help them recognize and manage their grief related emotions. Chapter 10 continues the discussion of attachment-informed techniques, illustrating the central role of meaning reconstruction in grief therapy and demonstrating the linkage between the ability to make meaning and the ability to mentalize. We conclude the book by commenting on the convergence of theory, research, and practice in the fields of thanatology, attachment, and neuroscience, and identifying what we see as the rich potential for communication and collaboration going forward.

What This Book Is, and What It Is Not

Attachment-Informed Grief Therapy is not a book about a new model of therapy, or even a new protocol or set of techniques for grief therapy. Indeed, most of the ideas in the book have been drawn from what others are writing about in the more general psychotherapy literature. Likewise, most of the techniques are "agnostic"—that is, they do not belong to any particular school or approach to therapy or grief therapy. What we have tried to do here is to weave together new ideas from several important clinical frontiers in psychotherapy, along with our combined experience as long time grief counselors, to offer a way of understanding grief and grief therapy that will be useful to others who are doing the same work.

It is worth noting that we see differences between therapy that focuses on chronic attachment based problems in interpersonal relationships (Holmes, 2001, 2010, 2013; Wallin, 2007), and the practice of attachment-informed grief therapy. These differences are inherent in the presenting problem of bereavement. Unlike dysfunctional attachment related patterns of thinking, feeling, and behaving that have their roots in early neglect, abuse, or trauma, the typical individual presenting for grief therapy has a real-time emotional injury, usually in the relatively recent past. It is the difficulty in managing their response to this event that is usually the focus of treatment. This is not to say that addressing characterological issues is something outside the scope of grief therapy. On the contrary, we spend a considerable amount of time working on these issues with clients, and we devote a good portion of this book to illustrating how bereavement is influenced by these difficulties. However, we also believe that clinicians must understand that the person in front of them is grappling with a real and unalterable challenge—the now permanent separation from someone who was important to the client. Ultimately, the goal of grief therapy is an adjustment to and acceptance of that change.

Another difference between grief therapy and conventional psychodynamic psychotherapy is the use of transference and counter-transference. Specifically, while we propose that the relationship between therapist and client is paramount in both types of therapy, an explicit focus on the patient's transference is a significantly less frequent occurrence in grief therapy than in other types of psychotherapy.

It is also worth noting here that many years ago, Worden proposed a distinction between grief counseling and grief therapy, with counseling referring to primarily supportive type interventions for mild to moderate bereavement related problems, and therapy referring to more intensive treatment for what today would be called complicated grief (Worden, 1983/2008). In the interest of simplicity, and because many of the examples provided in this book refer to complicated grief that has its roots in early attachment related dysfunction, we will use the term grief therapy throughout this book.

We also want to be clear about the extensive use of case material in our book. Of course, all of our case examples have been modified to protect the confidentiality of the individuals who are discussed. Some of the cases are, in fact, a composite of several people with whom we have worked, distilled into a single vignette that illustrates the ideas being discussed. Also, the gender of the client and the gender of the therapist have sometimes been changed. Readers should not assume that when the vignette refers to "she" it is referring to the first author, or "he" to the second.

To conclude, what we present here as an attachment-informed model of grief therapy is not meant to replace or supersede other approaches to grief therapy. Instead, our focus is on the value of adding attachment theory to our understanding of the practice of grief therapy. Our goal is not to reinvent grief therapy, but rather to expand the reader's ways of understanding their bereaved clients, and the work they do with those clients. We believe that knowing something about how a person has learned to relate to others, and tuning into the hopes, expectations, and needs that shape their attachments, can help us foster a healing experience for the bereaved person. It is our hope that what we share in this volume will provide the reader with a new lens through which to consider the nature of grief and the practice of grief therapy.

Part I

An Introduction to Attachment Theory and Research

The great source of terror in infancy is solitude.
William James, *The Principles of Psychology* 1980

Attachment theory has drawn increasing interest in recent years among researchers and clinicians in the field of bereavement (Boelen & Klugkist, 2011; Field & Wogrin, 2011; Mikulincer & Shaver, 2008b; Shaver & Fraley, 2008; Shear & Shair, 2005). Attachment style, and in particular the security or insecurity of early attachment bonds, has become a focus of research aimed at explaining the considerable variations that are observed in people's adaptation to the death of a significant other (Gaudet, 2010; Jerga et al., 2011; Mancini et al., 2012; Meier et al., 2013). In Chapters 1 and 2 we provide an introduction to the foundations of attachment theory, with particular attention to the role of early bonds in the development of attachment orientation or style, and associated aspects of social and emotional functioning across the lifespan. The impact of early relational experience on self-regulatory capacity will be further explored in Chapter 3, which focuses on contributions from neuroscience that are providing new insight into how the quality of caregiving in the first two years of life affects the development of the brain, particularly those parts of the brain that are most involved in emotional processing (J. R. Schore & Schore, 2014). Findings relating to the impact of early attachment experience on the capacity to respond flexibly in stressful situations rather than locking into rigid patterns of response will be highlighted, since these findings are directly relevant to emerging models of adaptation to bereavement (Mikulincer & Shaver, 2008b).

1 Foundational Concepts in Attachment Theory

Many of the most intense emotions arise during the formation, the maintenance, the disruption and the renewal of attachment relationships.

(Bowlby, 1977)

Mostly it is loss which teaches us about the worth of things.

(Schopenhauer, 1974)

No matter how much we value those we love, it is arguably only when we lose someone that the strength of our attachment becomes most fully, and painfully, apparent. Our relationships with others are the source of our greatest comfort and joy, and also the source of our deepest wounds. We come into the world with an instinct to attach, and this instinct propels us to form connections that, if we are lucky, provide us with protection and nurturance in infancy, with solace in old age, and throughout our lives, with the gift of being known and of belonging somewhere and to someone. As with any source of comfort and nourishment, we want to know that the people we depend on are available, and we become distressed when they are not. Whenever we open our hearts to others, we are primed for the pain of loss.

John Bowlby, a British psychoanalyst who was also interested in ethology, was the founder of attachment theory (Holmes, 2001). So many of Bowlby's ideas have become embedded in our understanding of the impact of separation and loss in childhood and beyond that we can easily lose sight of the extent to which his theories challenged what was then the dominant psychoanalytic paradigm. In classic psychoanalytic theory, the infant's drive to attach was considered a secondary drive, a behavioral response to the primary need for food, in infancy, and for sex, in adulthood (Bowlby, 1977). Bowlby's observations of the effects on personality development of deprivation of maternal care, along with his reading of research by Harry Harlow and others documenting the central role of attachment in the development of other species (Harlow & Zimmermann, 1959; Lorenz, 1957), led Bowlby to question the adequacy of the psychoanalytic model. He argued that attachment is "a fundamental form of behavior with its own internal motivation distinct from feeding and sex, and of no less importance for survival" (Bowlby, 2008, p.27). Although it is most evident in early childhood, the need to maintain a connection to a familiar and safe individual "can be observed throughout the life cycle, especially in emergencies" (Bowlby, 2008, p.27).

Bowlby's objections to the analytic approach taken by Freud, and by his own clinical trainer, Melanie Klein, were especially vehement concerning what he saw as their immersion in theory and an at times appalling lack of attention to the actual circumstances of children's lives. Bowlby made it his mission to advance an understanding of development based not only on drive theory, but on observation of the effects of lived experience—particularly adverse experience—on physical health, emotional well-being, and social functioning (Wallin, 2007).

Bowlby had the opportunity to gather evidence concerning the impact of early separation and loss on development and behavior when he worked as a psychiatrist in London's Child Guidance Center, where he spent three years studying delinquent boys. His report on "Forty-four Juvenile Thieves: Their Characters and Home-life" (Bowlby, 1944) documented the catastrophic effect of protracted early separation on development. Bowlby was subsequently commissioned by the World Health Organization to study the impact of homelessness on children in the aftermath of World War II (Bowlby, 1951). His observations led Bowlby to identify a sequence of responses that he interpreted as the bereft children's attempts to cope with a reality beyond their understanding or control. In the decades following this work, Bowlby identified a similar sequence of responses as characteristic of normal mourning in adults (Bowlby, 1977). These patterns of response became the centerpiece of Bowlby's writing on attachment and loss.

Fundamentals of an Attachment Perspective

The Attachment Behavioral System

The guiding assumptions of Bowlby's theory of attachment concern how a child attaches to her primary caregiver, usually the mother, and how the child responds when the caregiver is needed and not immediately available. Bowlby proposed that we have an instinct for attachment that can be observed from infancy. This instinct is part of what Bowlby labeled the *attachment behavioral system*, the goal of which is to provide protection and a sense of comfort and security for the child. That is, the nearness of the caregiver provides the child with physical protection, and with a psychological sense of safety that allows him to engage in play, exploration, and interaction with others, comfortable in the knowledge that the caregiver is nearby and available.

According to Bowlby, the attachment behavioral system is activated when the child feels uncomfortable or afraid and the caregiver is not immediately available or responsive. The resulting *"separation distress"* is expressed in behaviors that are designed to restore proximity and allow the child to return to a comfortable internal state (Bowlby, 1982). If proximity is not restored, the child will become increasingly agitated. In the event that the caregiver returns and comforts the child, the system is deactivated, or "resets," and the child resumes his activities. If the caregiver does not return, the child's protests will accelerate. Eventually, however, the failure of repeated attempts to create reunion will result in the abandonment of this strategy, and the child will begin to show signs of despair and disengagement. Bowlby labeled these three stages *protest, despair,* and *detachment* (Bowlby, 1960).

Attachment anxiety and related behaviors are

> part of the inherited behavior repertoire of man. . . . When they are activated and the mother figure is available, attachment behavior results. When they are activated and the mother figure is temporarily unavailable, separation anxiety and protest behavior follow. . . . [Finally,] grief and mourning will occur in infancy whenever the responses mediating attachment behavior are activated and the mother figure continues to be unavailable.
>
> (Bowlby, 1960, p.10)

The panic of a young child who needs and cannot find his caregiver is a corollary of his dependency. His sustained and high decibel attempts to restore proximity are an expression of the imperative to remain close to the person on whom survival depends. The subjectively felt, and objectively realistic need for a caregiver, and the protest that ensues when she is not available, are inborn features of our species. Once triggered, the child's need to reconnect with the caregiver takes precedence over any other activity. Play, exploration, and social interaction, all part of other behavioral systems that parallel the attachment behavioral system, are suppressed while the child frantically tries to reestablish contact. Security is not the only thing a child needs, but security is what frees a child to explore the world outside, as well as the world inside. A sense of security makes it possible for a child to be less vigilant about his environment and more attuned and responsive to his own thoughts, feelings, and needs.

Individual Differences in Attachment System Functioning

Beyond describing the basic elements and functioning of the attachment behavioral system, Bowlby was interested in identifying and accounting for differences in how this system operates in individuals. As a clinician, Bowlby wanted to understand how the quality of early attachment relationships factored into people's ability to manage their emotions, to form healthy relationships with others, and to cope with the variety of stressors with which life presents us. If early relational security frees us to engage with the world and to weather life's storms, how does the lack of security restrict engagement, constrict development, and compromise functioning in childhood and beyond?

Bowlby theorized that the attachment behavioral system is on standby as long as the child does not feel threatened or unsafe, at which time internal alarms sound and the child protests the caregiver's lack of availability. The nature of the caregiver's response at these times is a fundamental element in the alchemy of attachment development. *Bowlby focused attention on differences in the quality of caregivers' responses, and related these variations to observable differences in the child's subsequent attachment behavior.* Like little investigators, young children collect data about the likely outcome of their contact seeking behavior, learn to anticipate how different bids for attention will be met, and adjust their behavior accordingly. If it turns out that protest is a successful strategy for reestablishing proximity with the caregiver, the child will continue to employ this as his primary strategy in the future. However, if this strategy is not successful—if the caregiver does not return, or if she shows signs of being impatient, angry, or rejecting in response to the child's distress—the child will adopt secondary strategies in an effort to reduce discomfort (Bowlby, 1982).

Secondary Strategies

In circumstances where their initial cries for reunion have not brought about the caregiver's return, the child will employ one of two secondary strategies: *hyperactivating* (akin to what has just been described as protest, in Bowlby's vernacular) or *deactivating* (Main & Hesse, 1990; Mikulincer et al., 2003). Children who employ a hyperactivating strategy will escalate their attempts to restore proximity: they will cry louder and harder, and will thrash, pound, and in general, increase the intensity of their distress signals in an effort to attract the attachment figure's attention and care (Bowlby, 1982). When the caregiver returns, the child may attempt to maintain proximity by clinging, crying, and otherwise showing distress and protest at any signal of imminent separation. In contrast to these fervent attempts to hold onto the caregiver, deactivating strategies may be less apparent to an observer in that they involve the *suppression* of behavior and, in Bowlby's view, the suppression of affect. That is, deactivating strategies involve a shutting down of the awareness of discomfort when repeated attempts to seek comfort have not produced the needed response in the caregiver, as well as a shutting down of signaling behavior designed to produce a reunion with the caregiver.

The child's development of a secondary strategy represents their assessment of the best-case approach to restoring, or maintaining, proximity. A child who judges that his caregiver is responsive when available, but whose availability in an emergency cannot be counted on, is likely to employ a hyperactivating strategy, in effect pulling out all the behavioral stops to keep the caregiver close by (Cassidy & Kobak, 1987). In contrast, deactivating strategies are seen as a response to the consistent unavailability of the attachment figure as a source of reassurance or support.

> In such cases, a person learns to expect better outcomes if signs of need and vulnerability are hidden or suppressed, proximity seeking efforts are weakened or blocked, the attachment system is deactivated despite a sense of security not being achieved . . . The primary goal of deactivating strategies is to keep the attachment system turned off or down regulated so as to avoid frustration and distress caused by caregiver unavailability.
>
> (Mikulincer & Shaver, 2007)

Bowlby coined the term "defensive exclusion" for what he identified as the terminal strategy for avoiding the painful feelings associated with a caregiver's unavailability or unresponsiveness. Defensive exclusion involves the suppression of emotion *below the level of consciousness*. That is, the child, having concluded that protesting his fear and aloneness does not bring the desired response, not only stops expressing his dismay, he stops *feeling* it. Suppressing painful emotion becomes the primary way of surviving in an environment that does not provide the needed support and protection. When this approach to managing feelings continues into adulthood, the result is a kind of emotional confusion. Without the information provided by emotions, it is difficult for a person to know what she wants, to identify what is meaningful to her, to know whether a relationship is healthy or unhealthy. In a therapist's office, these are the clients whose response to any question about how they feel is "I don't know," who seem unable even to identify what they *might* be feeling, or what someone else might feel under the same circumstances (Kooiman et al., 2004). In some cases this may be an artifact of early defensive exclusion, a theme to which we will return when we discuss the role of emotion tolerance in coping with loss.

Through the ongoing collection and consolidation of information on the availability and responsiveness of their caregiver, a child develops an internal working model of that relationship. This will become the first, but not the only, model of relationship with another person. Bowlby believed that children formulate not just one, but multiple working models, depending on their experience with different people, and he proposed that these working models play an ongoing part in how a person interacts with others later in life. For example, a child who has a problematic relationship with her mother, but a positive and secure relationship with her father, may grow up to be a woman who is more at ease with men than with women. The working models developed early in life have a lasting, though by no means absolute, influence on the value people place on relationships, their feelings about what kinds of relationships they can expect to have or deserve to have, and their understanding of how to go about getting their need for connection with other people met.

In summary, Bowlby was the first to recognize the importance of early experiences of separation and loss on development and to suggest that these early experiences continue to have an impact on a person well into adulthood. *Further, the loss of a significant person in adulthood will evoke many of the same feelings that accompanied separation from an attachment figure in childhood.* Bowlby's ideas about the attachment behavioral system, the normative nature of a child's response to separation, and the parallels between separation distress in infancy and adult bereavement, have provided a conceptual framework for research into the role of early attachment experience in adult bereavement, which will be the focus of Chapter 4.

During the same period that Bowlby was doing his foundational work on attachment, another British psychiatrist, Colin Murray Parkes, was making observations about the course of normal and problematic grief in adulthood (Parkes, 1964, 1970). Parkes argued that although bereavement was not generally regarded as an "illness," it was associated with a range of physical and emotional symptoms. Among the bereaved psychiatric patients he treated, Parkes had found substantial evidence of serious and prolonged grief related symptomatology (Parkes, 1970, 1998). Parkes became convinced that the course of a person's bereavement was impacted by two sets of factors: those related to the nature of the bereaved's relationship with the deceased, and those related to the nature of the death (Parkes, 1998). Realizing the relevance of Bowlby's work on attachment to his own studies of bereavement, Parkes joined Bowlby's research unit at the Tavistock clinic in 1962. This collaboration led to the publication of a joint paper delineating four phases of grief during adult life (Bowlby & Parkes, 1970).

In later studies (Parkes, 1998; Vanderwerker et al., 2006), Parkes used retrospective data (collected through subject interviews) to investigate the role of early attachment security in bereavement. Parkes reasoned that a trusting and secure relationship with parents would be associated with trusting and secure relationships in adulthood, and would further be reflected in the nature of the individual's grief following the loss of these relationships. In short, Parkes, along with Bowlby, was among the first to suggest, and to substantiate, the life long impact of early attachment security and in particular, the connection between attachment and loss. The role of attachment security as a major influence on the response to loss continues to be a foundational construct in the research and thinking of Parkes (Parkes, 2013; Parkes & Prigerson, 2010).

Bowlby's hope was that attachment theory would bring attention to the dangers of separating young children from caregivers, and that it would attract clinicians interested in mitigating these effects. While it would be many years before it would be translated into practice, attachment theory has become the subject of substantial research and testing. Among the first and most prominent of researchers to investigate Bowlby's theories was the American psychologist Mary Ainsworth.

Ainsworth and the Development of an Attachment Classification for Infants' Patterns of Response

The approach to studying Bowlby's theories that Ainsworth developed involved a combination of naturalistic, in home observation of young children and caregivers, and observation in a laboratory setting that is known as the Strange Situation. Ainsworth's methods are still used in research settings where the goal is to observe and codify parent–child interactions and their effect on child development, and in research/clinical environments where the goals extend to modifying caregiver behavior to provide greater relational security to the infant (Steele & Steele, 2008).

Although she is best known for her collaboration with Bowlby and her laboratory studies, Ainsworth began her research in Uganda, in what was the first ever naturalistic, longitudinal study of infants in interaction with their mothers (Ainsworth, 1967). After returning to the United States, Ainsworth settled in Baltimore and enlisted 26 pregnant women who agreed, after the birth of their children, to be observed in their homes in four-hour sessions over the course of the first year (Ainsworth et al., 1978). From the age of 6 months, infants showed a clear preference for their mother over other adults, sought their mother when they were distressed, and in the majority of cases, required the security of her presence in order to engage in exploration and play. The connection between the mother's presence and an engaged, playful child did not hold in all cases, however. Some children appeared to cling to their mothers, while others appeared largely uninterested in her presence. Some children only wanted to play, while others could not tear themselves away from their mothers and showed no interest in exploring their environment.

Ainsworth began to formulate her own theory about the role of attachment in development. She posited that it was not only attachment *per se*, but the *quality* of the attachment relationship, mediated primarily by communication between the caregiver and the child, that accounted for the differences she observed in children's social and exploratory behavior. In order to test these assumptions, and with the children in the home based study now 12 months old, she created a laboratory environment, the Strange Situation, where she and colleagues could study the behavior of a mother and child together in a pleasant, toy filled room that could then be used to observe the behavioral response of the child when the mother left the room and the child remained behind in the care of a stranger; and the behavioral response of the child when the mother returned. Each of the 26 mother/child pairs was observed. The majority of the children in the Strange Situation played when the mother was present, cried when she left, were comforted and calmed when she returned, and soon resumed exploration and play after she was back. However, there were exceptions, just as there had been exceptions in the home observations. Some children collapsed when their mothers left the room, were inconsolable when they returned, and remained indifferent to their environment. Others seemed to be largely unaffected either by their mother's presence or her absence.

Ainsworth's classification of attachment patterns designated three categories (a fourth category would later be added by her student Mary Main). Ainsworth classified as *secure* those children who were able to tolerate separation, and to seek consolation and comfort from the mother. Their flexibility in moving between exploration and attachment was supported by a secure bond with their mother, the context of which was a sense that she would be there when needed, so that temporary separations did not cause unmanageable and sustained distress.

In contrast, two groups of children categorized as *insecure* in their attachment demonstrated rigid patterns of behavior that were described by Ainsworth as *anxious/ambivalent* or *avoidant* with regard to attachment. Anxiously attached children clung to their mothers and showed little or no interest in exploring their surroundings. When the mothers of these children were in the room, Ainsworth observed, they discouraged exploratory behavior, and the children complied. The children remained despondent for the duration of the brief separation, and upon reunion, clung harder and cried more, as though they wanted to do everything possible to avoid another separation. Avoidantly attached children paid little attention to their mothers when they were present and appeared uninterested in them when they returned after a brief separation. Ainsworth interpreted both of these patterns of behavior as adaptations to the mother's verbal and nonverbal cues. In the case of avoidantly attached children, what appeared to be indifference was actually the suppression of behavior that was ineffective or counterproductive in engaging a mother who communicated, with words, gestures, and body language, discomfort and disapproval of the infant's outward signs of distress. Subsequent studies, in which the physiological arousal of these infants was measured, supported Ainsworth's assumption, showing that the apparent calm of avoidant children does not accurately reflect their internal state (Cassidy & Shaver, 2008; Sroufe & Waters, 1977). Neither the anxious nor the avoidantly attached children appeared to be relieved by their mother's return. "It was as if, even in their presence, these infants were seeking a mother who wasn't there" (Wallin, 2007, p.20).

Strange Behavior in the Strange Situation: Mary Main

Based on her review of hundreds of hours of tapes from the Strange Situation (Main & Hesse, 1990), Main found confirmation of many of Ainsworth's observations. She also identified a group of young children whose behavior did not seem to fit any of Ainsworth's categories. Main noted that on the whole, insecurely attached children exhibited consistent patterns of behavior, reflecting either an avoidant or anxious attachment to the caregiver. For example, children who cried and clung to their mothers did this consistently; children who avoided their mothers also did this consistently, and did not cry or cling. The very rigidity of these behavior patterns, in Main's view, was a marker of attachment insecurity, and contrasted with the more variable and flexible behavior of securely attached children (Main, 1996). But what Main saw when she looked at the tapes was another category of children whose behavior was impossible to describe in simple terms; the behavior of these children was not rigid, but it was *odd*. This small subgroup, classified as *Disorganized*, did not employ any one, fixed strategy for getting their attachment needs met; sometimes they cried, sometimes they avoided the mother, and sometimes they engaged in a range of strange behaviors that had not previously been reported. A sample of 200 unclassifiable Strange Situation videotapes revealed an array of

> anomalous or conflicted behaviors in the parent's presence, as evidenced, for example, in rocking on hands and knees with face averted after an aborted approach; freezing all movement, arms in air, with a trancelike expression; moving away from the parent to lean head on wall when frightened; and rising to greet the parent, then falling prone.
>
> (Main, 1996, p.239)

These behaviors, Main proposed, were a response to the erratic and extreme behavior of the child's caregivers, which ranged from angry and punitive to overly intrusive and clingy. Having no access to coherent memories of interactions to guide their behavior, these children behaved in a seemingly random and often jarringly contradictory fashion. Unable to settle on a preferred strategy, and deprived of the external help they needed to regain emotional equilibrium, they remained agitated and upset, and had little energy or interest left over to devote to exploration or play. Main's interest in this group of children, and their comparably unsettled and overwhelmed caregivers, led her to a new way of thinking about, and studying, early attachment experience and the intergenerational transmission of attachment orientation.

Main: A Move to the Level of Representation

Until the 1980s, most attachment research had to do with attachment security in young children, and with the relationship between attachment security or insecurity and features of the parent–child bond observed in the Strange Situation. In 1985, Main and colleagues published a study that included assessment of adult attachment, and that used a newly developed research instrument, the Adult Attachment Interview (AAI). Although the AAI poses questions about the respondent's childhood, assessment is based *not on what the respondent says but on how they say it*, in other words, on qualities of discourse that have been shown to reflect a respondent's *internal representation* of attachment (Main et al., 1985).

Using the AAI in conjunction with Strange Situation observations, Main and her colleagues were able to make a connection between the behavior of *infants categorized as disorganized and the early relational experiences of their mothers.* Main found that a majority of the mothers of disorganized infants had experienced early relational abuse themselves as children, had a limited capacity to regulate their own emotions, and as a result were easily overwhelmed by their infants' distress and demands for attention. She concluded that these mothers were not only frightening *to* their infants, but frightened *of* them; of their crying, their neediness, and their vulnerability (Main & Hesse, 1990).

These observations signaled a change in Main's analysis, from an explanation of the transmission of attachment style based on maternal *behavior* to one emphasizing an *internal orientation to attachment on the part of the caregiver that derived from their own early childhood experience.* Notably, Main proposed that it was not the experience itself but the *adult's internal representation of that experience* that was reflected in their parenting behavior. Over the past 25 years the AAI has been used in hundreds of studies documenting this intergenerational transmission of attachment style. The AAI will be discussed further in Chapter 2.

Together, Ainsworth and Main provided the foundation for our understanding not only of variations in attachment style, but for individual differences in the capacity to tolerate painful emotions, the ability to cope in the face of stress, and the potential for recovery from significant loss. Subsequent research has identified the role of attachment in everything from general psychological health (Dozier et al., 2008), to romantic attachment (Hazan & Shaver, 1987), to the degree to which a person believes that life has meaning (Mikulincer & Shaver, 2012). Much of this research has served to strengthen Bowlby's claims about the critical importance of good early care for infants and children, and of a social environment that supports parents' ability to provide children with the best, most secure base at their most tender stage of development.

Adult Bereavement through the Lens of Attachment

We move now from an overview of what factors impact attachment orientation and behavior in children and adults, as conceptualized by Bowlby, Ainsworth, Main, and others, to consider what Bowlby had to say about the nature of bereavement in adults. Although Bowlby was initially interested in understanding the impact of attachment and loss of attachment in infancy and childhood, he believed that the instinct for attachment persisted throughout life, and with it, the distress occasioned by separation. Bowlby devoted the third volume of his trilogy *Attachment and Loss* to bereavement and grief (Bowlby, 1980). In this volume Bowlby articulated two ideas that are particularly relevant to an attachment perspective on grief therapy, and to which we will return in the chapters that follow. First, he argued that the seemingly irrational or immature behavior exhibited by many people in reaction to the loss of an attachment figure was in effect rooted in the same behavioral system that drives infants to maintain proximity to caregivers. In infancy this drive provides a survival advantage to those who can attract and hold onto the attention of caregivers. In other words, we come into the world with a strongly felt sense of the importance of keeping track of our primary attachment figures, and a biologically encoded propensity to panic when they become unavailable. Seen in this light, the protest and searching behavior of many bereaved people takes on a deeper and clearer meaning.

In addition to describing the normative aspects of adult response to loss through death (Bowlby & Parkes, 1970), Bowlby proposed a framework to account for atypical, disordered forms of mourning, describing a continuum from "chronic mourning" to "prolonged absence of mourning" (Bowlby, 1980; Parkes, 1975). According to Bowlby, chronic mourning is characterized by an inability to move from a state in which awareness of the death, with its attendant fear, pain, and yearning, interferes with the mourner's ability to engage in his normal, everyday tasks. This description of chronic mourning, and the characteristic suppression of functioning associated with it, may remind the reader of Bowlby's description of an infant who is preoccupied with reestablishing a tolerable level of proximity to a caregiver. While such a reaction is normal in the early stages of grief, it becomes problematic when it interferes with reengagement with life to the point where the bereaved individual becomes increasingly isolated and hopeless about the prospect of recovery (see the discussion of continuing bonds with the deceased in Chapter 5 for more on this). Here too, the parallel to an infant's response to separation is apparent. The chronically bereaved person, determined to regain connection with the deceased and unwilling to accept that this is impossible, puts all her energy into denial, protest, and despair, leaving little available for the tasks of reconciliation and rebuilding that are intrinsic to adaptive grieving. With reference to the discussion of hyperactivating and deactivating strategies previously, the chronic mourner can be seen as engaging in activating strategies, motivated by a seeming conviction that if they protest long and loudly enough, the deceased will return (Mikulincer et al., 2013).

Another version of what can be seen as an activating strategy is described by novelist Joan Didion in her account of the sudden collapse and death of her husband. Didion's "year of magical thinking" (Didion, 2007), involved exhaustive efforts to uncover the details of her husband's final hours, his condition on arriving at the hospital, the observations of everyone who worked on him, and the precise cause of his death. Retrospectively acknowledging the futility of these efforts, Didion sees them as her way of refusing to accept her husband's death, and instead focusing on the possibility of bringing him back:

> Whatever else had been in my mind when I so determinedly authorized an autopsy, there was also a level of derangement on which I reasoned that an autopsy could show that what had gone wrong was something simple . . . It could have required only a minor adjustment – a change in medication, say, or the resetting of a pacemaker. In this case, the reasoning went, they might still be able to fix it.
>
> (Didion, 2007, p.37)

In contrast, a person using a deactivating strategy will do whatever she can to avoid being reminded of the loved one, will deny strong feelings about the loss, and will suppress these thoughts when they arise. She may deny the importance of the relationship and reject any suggestion that the loss is affecting her in any significant way. Any suggestion that she may want to take some time from her normal schedule of activities will be rejected, as will any overtures of sympathy or offers of help. The level of disengagement from feelings about the loss may be so complete that the person does not in fact experience them on a conscious level, although they continue to affect her state of mind, and could be triggered without warning by reminders of the deceased (Bowlby, 1980). Bowlby believed that sustained suppression of emotions relating to grief had the potential to manifest itself as negative emotional or physical symptoms. As discussed in Chapter 4, this supposition is supported by research and clinical reports (Meier et al., 2013), although other researchers have challenged the assertion that every grieving person must experience and work through bereavement related distress (Bonanno & Boerner, 2008).

Summary

Bowlby's theories about attachment grew out of his observations of children who were separated from their caregivers for medical reasons, for purposes of behavioral reform, or as a result of war or other extreme circumstances. What he observed led him to conclude that such separations deprived children of an essential source of security and comfort, the need for which was as basic as the need for food and shelter. A fundamental tenet of attachment theory is that children have an instinctive need to maintain connection with their primary caregiver, most often (but not always or exclusively) their mothers. Loss of that connection triggers behavioral responses that vary in intensity and form, but have the common goal of reconnection. The same instinct to maintain connection is present in adults, and the same response to loss of connection that causes such distress in young children is manifested in bereaved adults.

Bowlby's views regarding the importance of attachment in early childhood development, and in the mental health and relational capacity of adults, have inspired generations of researchers, many of whom have looked at questions that bear directly on our understanding of the nature of grief and its complications. How does maternal caregiving impact attachment security? Is attachment style in childhood predictive of attachment style in adulthood? Can attachment orientation change over time? Does insecure attachment create problems in cognitive, emotional, or social functioning that might complicate adaptation to grief? These are some of the questions we will explore in the next chapters.

2 Building on the Foundation

The Second Wave of Attachment Theory and Research

> We would do well ... to consider that much of the thinking, feeling, remembering, and behaving that we observe in our patients (and ourselves) has arisen and persists in order to preserve outdated – but all too enduring – internal working models of attachment.
>
> (Wallin, 2007, p.36)

The experiences of childhood are the primordial soup of our identity. Ill equipped as we are in the first years of our lives to make sense of what is going on around us, or to distinguish what is real from what is imagined, we stumble through, dependent on the direction and attention of others. Given the depth of our dependence, the unrivaled intimacy of our first human relationships, and our own very limited ability to understand the behavior of our caregivers, it is not surprising that so many of our childhood memories are as incomprehensible as they are indelible.

Many therapy clients, including those who seek help following a significant loss, find that the difficulty they had making sense of their surroundings and the behavior of the people closest to them has persisted into adulthood. They may be able to recognize, but not to explain, their fear of intimacy, their extreme reaction to being criticized, and, if they are bereaved, why the prospect of living without a partner or sibling is so terrifying. In Bowlby's view, problems of this sort can often be traced to a person's early attachment experience. While the first lessons we learn about ourselves and others can be reworked and modified, they are never entirely forgotten.

In the first part of this chapter, we will look at the work of developmental psychologists, notably Mary Main and Peter Fonagy, whose research efforts have been directed toward enhancing our understanding of the intergenerational transmission of attachment orientation, and the adverse effects of early relational trauma. Attachment scholars in the developmental psychology tradition have used interview based methods, such as the Adult Attachment Interview (AAI), as their primary methodology. In the second part of the chapter we will introduce the work of social psychologists, including Hazan and Shaver (Hazan & Shaver, 1987) and Bartholomew and Horowitz (Bartholomew & Horowitz, 1991) whose investigation of attachment, in terms of focus and methodology, went in a different direction. Social psychologists focused on adult attachment, particularly intimate peer relationships, with self-report measures such as the Experiences in Close Relationships inventory as the methodology of choice. This branch of attachment research has produced a substantial body of evidence concerning the impact of attachment orientation on a range of cognitive, emotional, and social processes (Fraley et al., 2013), as well as on the links between parenting and attachment style. In their recent review of 60 studies conducted by social and personality psychologists on parenting and attachment style since the 1990s, Jones and his colleagues argue that this research "has received less attention than AAI research on the same topic" (Jones et al., 2015), an imbalance we will endeavor to avoid in the discussion that follows.

Research and theory from developmental and social psychology together have taught us a great deal about how relationships form, how people cope with the loss of significant people in their lives and what factors contribute to the ability to heal, and what constitutes effective treatment for people suffering from prolonged grief (Jordan & Neimeyer, 2003). In bereavement therapy, as in other areas of clinical practice, there is often a considerable lag between reports of new information or theory and the utilization of this information by practitioners (Jordan, 2000). With respect to attachment theory and research in particular, Lopez suggests that the scope and complexity of the literature has created confusion regarding the conceptualization and assessment of adult attachment (Lopez, 2009). Thus, another purpose of the discussion in this chapter is to provide an orientation to the attachment literature for readers who are not familiar with it, as well as an explanation of the terms we will be using in the remaining chapters.

The scope of research concerning attachment is suggested by the length—over 1,000 pages—of the second edition of Cassidy and Shaver's *Handbook of Attachment* (Cassidy & Shaver, 2008). Beyond its function as the mechanism by which babies elicit essential care, attachment, and the quality of early attachment interactions, are crucial influences on the development of the young child's ability to regulate emotion, manage stress, and experience a sense of self agency (Fonagy et al., 2014). Secure relationships with caregivers support the development of these core capacities. Conversely, adverse early attachment experiences compromise the development of these capacities. This being the case, we would expect the incidence of mental disorders, and an array of lesser problems in living, to be higher among people with adverse early attachment experiences. In the third part of this chapter we will discuss some of what researchers have reported concerning the effect of early attachment experience on the development of core capacities for emotion regulation, capacities that we see as requisite to healthy adaptation to loss. The implications of this connection between early attachment experience, emotion regulation, and adaptation to loss will be revisited throughout the remainder of this book.

Developmental Psychology: Mary Main and the AAI

Main began her investigation of attachment as a graduate student of Ainsworth, during which time she spent many hours observing infants and mothers and viewing tapes of their behavior in the Strange Situation lab. But she is best known for the development of the AAI, the creation of which can be seen as marking the beginning of a second wave of attachment theory that focused on identifying the roots of disorganized attachment. Main believed that parents' secure or insecure states of mind with respect to attachment are transmitted to children through the manner in which they care for their children, and she developed a methodology for testing this hypothesis that was unlike anything previously used in attachment research.

As discussed in Chapter 1, Main believed that taking a straightforward history of a mother's childhood would not allow the interviewer to assess her *internal representation* of that experience. And it was that internal representation that Main considered crucial in shaping the mother's, and ultimately the infant's, state of mind with regard to attachment. Main knew that people with similar kinds of childhood stories can turn out to be very different as adults. She knew that some people who experience early abuse or neglect grow up to be calm and capable people who raise healthy, well-adjusted children, while others cannot seem to break free of destructive bonds to the past: what she wanted to understand was *why*. Main reasoned that what influenced adult attachment behavior was not simply a person's history, but their internal narrative of that history. Her goal, then, was to devise a method of gathering information that would allow her to assess not what the person had experienced, but *what meaning they had made of that experience*.

Working Models of Attachment in Adulthood

The question of how to assess an individual's state of mind regarding attachment is a bit like the question of how to measure the distance to the stars. Direct measurement is impossible, and the investigator must instead rely on ingenuity and invention to make an indirect assessment. Main's invention, the AAI, was conceived as a way to capture indirectly, by reflection and inference, the nature of adults' internal working models regarding attachment in past and present relationships (Main, 1996). Although the AAI is used to gather information about the respondent's childhood, what is being evaluated is not the security or insecurity of childhood relationships but rather the individual's "*current overall state of mind with respect to attachment*" (Allen, 2013, p.14).

The AAI is a semi-structured interview in which respondents are asked to characterize their relationships with primary caregivers, to recall early experiences of loss and trauma, and to reflect on how they see their early experiences as having affected their development. The content and organization of the AAI are designed to slip past the respondent's conscious filters, to "surprise the unconscious" (Steele & Steele, 2008, p.8), so that what emerges is something more than a well-rehearsed narrative. The AAI was developed as a research instrument, and its use in research requires extended training by a small number of qualified instructors (Hesse, 2008). However, the questions contained in the interview have proven extremely valuable as a guide to gathering information about early attachment experiences, as well as experiences of loss and trauma, which makes it particularly relevant to work with the bereaved (Thomson, 2010). While a basic familiarity with the manner in which the interview is to be conducted is recommended, formal training is not required to use the AAI in this manner (Levy & Kelly, 2009; Steele & Steele, 2008).

In the first section of the AAI, the respondent is asked to list five adjectives they would use to describe their relationship with their mother. This list of adjectives is read back one at a time to the respondent, who is asked to provide the interviewer with memories that illustrate each adjective chosen. This procedure is then repeated for the relationship with the father, and for any other significant attachment figures (for example, a grandparent or stepparent). The protocol next contains questions about which parent the subject felt closer to and why, what the subject would do when emotionally upset, or physically hurt or ill, and how the parent (mother first, then father) responded at such times (Hesse, 2008). The next section includes questions about experiences of rejection, separation, and discipline. Once these events are recorded, the respondent is asked to reflect on the effects of these experiences on his or her adult personality, whether they believe any of them had a negative impact on their adult development, and why they believe their parents may have behaved as they did. Further questions explore whether a person has lost a family member or someone else who was close to them, and if so, how the death occurred, their reactions to it at the time, their feelings about it then and in the present, and other details. Similarly detailed follow up questions are posed regarding any experiences of abuse or trauma mentioned in the interview.

In a research setting, the AAI is recorded and transcribed, and a trained coder classifies respondents into one of three categories of attachment that parallel (but are not the equivalent of) Ainsworth's infant typology: "Secure-autonomous" (corresponding to Secure); "Dismissing" (corresponding to Avoidant); or "Preoccupied" (corresponding to Anxious/Ambivalent) (Main, 1996). A secondary classification captures the extent to which respondents are "Unresolved" with respect to trauma or loss. This second classification has particular significance for clinical work with the bereaved, in that it appears to overlap to a considerable extent with descriptions in the bereavement literature of complicated grief (Thomson, 2010).

Interpreting the AAI

The AAI coding system is based on a set of assumptions about *how* information is communicated, rather than the information itself (Hesse, 2008; Main et al., 1985; Main et al., 2008). The coder focuses not so much on what the person says as on the way they say it, and how their thoughts are ordered. The primary element the coders look for is the degree to which the narrative contained in the subject's answers is coherent, internally consistent, and responsive to the questions posed. Coherence in the narrative is closely related to the concept of *behavioral flexibility* in the Strange Situation (Main, 1996, 2000). As previously noted, Main proposed that the rigid patterns of behavior exhibited by some infants were evidence of insecure attachment. She contrasted this with the more flexible responses observed in securely attached infants. Main made a similar assumption about the connection between attachment security and *attentional flexibility* in adults, and this assumption is reflected in the AAI coding system. Adults classified as secure-autonomous are those who are able to fluidly shift their attention from describing attachment related experiences, to responding to requests to evaluate the influences of these experiences. In contrast, *attentional inflexibility*, as evidenced in a subject's dismissal of the importance of past attachment experiences, or their preoccupation with these experiences, is evidence of an insecure state of mind with respect to attachment (Hesse, 2008).

In addition to classifying an individual as secure, insecure-dismissing, or insecure-preoccupied, the AAI and coding scheme are designed to elicit evidence regarding experiences of loss and trauma, and to determine the extent to which these experiences continue to impact the subject's thinking and behavior. A classification of "unresolved with respect to loss" is assigned when a respondent's narrative of early loss and/or trauma is disjointed, tangential, and otherwise lacking in coherence and consistency (Hesse, 2008). This classification is associated with a range of psychological difficulties, including problems in recognizing and regulating emotion (DeOliveira et al., 2005), personality disorders (Fonagy et al., 2000; Liotti, 2014), and complicated grief (Thomson, 2010). In sum, the AAI "examines whether adults have developed a psychologically mature account of early attachment experiences and their ongoing impact on personality" (Roisman, 2009, p.122)—something that we will later describe as a "reflective" stance on experience, and in particular, the experience of loss.

By administering the AAI to mothers of infants observed in the Strange Situation, Main was able to establish a strong correlation between the attachment security of a mother and that of her child (Main et al., 1985). Main reported that the parent to infant match across the secure versus insecure categories averaged 75% (Main, 1996, p.240). Similarly noteworthy was the finding that infant behavior in the Strange Situation could be predicted based on a mother's responses to the AAI *before the child was born* (Fonagy et al., 2000). As fascinating as these early results were, they were only the beginning, as Main and her colleagues continued to look for a way of explaining why some children of mothers who report early abuse or neglect develop a secure attachment orientation, while others behave in a way that suggests insecure, and even disorganized, attachment.

Main employed the terms *meta-cognition* and *meta-cognitive monitoring* to describe the processes by which we examine our own minds and the minds of others. She proposed that a speaker with the ability to monitor and correct their speech in the course of the conversation is able to reflect on a traumatic experience in a coherent manner, without the lapses in monitoring of reason or discourse illustrated in the examples given. Analyzing the transcripts of mothers whose infants demonstrated the kind of unusual behavioral patterns that have been described, it became increasingly clear that what the parents of disorganized infants had in common were indications of what were termed "lapses in the monitoring of reasoning or discourse" (Hesse, 2008, p.57). The narratives given by these respondents have their own kind of strangeness, including breaks in logic or coherence that suggest "temporary alterations in consciousness or working memory" (Hesse, 2008, p.570). Lapses in the monitoring of *reason* are manifested in statements that violate our usual assumptions about causality or time and space, as when a speaker makes a statement indicating that a "person is believed simultaneously to be dead and not dead in the physical sense" (Hesse & Main, 2000, p.112).

> "It was almost better when she died, because then she could get on with being dead and I could go on with raising my family" (Hesse & Main, 2000, p.112). "This statement," the authors note, "implies that death is an activity that can be 'gotten on with'" (Hesse & Main, 2000, p.112).

Lapses in the monitoring of *discourse* are cited when the narrative is hard to follow, disjointed, excessively detailed, or metaphorical, suggesting that the speaker has entered into "peculiar, compartmentalized or even partially dissociated/segregated states of mind":

> We went to the hospital, let's see. I think it was the grey Buick, and I sat in the back to the right of my mother. I was wearing jeans and polo shirt, well not jeans, but you know, khakis, and we turned first down West Street, and then there was a kind of a lot of traffic, so we took . . .
>
> (Hesse & Main, 2000, p.113)

The authors suggest that this kind of fragmented narrative is evidence of unresolved trauma, and they propose that in these cases, the interviewer's questions "may have sparked or induced a momentary but dramatic alteration in the speaker's mental state" (Hesse & Main, 2000, p.113). In explaining the significance of this observation with respect to the attachment experience of the infant, Hesse and Main suggest that it is reasonable to assume that parents who respond in this fashion in the interview setting are also apt to experience "state shifts" when caring for their children. These state shifts, they further suggest, affect the child's mental state and attachment security.

> [These parents] . . . may at times become peculiarly frightened in response to aspects of the environment that are unconsciously associated with a traumatic event. Having entered such a state, the parent might exhibit anomalous forms of threatening, frightened, or overtly dissociated behavior, and the apparent inexplicability of such behaviors may, like overtly agonistic threats or direct maltreatment, be alarming to the infant.
>
> (Hesse & Main, 2000, p.113)

Research employing the AAI has provided a great deal of support for Main's hypotheses concerning the association between unresolved trauma, as evidenced by breakdowns in meta-cognitive monitoring and disorganized attachment in infants (Hesse, 2008). There is now little question of the link between the attachment security or insecurity of mothers and that of their children. Must we conclude then, that there exists an inviolable cycle in which insecure mothers transmit their insecurities to their children, who grow up to be insecure parents? Thanks to Main, and others who built upon her work, we know that this is not the case. But why not?

Earned Security: Accounting for the Differential Impact of Early Neglect and Trauma

The answer, Main proposed, lies in the evidence provided by the mother's responses to the AAI, and in particular, her ability to speak coherently and logically about her early life, including incidents of loss and trauma. Main noted that some mothers who reported significant early neglect and trauma were able to describe these experiences without lapsing into disorganized or illogical discourse; they were able to stay present, avoiding the lapse into an altered state as described earlier. In effect, these women had been able, by the time they reached adulthood, to develop a more secure attachment orientation— what Main termed "earned security" (Main, 1996). As an example, Main reasoned that if a person can understand that their mistreatment in childhood was not their fault, if they can understand that the harsh words and punitive actions of a parent did not reflect who they were as a child or who they are as an adult, this may serve to moderate what might otherwise be the damaging impact of early neglect or abuse. Moreover, if someone is able to understand some of what drove a parent to behave as they did, the overall sense of unfairness, resentment, and anger can also be moderated, and therefore may not be carried over into other relationships later in life. A person who has learned to reflect on and consider the thoughts and motives of others is a person who is less likely to react impulsively at the smallest hint of another person's apparent disregard or anger. As one researcher puts it, adults who have developed a "psychologically mature account" of their early attachment experiences and how they continue to impact their personality are better equipped than those who have not done so to manage a variety of stresses, including the stress of parenthood, and to remain present and in control when responding to what can be the challenging behavior of young children (Roisman, 2009, p.122).

As an example, consider a woman who has spent several years thinking and talking about her childhood trauma as she shares what has come to be her understanding of the circumstances that contributed to her father's violent behavior. Note that she is able to reflect in a coherent manner on the events that precipitated her father's descent into alcoholism and violence:

Lorraine

"After my brother died, my father was never the same. He started drinking more than ever, coming home drunk. They had another baby—my sister. My father was terrible to her, hit her, yelled at her, and she's had problems with drugs and alcohol her whole life. I always blamed him. But as I think about it now—my brother was 4 years old. And my dad and he were really close. I can't imagine how it must have devastated him to lose his only son. Maybe if my sister had been a boy, things could have been different in my family."

Another important development in attachment research was the introduction, by Peter Fonagy and his colleagues, of an approach to *operationalizing and measuring meta-cognition in the mother.* This was work that established the crucial role that a mother's capacity to *understand what is in the mind of her child* plays in providing a secure base (Fonagy et al., 2000).

Fonagy: From a Theory of Mind to a Theory of Other Minds

Fonagy introduced the term *reflective functioning* to describe the psychological processes underlying the capacity to be aware of the internal mental states and affective experiences of others, a capacity he referred to as *mentalizing* (Fonagy et al., 1998). Drawing from the questions included in the AAI protocol, Fonagy and his colleagues constructed and validated a sub-scale, the Reflective Functioning Scale, which yields an assessment (RF) from -1 (totally lacking in mentalization or grossly distorting the mental representations of others) to 9 (exceptional RF, in which interviews show unusually complex, elaborate, or original reasoning about mental states).

Fonagy and his colleagues proposed that a mother's ability to mentalize is crucial to the development of attachment security in her child. They reasoned that a mother who is able to hold in mind the thoughts and feelings of her child is more likely to be able to understand her child's intentions and behaviors. This understanding enables her to respond in a measured way to the child's behavior. The child whose mother responds with warmth and understanding rather than with anger is more likely to be securely attached, and this relational security provides a fertile ground for the development of the child's own capacities for mentalization and self-regulation (Fonagy et al., 1991).

The work of Fonagy and his team established mentalization/reflective functioning as the *core capacity* that enables caregivers to provide a secure base for their children, even if their own early attachment experiences were insecure or traumatic (Fonagy et al., 2000). In a study examining the role of parents' reflective functioning in relation to their children's attachment orientation, Fonagy found that among parents whose self-narratives led to a classification of "insecure" on the AAI, those with high RF scores were more likely to have securely attached children than those with low RF scores (Fonagy et al., 2000). In accounting for this finding, the investigators suggest that mothers who are high in reflective functioning are able to make sense of their own attachment experience and also to hold their child's internal affective experience in mind. The combination of coherence of their own childhood narrative and *the capacity to understand their child's behavior with respect to his or her feelings* supports the mother's ability to respond empathically, thereby providing her child with a sense of security and safety.

Researchers continue to find evidence of the importance of mentalization as a factor in mental health and in the development of meaningful, sustaining relationships (Allen, 2013; Fonagy et al., 2014). We will have more to say about mentalizing in relation to bereavement in Chapter 4, and in Part III we will discuss restoration of mentalizing capacity as a therapeutic goal in work with the bereaved, and closely related to the process of meaning reconstruction after loss.

Social Psychology: Investigations of Adult Attachment

Hazan and Shaver: Adult Romantic Relationships

In Bowlby's writing, the term "attachment relationship" refers to the child's relationship with a primary caregiver, the person most depended on for nurturance and protection (Bowlby, 1977, 2005). In the 1980s, Hazan and Shaver advanced the idea that this term can also be used to characterize emotionally intimate ("romantic") relationships between adults (Hazan & Shaver, 1987).

In support of this view, Hazan and Shaver identified what they saw as the many similarities between infant/caregiver relationships and the relationship between adult romantic partners: the feeling of security felt by each member of the dyad when the partner is nearby and responsive; the discomfort experienced when the other is inaccessible; and what the authors describe as the mutual fascination and preoccupation of romantic partners, a state of absorption that is comparable to the sustained, intense gaze shared by a mother and her infant (Hazan & Shaver, 1987). According to Hazan and Shaver, if romantic relationships qualify as attachment relationships, we would expect to see the same kinds of variation in adult response to separation that Ainsworth observed in infant–caregiver relationships. That is, an attachment model of romantic relationships would predict that some adults are secure in relation to their partners, others are insecure, and when separated, these insecure adults will behave in either an anxious or avoidant manner similar to the infants observed by Ainsworth in the Strange Situation.

To investigate their suppositions about adult romantic relationships, Hazan and Shaver asked subjects to choose from among three statements the one that best represented their feelings and behavior in close relationships (for example, "I want to be completely emotionally intimate with others, but I often find that others are reluctant to get as close as I would like" (Bartholomew & Horowitz, 1991)). Based on their responses, Hazan and Shaver identified three categories of attachment (Secure, Avoidant, and Anxious/ Ambivalent), the distribution of which was comparable to that found among infants and children in the Strange Situation. That is, 60% of adults chose the statement representing secure attachment, about 20% identified with the avoidant statement, and the same percentage identified with the statement that emphasized anxiety as a corollary of intimacy with others.

In their initial studies, Hazan and Shaver found that respondents' self-reported attachment patterns in adult relationships were related to a number of variables referenced in attachment theory, including beliefs (working models) about love and relationships and recollections of early experiences with parents (Hazan & Shaver, 1987). For example, people who identified themselves as secure in romantic relationships were more likely to report warm relationships with their parents, as well as harmonious relationships between their parents, whereas anxious/ambivalent adults were more likely to report conflicted relationships with and between their parents. People self-identified as avoidant in their romantic relationships were more likely to describe their mothers as cool and rejecting, they reported a fear of intimacy, and expressed a general view that romantic love does not last (Hazan & Shaver, 1987).

Hazan and Shaver's research was followed by hundreds of studies of adult attachment, the results of which led the authors to revise their theory. Their original formulation assumed that all romantic relationships were attachment relationships, an assumption that was not supported by research. Additionally, research by Bartholomew and Horowitz indicated that individual differences in adult attachment reflected two underlying dimensions: *attachment related anxiety* and *attachment related avoidance* (Bartholomew & Horowitz, 1991). Bartholomew and Horowitz also interpreted their findings as indicating that the working models of adults consist of two parts: one dealing with thoughts about others, and the other dealing with thoughts about the self. The four categories of attachment proposed by Bartholomew and Horowitz are shown in Figure 2.1.

Note that in this model, the avoidant category in Hazan and Shaver's model breaks into two categories: "Fearful" and "Dismissive." Whereas people in the first category avoid close relationships with others because they are afraid of being hurt, people in the second category do so because they prefer not to rely on others for comfort or help. Bartholomew and Horowitz's model also includes a category of people who are high in dependence and low in avoidance ("Preoccupied"); these individuals worry about the availability of others in close relationships. Bartholomew and Horowitz used this model to create the Relationship Questionnaire (RQ-CV), which consists of four sets of statements similar to those used by Hazan and Shaver. An updated version of this scale, the Experiences in Close Relationships (Revised) Scale (ECR-R) (Wei et al., 2007), is among the most widely used self-report measures of attachment.

Evidence Regarding the Impact of Early Attachment Experience

We return now to questions regarding the origin, transmission, and maintenance of attachment orientation. In the past 10 years, the availability of large data sets and the

MODEL OF SELF
(Dependence)

	Positive (Low in dependence)	Negative (High in dependence)
Positive (Low in avoidance)	**CELL I** SECURE Comfortable with intimacy and autonomy	**CELL II** PREOCCUPIED Preoccupied with relationships
Negative (High in avoidance)	**CELL IV** DISMISSING Dismissing of intimacy Counter-dependent	**CELL III** FEARFUL Fearful of intimacy Socially avoidant

MODEL OF OTHER
(Avoidance)

Figure 2.1 Attachment styles: The four category model. Adapted from Bartholomew and Horowitz (1991, p.244). Copyright 1991 by the American Psychological Association (APA).

development of increasingly sophisticated methods of data analysis have enabled researchers to offer new insight into the mechanisms of attachment, their operation, and the stability of relational models established in the earliest years of life. Two related questions that have continued to attract the attention of researchers are:

- Does attachment orientation in childhood tend to persist? Is it predictive of attachment style in adulthood?
- What effect does attachment security or insecurity have on people's ability to establish and maintain relationships?

As previously noted, research on attachment has been conducted by investigators with diverse interests, using different methods and employing methods of analysis that vary considerably in their complexity (Bornstein, 2014). Differences between developmental research, much of it using interview methods, and research by social psychologists, who have continued to favor self-report measures, and the divergent systems of categorization used in these two branches of study, make it difficult to compare or combine results into a cohesive portrayal of the state of our knowledge of attachment. In an effort to address this problem, Lopez (Lopez, 2009), has consolidated developmental and social psychological research on attachment into three domains of inquiry: Developmental and Family Histories; Cognitive–Affective Patterns and Coping Processes; and Types of Interpersonal Problems and Relationship Difficulties. These domains "parallel likely arenas of therapeutic exploration, and as such may hold particular promise as guideposts for the differential assessment of clients' adult attachment organization" (Lopez, 2009, p.99).

Developmental and Family History Correlates

> The start does not fix the course or outcome of development, but it clearly exerts an impact on both.
>
> (Bornstein, 2014, p.145)

A fundamental assumption of attachment theory is that responsive, attentive, and loving caregiving promotes attachment security in children. This assumption has been supported by decades of research (Fonagy et al., 2014; Mikulincer & Shaver, 2007), and by several longitudinal studies (Fraley et al., 2013; Grossmann et al., 2005). The question of whether attachment security or insecurity in childhood persists into adulthood is more complex. As Bornstein suggests in his recent research review, the experiences of childhood constitute a significant, but not exclusive influence on identity and functioning in adulthood (Bornstein, 2014).

That said, the advantages of a good beginning are undeniable; children who have the kind of secure base that Bowlby describes develop internal resources that help them learn, interact, and productively manage their feelings in the short term, and in many cases, for the rest of their lives. Children who are secure in their attachment relationships tend to feel more secure in their adult relationships (Shaver et al., 2005), are less likely to report higher levels of depressive symptoms (Hankin et al., 2005), and tend to cope more effectively in response to stressful events (Berant et al., 2008).

As noted, early attachment experience has traditionally been the research domain of developmental psychologists, who have employed interview based measures such as the AAI to assess parents' *state of mind with respect to attachment*. Recently, however, social psychologists have become interested in parents' *attachment style* as an influence on various aspects of parenting, and they have used self-report measures to study the role of attachment in parenting behaviors, emotions, and cognitions. A recently published review of research on the relationship between parents' attachment styles and self-reported and observed parenting behaviors (Jones et al., 2015), includes a number of findings that are highly relevant to our understanding of the development of core capacities for social and emotional functioning. These capacities have a great deal to do with how people form, and later cope with the loss of, close relationships. For example, several of the studies reviewed suggest that secure mothers are better able to cope with the demands of parenting than are insecure mothers, are more likely to seek support when needed, and in general, report less stress than parents with an anxious or avoidant attachment style (Jones et al., 2015). These studies complement AAI based research on the impact of attachment security or insecurity on maternal attunement and responsiveness. The authors suggest that it would be "interesting to examine how parental state of mind in the AAI relates to these specific feelings related to parenthood and to compare these findings to those in the attachment style literature" (Jones et al., 2015, p.17).

At the time of his review, Lopez described research correlating AAI classifications with independent measures of family history or parental representations as limited, and inconsistent with respect to findings (Lopez, 2009, p.100). Studies using self-report measures have provided more consistent evidence linking early family environment to attachment in adulthood (Lopez, 2009). Adults with secure attachment styles report more positive early bonds with parents (Collins & Feeney, 2004), and fewer experiences of childhood adversity (Mickelson et al., 1997). When compared to respondents with a secure attachment orientation, insecurely attached individuals describe one or both of their parent's behavior as hostile (Gallo et al., 2003). Researchers have also looked at contextual factors that may impact the quality of the caregiving environment. Maternal depression, for example, interferes with the parent's ability to provide a supportive environment for the child (Mickelson et al., 1997). Parental divorce, father absence, and low socioeconomic status are also related to insecure attachment in adulthood (Chisholm et al., 2005).

Cognitive–Affective Correlates

> The more favorably organized internal working models of people with a secure attachment style or state of mind are also presumed to optimize their capacity for open, flexible cognitive processing and memory retrieval of attachment information, thereby facilitating more competent affect regulation.
>
> (Lopez, 2009, p.101)

Questions about how variations in attachment security correlate with variations in cognitive and affect regulating functions have also been the subject of ongoing investigation. Findings from these studies bear directly on a central question posed by bereavement researchers, namely, how to account for variations in the nature of people's adaptation to significant loss. One possible explanation, as Lopez's comment suggests, is that adverse early experience inhibits access to information about feelings and results in a diminished ability to cope with stressful, emotion generating situations. Lacking an internal sense of direction with regard to feelings, these individuals would find such situations challenging and even frightening. The ability to experience emotion and to reregulate in the wake of emotional upset is a capacity that is important, if not essential, to adaptive grieving (Mikulincer & Shaver, 2013; Mikulincer et al., 2013). What brings many of our clients into treatment is the breakdown, or underdeveloped nature, of these capacities.

Main, Fonagy, and researchers in the developmental tradition have emphasized the correlation between attachment orientation and cognitive functioning (meta-cognition and meta-processing, mentalization, and affective regulatory capacity) (Fonagy et al., 2014; Main, 1996). The AAI classifies as having a secure-autonomous state of mind with respect to attachment respondents who are able to access, retrieve, and appropriately describe both positive and painful attachment related memories without becoming overly emotional or lapsing into tangential or excessively detailed narratives. It is assumed that their ability to engage in this way is grounded in an integrated, resilient self structure that enables the individual *to move fluidly between self-reflection and self-soothing, when necessary, and reorientation to the interview questions when equilibrium has been regained.* This capacity for flexible attention, as we will see in Chapter 4, is associated with adaptive coping in response to loss, as is the ability to access painful memories.

Support for the role of attachment security in cognitive functioning and affect regulation has also come from social psychological studies of adult attachment. In one early study Mikulincer and Florian (Mikulincer & Florian, 1998) concluded that secure attachment functions as an "inner resource" that helps to cushion the blow of stressful events, including interpersonal losses. Other investigators have reported that securely attached adults are more likely to seek support from others than avoidant adults (Davis et al., 2003). This finding is directly relevant to adaptation to bereavement, since there is an established link between the availability of social support and the positive trajectory of healing from loss (Kaniasty, 2012).

These variations in cognitive and affective functioning may in part reflect important differences in people's access to and management of attachment related memories, as theorized by Main (Main, 1996). In fact, studies have found that those with a secure attachment orientation have easier access to negative memories than their insecure peers. Preoccupied persons, while capable of accessing these memories, tend to be thrown off by intense emotion in the telling; and avoidant individuals demonstrate low accessibility to negative affects (Mikulincer & Orbach, 1995).

Lopez reports that overall, research studies are in accord regarding the advantages of early attachment security in the development of an array of capacities related to stress management, constructive coping, and optimal adjustment, with the opposite results being observed in individuals with avoidant or anxious attachment styles (Lopez, 2009). Davis and colleagues, in a study of physical, emotional, and behavioral reactions to relationship breakup, found that in general, stressed, secure adults demonstrate adaptive forms of coping and, when necessary, enlist the emotional support of others (Davis et al., 2003). In a complementary finding, Mikulincer and Shaver found that when faced with attachment related distress, preoccupied adults are more likely to ruminate on their emotions, thereby exacerbating their distress, while avoidant adults tend to engage in distancing coping behaviors such as denying the distressing impact of a negative event, minimizing their need for help from others, and inhibiting emotional displays (Mikulincer & Shaver, 2007).

Social Competencies and Relationship Problems

Attachment theory and research offer insights regarding many of the interpersonal problems that bring people into treatment, including the loss of a loved one. As suggested by the preceding discussion of cognitive and emotional capacities, people with a secure attachment orientation are able to behave flexibly with regard to attachment, such that they neither avoid nor anxiously pursue intimacy with others (Lopez, 2009).

In contrast, findings from both interview and self-report studies confirm that the excessive demands for reassurance and support that people with a predominantly preoccupied, anxious orientation may make can cause problems in their relationships, leading to the very loss of connection that they most fear (Shaver et al., 2005). The problems reported by avoidantly attached people, as might be expected, have to do not with excessive dependence, but with what others see as their aloofness and indifference to partners (Bartholomew & Horowitz, 1991; Gross & John, 2003).

Based on his review of findings from developmental and social psychology across these domains, Lopez proposes four "Profiles of Adult Attachment Organization: Secure, Preoccupied, Dismissing and Fearful," shown in Table 2.1 (Lopez, 2009). These categories roughly correspond to the categories of Secure, Anxious, Avoidant, and Disorganized, which for simplicity's sake, will be consistently used in the remainder of this book.

Table 2.1 Summary of Adult Attachment Organization Correlates across Three Clinically Relevant Domains From Lopez, in Obegi and Berant (2009). Reprinted with permission

Developmental/ family history	Cognitive–affective processes	Social competencies/ relationship problems
Secure attachment organization		
• Favorable early parental bonds; positive, differentiated parental representations • Stable, satisfying relationship histories • Less childhood adversity • Mature, integrated personality orientation	• Enhanced capacity for self-reflection; flexible cognitive processing of attachment information • Greater access to both positive and negative affect, memories; more adaptive coping • More resilient, coherent, positive self-structure	• Higher-quality self-disclosure • More collaborative problem-solving orientation • More stable, satisfying intimate relationships • Need-contingent support seeking, caregiving
Preoccupied attachment organization		
• Less warm, more enmeshed parental relationships • Parental representations as both punitive and benevolent • Dependent personality orientation	• Reflective capacities impaired by negative associations • Reactive, emotion-focused coping; low self-esteem • Less open to assimilating new information about others	• Excessive reassurance seeking; controlling • Seeks but devalues social feedback • Poor caregiving skills
Dismissing attachment organization		
• Early parental bonds as less warm and caring • Less differentiated, more punitive parental representations • Counterdependent personality orientation	• Poor recall, integration of attachment memories • Distancing, denial, and distraction as coping strategies • Suppresses attachment-related affect; defensive self-esteem	• Low self-disclosure; viewed as aloof, detached • Unlikely to seek social support when stressed • Neither seeks nor values social feedback
Fearful attachment organization		
• More disrupted, traumatic early bonds • Well-differentiated, malevolent parental representations • More likely exposure to physical/sexual abuse • Socially avoidant personality orientation	• Chronic vulnerability to stress • Tendency to dissemble, dissociate when faced with attachment-related threats • Self-critical depression; low self-esteem	• Passive, unassertive, exploitable • Poor social and support-seeking skills • Less satisfying and stable intimate relationships

Summary

Attachment theory began as a template for understanding the impact of early relational experience on human development and functioning. It has been extended to studies of relationships in adulthood, and to the investigation of how people cope under conditions of extreme stress. Some writers have suggested that the diversity of the literature on attachment, the variety of questions posed, the multiplicity of methods used, and the often complex analysis of data presented, have prevented clinicians from accessing and utilizing this information. While that may have been the case in the past, recent efforts to translate and consolidate attachment theory and research have gone far to bridge the gap that separates investigation from practice. At the same time, the field itself has become more integrated, as evidenced by the growing convergence and complementarity between theory and research in developmental and social psychology regarding attachment. All in all, we have substantially more information, and more coherent and accessible information about attachment, than we did even 10 years ago.

This is not to say that we have clear answers to many of the most basic questions about attachment as a factor in human development and the long term impact of early attachment on lifelong mental health. For example, there is still much to be learned about the continuing influence of early working models on adult attachment style. While research demonstrates that the effects of early experience can be detected well into adulthood, this does not mean that there is a straight line trajectory between attachment in childhood and in adulthood. Indeed, it would be surprising, and even disheartening, if we could predict with confidence that anxiously attached children grow up to be anxiously attached adults. As clinicians, we want to believe that corrective emotional experiences—including the experience of therapy—can modify, if not override, the negative messages transmitted to people as children, and there is evidence to support this belief. But the capacity of people to unlearn old lessons and learn new ones is variable—some beliefs, bred in the bone at an early age, are harder to change than others.

Within the expansive intellectual enterprise that is attachment studies, certain aspects of theory and research are of particular relevance to our understanding of the ways in which people respond to loss. In this chapter we have discussed Main's theoretical work on the role of parents' own attachment experiences in the attachment orientation of their offspring, Fonagy's identification of the role of reflective functioning in the development of attachment security, evidence concerning the development and stability of attachment patterns from infancy to adulthood, and findings concerning the impact of attachment orientation on adult relationships. This literature provides a foundation for the remainder of the book with regard to the role of attachment in emotion regulation, and the connection between early attachment security and the ability to reflect on one's loss experiences and cope with the death of a loved one.

One thing that has not changed since Bowlby introduced attachment theory is the recognition that the quality of early caregiving matters. Our understanding of the critical role of early caregiving has been greatly extended by research into the development and functioning of the brain. In the following chapter, we will look at evidence from neuroscience regarding the ongoing effect of early experience on the development of mentalizing and other core capacities related to how people form relationships, how they manage stress, and how they are able to regulate affect. We will look at what neuroscientists are teaching us about optimal and non-optimal human development, secure and disordered patterns of attachment, and what this new knowledge tells us about the nature and process of therapeutic change.

3 Attachment Theory in the Decade of the Brain

> The self-organization of the developing brain occurs in the context of a relationship with another self, another brain.
>
> (A. N. Schore, 2003a, p.5)

> When one or more neural networks necessary for optimal functioning remain under developed, under regulated or under integrated with others, we experience the complaints and symptoms for which people seek therapy. We now assume that when psychotherapy results in symptom reduction or experiential change, the brain has, in some way, been altered.
>
> (Cozolino, 2010, p.13)

Why Should Neuroscience Matter to Grief Therapists?

As much as their interests may diverge, researchers and clinicians in the field of death and dying share a desire to account for the variation in people's responses to loss, and questions about the source of these differences have been a major focus of study. Attachment theory suggests that the answers to these questions can often be found in the details of people's early environment, and in particular, the quality of care they received as infants and young children. Ideally, the environment in which a child first becomes aware of the existence of other people promotes a sense of security that encourages exploration and engagement with others. An essential component of this environment is the child's relationship with a primary caregiver who is more or less consistent in providing the child with responsive nurture in times of emotional distress. Through this relationship with an attentive caregiver, a child learns that difficult thoughts and feelings can be managed and stressful situations mastered, first with the help of the caregiver and eventually on his own.

The processes through which self-regulatory capacity develops are relational, experiential, and neurological. Along with transmitting worldviews about how to understand the self, others, and events, parents help children develop the neurological substructure that supports healthy emotional and social functioning (A. N. Schore, 2003a, 2009). In this sense, a person's ability to manage difficult feelings is a window into the past, a clue to the quality of care they received as a child. In this chapter we will discuss findings from neuroscience that help explain the connection between early relational experience, neurobiological development, and the capacity for emotion regulation, meaning-making, and adaptation to loss in adulthood (Porges, 2011; A. N. Schore, 2009).

Much of what we have come to understand about brain development and functioning is the result of research that has been made possible by advances in technology over the past two decades (O'Connor, 2005). Computerized tomography (CT), magnetic resonance imaging (MRI), and most importantly, functional magnetic resonance imaging (fMRI), have enabled neuroscientists to produce dimensional pictures of the brain and to explore complex activation–deactivation patterns of brain activity in subjects performing cognitive, emotional, and behavioral tasks (Cozolino, 2010). Using these methods, researchers have mapped functional responsibilities to different brain regions and augmented earlier studies about learning, memory, emotional processing, and behavioral responses associated with forming and maintaining bonds.

Our appreciation of the role of attachment bonds and emotion in the growth and development of our brains has also deepened as a result of research made possible by advances in technology. Neurological development, it is clear, occurs in the context of our relationships with others, from our earliest caregivers to the people with whom we form close connections as adults (Cozolino, 2014; D. J. Siegel, 2012a). This perspective is part of the emerging field of *interpersonal neurobiology*, an interdisciplinary approach to understanding brain development, the impact of trauma on brain structure and function, and the mechanisms of therapeutic change. Insights from neuroscience have been incorporated into models of psychotherapy that are designed to take advantage of what is now seen as the essential contribution of the therapeutic relationship to emotional healing (A. N. Schore, 2012; D. J. Siegel, 2012b).

The idea that it is the therapeutic relationship, rather than the particulars of theory or technique, that makes change possible is not new (Norcross, 2011). What *is* new is our understanding of the mechanisms by which change occurs and the essential elements of the therapeutic relationship that make it possible. The work of Eric Kandel, the first American psychiatrist to win the Nobel Prize in physiology or medicine, has gone far toward advancing the view that when psychotherapy results in symptom reduction or experiential change, *the brain has in some way been altered* (Kandel, 1998; Kandel et al., 2013). The primary mechanism of this kind of change is the therapeutic relationship, and specifically, *right brain to right brain emotional processes* not unlike the process through which the brain develops early in life (A. N. Schore, 2009). Effective psychotherapy, then, is that which engages the client's *emotion focused right hemisphere* as well as the language focused left hemisphere, and promotes the development of the individual's ability to manage emotion. Interdisciplinary research and updated clinical models suggest that "the right hemisphere is dominant in treatment" and that psychotherapy is not so much a "talking cure" as it is an "affect communicating and regulating cure" (A. N. Schore, 2009, p.128). We will return later to Schore's model and the research on which it is based, and its implications for psychotherapy. But first things first: to lay the foundation for this discussion, it is necessary to begin with a brief, orienting review of the organization and development of the brain.

Advances and Limitations in Our Understanding of the Brain

While our models of the brain, processes in the brain, and brain–body functioning have grown increasingly sophisticated, it is important to recognize that these models are supported by varying degrees of scientific evidence, and as such, are continually being challenged and revised. The enormous complexity of the brain and the highly integrative nature of brain functioning, as well as fundamental differences of opinion about research methods and the interpretation of results, make it difficult to arrive at a consensus about how the brain develops and operates (Parens & Johnston, 2014).

One of the factors that limit our ability to make definitive statements about the location of specific activities within the brain is the sheer number of operating parts it contains. The human brain has an estimated 86 billion neurons, each of which establishes thousands (estimates range from 1,000 to 10,000) of synapses or connections with neighboring cells (Azevedo et al., 2009). Neuroscientists talk about the organization of these cells in terms of bounded segments, "regions" of the brain, much as we might discuss "regions" of a country. In reality, neurological boundaries, like governmental boundaries (for instance, state borders), are not naturally occurring, but arbitrarily established. They serve a purpose, to be sure. But particularly with respect to the brain, when we talk about the "functions" of these "regions" we do not want to lose sight of the discrepancy between our representation of the brain, and the brain as it actually exists.

The functioning of the brain is thus more accurately represented as being simultaneously holistic and distributed. That is, the activity that is related to end functions (e.g., vision and hearing) occurs across many areas of the brain, including some that are very old in a phylogenetic or evolutionary sense and are typically more emotional and action oriented, and some relatively new parts of the brain that are involved with thinking or executive functioning. These newer parts of the brain have more to do with our capacity to make reasoned decisions and to inhibit impulses to act that arise from phylogenetically older parts of the brain. The distributed nature of information processing means that healthy functioning depends not only on the integrity of discrete areas of the brain, but also on the integrity of the brain's connective circuitry. The more complex the task, the greater the need for integration and the greater the potential for compromised functioning if this circuitry is impaired or damaged (Riva et al., 2011). *The role of integration in healthy brain functioning is a basic premise of interpersonal neurobiology* (D. J. Siegel, 2012b)*, and it informs our understanding of psychological and neurological integration as the goal of all psychotherapy, including grief therapy, as discussed in Part III.*

Brain Organization

As Siegel has helpfully pointed out, the major (Figure 3.1) regions of the brain can be visualized by using the human hand as a physical metaphor (D. J. Siegel, 2012b).

With the hand open and the thumb folded over the palm, the tips of the fingers represent the middle prefrontal cortex, and the thumb represents the limbic system, which includes the amygdala and the hippocampus. With the fingers closed over the thumb, the top of the hand (the middle joint of the fingers) represents the cerebral cortex, which is now enclosing the limbic region. The soft, meatier part of the palm below the thumb corresponds to the brainstem. The very top of the wrist corresponds to the base of the skull and the wrist corresponds to the top of the spinal column.

Staying with this model for a moment, we can say that the evolutionary development of our brains occurred from the "wrist up." The brainstem is the oldest part of the brain in terms of evolutionary development, i.e., phylogenetically. Broadly speaking, it is

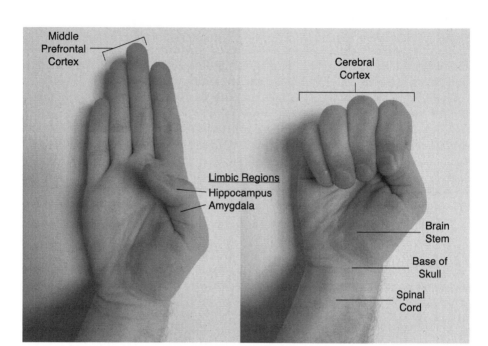

Figure 3.1 Hand model of the brain. Based on D. J. Siegel (2012a), *The developing mind: How relationships and the brain interact to shape who we are*, p.20, Guilford Press

concerned with mediating states of arousal and regulating automatic functions like breathing and heart rate. The brainstem also houses neurons that trigger the "fight, flight, or freeze" response when we perceive danger.

The next part of the brain to develop was the limbic system, which is generally involved in the generation and regulation of emotion. It also has an important role in our ability to interpret social cues and make sense of other people's behavior. All of these functions make the limbic system particularly important in mediating the response to loss and separation. Researchers interested in how early attachment affects emotional functioning have paid particular attention to the development of the limbic system, and as we will see shortly, this research is relevant to our understanding of the impact of early attachment on adaptation to loss, and to the response to trauma at any developmental point in life.

Last to develop was the cerebrum (cerebral cortex), also called the upper brain. The cerebral cortex is responsible for the cognitive skills of logic, creativity, intuition, and decision-making, and it also has a central role in the ability to understand and narrate emotional experiences. The cerebral cortex is further divided into four lobes: frontal, parietal, occipital, and temporal. The frontal lobe is necessary for higher level functions, including thinking, planning, and emotional reflection. The parietal lobe is broadly associated with motor control, the occipital lobe with visual processing, and the temporal lobe with memory formation and sensory processing. The temporal lobe of the left hemisphere is particularly important for speech recognition.

As a researcher, clinician, and educator, Siegel has been at the forefront of efforts to bring knowledge of the brain to the practice of psychotherapy. But his belief in the importance of understanding how our brains work extends beyond psychotherapy to how we parent, how we form relationships, and how we understand our own behavior and emotions (D. J. Siegel, 2012a). When we understand how the brainstem operates, for example, we can be more forgiving of our automatic responses in situations that threaten or upset us. This knowledge, shared with clients who have blamed themselves for actions taken under extreme circumstances, can help alleviate ruminative guilt and self-criticism. One of the most important and life enhancing impacts of an understanding of the brain, Siegel proposes, is that it supports a more compassionate view of the self: "'This may not be my fault because my brain did this, but it is my responsibility to make a change' is a common response from those who are taught about the brain" (D. J. Siegel, 2012b, p.3–2).

This same principle—that there will be situations in which more evolved systems for decision-making and action are overridden by more primitive neurological functioning—is also a feature of the triune model of the brain introduced in the 1960s by the neuroscientist Paul MacLean (MacLean, 1990). In concordance with Siegel's tripartite "hand metaphor" model, MacLean also argued that our brain is actually three brains in one, and incorporates structures found in reptiles (the reptilian brain), in mammals (the paleomammalian brain), and uniquely, in humans (the neo-mammalian brain). As a result, we have a variety of sometimes conflicting ways of responding to environmental stimuli—in particular, our response may come from an older part of our brain when we feel threatened or angry. While the triune brain model has been criticized by some writers who find it to be an oversimplification of brain structure and functioning (Reiner, 1990), others see it as a useful metaphor, one that can be introduced to clients to help them understand the range of human behavior, from the lowest forms of "mindless" aggression to the upper reaches of creativity and concern for others (Hanson, 2013).

The development of an individual's brain over the course of his or her life mimics the evolutionary development of the human brain over many thousands of years, beginning first with regions involved in simple survival functions (respiration, digestion, movement), moving on to emotional processing, particularly of danger (e.g., from a predator) or possible reward (e.g., a food source or sexual partner), and continuing on with those involved in higher order cognitive functions such as thinking about, reflecting upon, and deciding about. At birth, the reptilian brain is fully functional and the paleomammalian brain is coming online; the cortex, however, is only just beginning to form. As a result, much of what we learn early in life is "organized and controlled by reflexes, behaviors, and emotions outside of our awareness and distorted by our immature brains" (Cozolino, 2010, p.9). Regardless of the quality of our early experience, we carry with us into adulthood implicit (unconscious) memories of feelings, interactions, and events from personal experiences before our brains were fully developed. This includes positive emotions of pleasure and security, and negative emotions of pain and/or threat. Also significant is the fact that these very early experiences occur before our brain's capacity for the use of language to understand and communicate our inner states comes online.

Brain Function and Functional Systems

The brain is comprised of a left and a right hemisphere, and most parts of the brain come in twos: two amygdalae, two hippocampi, etc. This is to be kept in mind in the discussion that follows, in which we refer to these parts in the singular (e.g., "the amygdala") when describing their function. Despite their essential structural symmetry, we now understand that the two hemispheres diverge considerably with respect to their primary functions. The left side of the brain generally controls conscious, cognitive, and verbal mental states while the right side has the lead role with regard to emotion and nonverbal cues, mostly below the level of consciousness. In the simplest (and unavoidably oversimplified) terms, the left brain deals with words and thoughts, the right brain with form and feelings. Evidence of the right brain's involvement in emotion processing, and the discovery that this part of the brain becomes operational earlier in a child's development than many left hemispheric language and reasoning functions, has fueled a major shift in the focus of psychotherapy from left to right brain processes (Cozolino, 2010, 2014; Cozolino & Santos, 2014; Montgomery, 2013; A. N. Schore, 2012; J. R. Schore & Schore, 2014). Although the two halves of the brain are specialized, optimal brain functioning requires integration through communication between the left and right hemispheres of the brain. The corpus callosum, a thick bundle of neural fibers that connects the two hemispheres, is the structural foundation for the flow of information between the two halves of the brain. As the brain matures, the corpus callosum becomes increasingly efficient, allowing for a more fluid integration of the two hemispheres.

The brain can be further divided by visible tissue markers, functional boundaries, or a combination of the two. Many systems for subdividing the brain have been proposed, and each of them is useful within particular contexts. Some of these systems, for example, the limbic system, are more widely accepted within the field of neuroscience than others of more recent origin. These newer systems, for example, the social engagement system (Porges, 2011) and the primal emotional systems (Panksepp & Biven, 2012), are essentially models about the operation of various complex brain functions that, as we noted previously, involve multiple regions of the brain acting in concert.

The Limbic System

The limbic system is a group of structures in the brain that play a major role in our experience of emotions, particularly the management of distressing emotions such as anger, fear, separation distress, and shame (Cozolino, 2014). The limbic system is usually described as including the prefrontal cortex, which along with the amygdala and hippocampus is crucial to the process of creating meaning and emotion.

The major functions of these structures are summarized here:

> **Amygdala:**   The amygdalae are two almond shaped masses on either side of the thalamus. Often referred to as the brain's "fear hub," the amygdala activates the brain's fight or flight response and is also involved in emotions and memory.
>
> **Hippocampus:**   Involved in creating and filing new memories. If the hippocampus is damaged, a person cannot build or store new memories.

Prefrontal Cortex: Closely linked to the limbic system, the prefrontal cortex appears to be involved in thinking about the future, making plans, and taking action.

The limbic system is what we rely on to interpret the facial expressions, moods, and intentions of other people. The signals we receive from this area of our brain are crucial for making us aware of danger and triggering an appropriate, self-protective behavioral response (Braun, 2011). The limbic system is also tightly linked to the autonomic nervous system (ANS) and, via the hypothalamus, regulates certain endocrine functions, such as the hormonal responses that occur when we are under stress. The central role of the limbic system in emotional and social functioning has made it the focus of research into the genesis of maladaptive patterns of development and the etiology of mental disorders (Braun, 2011). Given its involvement in emotional processing and the interpretation of interpersonal cues, the limbic system is a key player in the attachment system, the elaboration of which has been one focus of Allan Schore's contributions to interpersonal neurobiology.

The Attachment System and Right Brain Regulation: Allan Schore

Allan Schore is a psychiatrist and neuroscientist whose work has been singularly important in documenting the role of the right hemisphere, and the limbic system in particular, in the formation of attachment bonds in childhood. As the Schores have reported (A. N. Schore, 2012, 2013; J. R. Schore & Schore, 2008, 2014), recent research has substantiated the role of the right brain in affect regulation, and has also demonstrated how right brain development is affected by the quality of early care. In the best case, the process of dyadic, mutual regulation between child and caregivers fuels positive emotions, promotes mutual understanding, and fosters psychological intimacy, all elements of what Bowlby defined as a secure base (Bowlby, 2008). The child comes to depend on the parent as a source of comfort and safety; that is, he develops an internal model of the caregiver as responsive and protective. Thus supported, the child gradually develops an independent capacity for self-regulation (A. N. Schore, 2003a, 2003b, 2009).

Like Bowlby, Schore emphasizes the positive impact of a secure bond, and the influence of quality of care on identity formation, emotional functioning, and ultimately, on the ability to establish and maintain healthy relationships with others. Schore has also brought attention to the physiological consequences of early caregiving, and the advantages of moderate stress. Life itself is unavoidably stressful; episodic exposure to manageable levels of stress, accompanied by responsive caregiving from engaged and loving attachment figures, not only teaches the child that difficult feelings can be managed, but also enhances that capacity by stimulating the development of a healthy and stress resistant brain (A. N. Schore, 2009). For example, moderate stress increases the production of myelin, an insulator that enhances communication efficiency between neurons, in the orbitofrontal cortex, a region of the brain that controls arousal regulation and resilience (Katz et al., 2009).

Even more important than these results suggesting the benefits of moderate stress are alarming findings concerning the harmful impact of excessive stress, the kind to which infants are exposed in situations involving neglect, abuse, and trauma (Lanius et al., 2010). Researchers have documented that repeated traumatizing interactions between caregiver and child (including traumatizing separations) leave the child's stress response system (primarily the sympathetic nervous system (SNS) and hypothalamic-pituitary-adrenal (HPA) axis response) in a persistent state of hyperactivation. When this state persists over time, there is, in effect, a system overload, and the hyperaroused state gives way to a hypoaroused state, reflected in low energy and flattened affect. This "shutdown and withdraw" behavior is what mammals engage in when they are trapped in a threatening or stressful situation from which they cannot escape (Porges, 2011). Psychologically, this shutdown involves defensive dissociation to protect the person from a deeply distressing affective arousal that cannot be externally controlled. Schore maintains that this dissociative response, which he calls the "bottom line defense" (A. N. Schore, 2012, p.60), is the foundation of most forms of severe psychopathology.

Schore is one of a number of researchers whose contributions to the field of affective neuroscience cross disciplinary lines, bringing together biology, psychology, and physiology. Another contributor is Stephen Porges, whose work has provided a compelling explanation of how humans evolved a capacity for social engagement and how that capacity is impacted by early relational experience.

The Social Engagement System: Polyvagal Theory, and the Work of Stephen Porges

Porges' Polyvagal Theory refers to the vagus nerve, the tenth cranial nerve. The vagus nerve plays a crucial role in regulating activation and deactivation within the central nervous system, which is composed of the brain and spinal column (Figure 3.2).

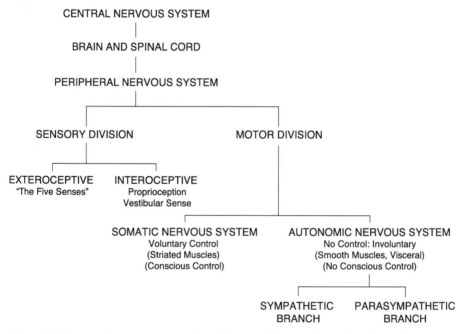

Figure 3.2 The central nervous system. From "Figure 1.0 Organization of the Central Nervous System," in Montgomery (2013), *Neurobiology essentials for clinicians: What every therapist needs to know.* Copyright 2013 by Arlene Montgomery. Used by permission of W. W. Norton & Company.

The rest of the nervous system is known as the peripheral nervous system, and is classically divided into the somatic or voluntary nervous system and the ANS. Note that the "voluntary" vs. "involuntary" divide is arguably less clear than it was once, since it has been demonstrated that people can be taught, through techniques like biofeedback or meditation, to regulate brain/body functions that were previously seen as involuntary (Baumann et al., 2011). The ANS has two branches: the SNS, which activates the "fight or flight" response, and the parasympathetic nervous system (PNS), which inhibits this arousal and triggers the "rest and digest" response. The vagus nerve has a central role in regulating the balance between the SNS and PNS. It also links the brain to other key organs, including the heart, brain, lungs, throat, and digestive system.

Of particular interest here is the fact that the vagal system is centrally involved in our response to threat. This system, shared by all mammals, originally evolved to allow an organism to respond to predators. Although most people no longer have to deal with life-threatening encounters with predators, this system continues to serve us (and potentially cause problems for us) whenever we are faced with a challenge or danger of any kind. This includes both physical and psychological threats, such as the threat inherent in the loss of a loved one to whom we are attached, or toward whom we feel caregiving responsibilities.

When we are faced with a sufficient amount of perceived threat, the SNS is activated, and our bodies prepare to attack the threat, or to flee from it. For example, blood is shunted from the digestive organs to large muscles in the arms and legs, so that we can make a more effective attack or a faster escape. When threat is present but neither fight nor flight will work, a third option is the "freeze" response. In its most primitive (and phylogenetically oldest) form, the freeze response involves feigning death so as to "trick" the predator into leaving us alone, and instead pursuing "live" prey. It is illuminating to realize that all of these responses have corresponding subjective feelings associated with them. Thus, "fight" is usually associated with angry, hostile feelings, and the desire to physically or verbally attack. "Flight" is associated with anxiety, fear, and a desire to hide or run away. "Freeze" is connected with psychological dissociation and numbness (Montgomery, 2013; A. N. Schore, 2012).

As Porges explains, the vagal system in humans evolved to allow for two different approaches to deactivation, or down-regulation of the SNS. These two vagal circuits, one "old" and one "new," correspond to the dorsal and ventral portions of the vagus nerve respectively. This differentiation of the vagal system provides for a more nuanced response from our peripheral nervous system to perceived threat in the environment— what is in effect a middle ground between SNS activation (all out fight or flight) and PNS activation (which leads to passive shutdown and withdrawal). Rather than running away, fighting, or becoming immobilized (what Porges calls "immobilization with fear") we have the ability to stay present when threatened by something without attacking or shutting down. Porges suggests that this *ability to stay put without shutting down is essential for social engagement.* The dorsal vagal circuit, which is not myelinated and which we share with more primitive species (e.g., reptiles), is involved with adaptive reactions characterized by immobilization and decreases in arousal and metabolic output (the "freeze" response of a mouse trapped in the mouth of a cat). In contrast, the myelinated ventral circuit down-regulates activation of the SNS. Thus, the newer ventral circuit is involved in producing the calm but alert state that allows for social engagement by balancing sympathetic and parasympathetic activation (Porges, 2009, 2011). Porges calls this capacity to modulate our response to interpersonal threat and to engage socially with others, "vagal tone." Vagal tone refers to our ability to make realistic and appropriate appraisal of threat (particularly interpersonal or social threat), and to make nuanced, rather than blunt, responses to the threat or the safety of our social environment.

How does our nervous system "know" whether or not we are safe? According to Porges, we make this determination based on cues received through *neuroception*, "a neural process that is distinct from perception and that is capable of distinguishing environmental features and visceral reactions that are safe, dangerous, or life threatening" (Porges, 2009, p.45). Foremost among these cues are the signals read from another person's nonverbal behavior, such as facial expressions and tone of voice. This explains why Porges calls this sophisticated vagal circuit the "social engagement system." This system also provides us with feedback about our own, internal physiological state, particularly our heart rate, lung functioning, and digestive processes. Neuroceptive cues from the body are implicitly or unconsciously processed by the brain, and result in the "gut feeling" we have about their relative emotional safety or threat when we meet someone new or who, in the past, has represented a threat.

We can link these ideas to attachment theory by noting that our earliest experiences serve as the basis for our learned ability to interpret all manner of interpersonal signals, including information about safety vs. danger (including social acceptance vs. rejection, and curiosity/exploration vs. fear/avoidance). Put differently, our earliest experiences shape our vagal tone, which is also likely related to our evolved attachment styles and strategies. We have all worked with, or known, people who have overactive "threat detectors." These people are hyper-vigilant for and reactive to the smallest sign of interpersonal rejection and see danger in every social situation. This is often an indication of early relational trauma (Van der Kolk, 2014). According to Porges, the persistent or frequent experience of too much stimulation (hyperarousal) or too much inhibition (hypoarousal or dissociation) that results from abuse or neglect in early life sets our vagal tone, compromises the brain/body communication system, leads to faulty neuroception, and has an overall negative effect on social and emotional functioning in adult life.

Let us summarize the contributions of Porges' model. The peripheral nervous system is classically divided into the voluntary somatic nervous system and the involuntary ANS, which is further divided into the sympathetic and parasympathetic branches. The SNS excites, triggering the "fight or flight" response, while the PNS inhibits, triggering the "rest and digest" (or in extreme form, the freeze) response. Ideally, these two systems operate to maintain a state of balanced physiological arousal. Porges proposed that this balanced state of arousal can be disrupted, with the result being either too much excitement (hyperarousal) or too much inhibition (hypoarousal or dissociation). *If this state of imbalance persists or occurs frequently, as in the case of early relational trauma, the normative interplay of the two branches may be compromised* (Porges, 2011). The significance of Porges' theory as it relates to grief therapy will become clear in the next section and in the chapters to follow, where we will elaborate on the neurobiology of the stress response (Chapter 6), and the role of grief therapy in helping the bereaved person return to a regulated state (Chapters 7–10).

The Social Motivation System and Core Affects: The Work of Jak Panksepp

Panksepp has described what he calls a *social motivation system* modulated by oxytocin, vasopressin, and endogenous endorphins and other neurochemicals related to reward, decreased physical pain, and increased feelings of well-being (Panksepp, 2011; Panksepp & Biven, 2012). The neurochemicals involved in this system are thought to regulate attachment, pair bonding, and other relational behaviors. Different chemicals are believed to regulate different categories of activity: for example, bonding and attachment are regulated by peptides, vasopressin, and oxytocin; attraction is regulated by dopamine; and sex drive is regulated by androgens and estrogens. The production of these biochemicals, as well as the creation of their receptors, is subject to the impact of early life experience.

More recently, Panksepp has proposed that mammalian brains have been "hard-wired" through evolution with seven primal emotional systems (or "core affects") (Panksepp & Biven, 2012, p.562). In the language of behavioral learning theory, these are unconditioned responses (UCR) in that mammals have the rudiments of these emotional systems at birth. They are the result of both central and peripheral nervous system development, and of brain hormones (such as oxytocin and testosterone) that affect neurological functioning, emotions, thinking, and behavior. Panksepp capitalizes the labels of these prime emotions to differentiate them from "secondary" emotions, which are conditioned responses (CR), i.e., learned emotional responses that have become associated with UCRs. The seven core affects are SEEKING, FEAR, LUST, RAGE, CARE, PANIC/GRIEF, and PLAY. Each of these, like other neurological systems, cuts through lower and higher anatomical regions of the brain, as well as other systems, such as the endocrine system.

Several elements of Panksepp's model correspond to Bowlby's representation of the attachment system. Behavior associated with the CARE system, for example, closely matches caregiving behavior that Bowlby theorized was the mirror image of attachment behavior (J. Solomon & George, 1996). The CARE system motivates parents to bond with their offspring, and it also motivates adults to engage in the "tend and befriend" behaviors seen between partners and friends. Panksepp suggests that the CARE system is one of three emotional systems that comprise the foundation of our non-sexual social bonds. The other two are the PANIC/GRIEF (P/G) system and the PLAY system. The P/G system correlates very closely with the attachment system postulated by Bowlby. It is called the P/G system because it is activated by separation from attachment figures, and results in separation distress when the attachment figure is temporarily unavailable (panic), and mourning when the attachment figure is permanently unavailable (grief). Lastly, the PLAY system forms the basis of juvenile and adult peer friendship, and is manifested in shared activities with siblings and peers that are mutually enjoyable.

Panksepp has also argued that many psychiatric disorders can be understood in terms of dysregulation of these core biologically based affects. For example, he suggests that hyperactivity of the P/G system, which is subjectively experienced as separation distress, is the foundation of "social" pain in response to rejection, abandonment, and separation through death by other people. Panksepp also postulates that this is the source of major depression, which involves hypoactivation of the SEEKING system (Panksepp et al., 2014).

How the Brain Develops

The development of the brain can be described as the integration of neurons into increasingly complex functional neural networks. Although the brain is functional upon birth, its full potential for growth is only realized when we come into contact with other people. It is not only that people need other people, but also that brains need other brains, to survive and flourish.

Development in the First Year

While brain development can and does occur throughout life, the first year after birth is a critical period with respect to the development of the right brain, and consequently, a critical period with respect to the development of affect regulation and attachment. For optimal functioning, the neural networks involved in balancing hyper and hypo levels of emotional arousal, and particularly the management of negative affect, need to be fully developed and integrated over time, and the first year after birth is the critical beginning of this process. Optimal affect regulation, in turn, promotes neurological (and psychological) growth (Cozolino, 2010, 2014; D. J. Siegel, 2012a). In other words, brain development supports the development of affect regulation, the capacity for which then allows for further cortical development. As affect regulation increases, the growing child gradually comes to rely on their own capacity for internal modulation of emotion, and less on external regulation from their caregiver—a process that is central to physical, emotional, and psychological maturation.

Arousal that disrupts this balancing act between the sympathetic and parasympathetic systems is actually necessary for an infant to learn to regulate his or her affect—in a sense, a child needs "practice sessions" to learn how to handle emotional distress. However, it is essential that the infant's growing brain not be subjected to an overload of emotional arousal, particularly negative stimulation, since stress results in an internal biochemical environment (reduced levels of endorphins and dopamine and increased stress hormones) that inhibits brain development and learning (A. N. Schore, 2001a, 2001b, 2002b, 2002c, 2003a). Chronic exposure to negative emotional arousal (primarily fear or separation distress) can have effects on neurological development and psychological functioning literally throughout the rest of life (Hart & Rubia, 2012; Lanius et al., 2010). These changes have been linked to the development of many psychiatric disorders in adulthood (Lanius et al., 2010). The important point here is that it is repeated experiences of moderate, *regulated* arousal that stimulate the development of neural circuits that support an increased capacity for emotion regulation. As we shall discuss later in the book, this principle of titrated emotional arousal is also central to the skillful conduct of psychotherapy, including grief therapy.

Development in the Second Year

During the second year of life, a growth spurt in the left hemisphere is announced by the emergence of language skills and increased locomotion. More than ever, the child is able to move about and interact with her environment. Given the extravagant growth in neural integration occurring during this time, the quality of care the infant receives is critical, not only for the infant's physical and emotional health, but also for the child's long term development and functioning. The development of budding language skills, the ability to interact with peers and teachers—these and other rudimentary abilities are coming online, establishing a foundation for neurological and personality development to come. Research over the last three decades has demonstrated that development in any or all of these areas can be compromised not only by outright abuse, but also by a lack of responsive and attuned nurturing (Trevarthen, 2009). More severe adverse early childhood experience produces an increased vulnerability to psychiatric disorders in adulthood (Lanius et al., 2010). It seems reasonable to suppose that this vulnerability might extend to a vulnerability to the development of complicated grief after the loss of an attachment figure in adulthood. This possibility will be further explored in Chapter 4.

The Role of Attachment in Brain Development: Empathic Attunement, Neural Integration, and Affect Regulation

Motherhood, as many women have long suspected, changes the brain. The release of oxytocin and other endogenous brain chemicals increases the mother's sensitivity to her infant's emotions and affects her behavior, including how she looks at her infant and the tone of her voice (Ammaniti & Gallese, 2014).

These features of maternal caregiving in turn have an impact on the development of the infant's brain. In discussing the fundamentals of attachment theory, writers often observe that human beings are predisposed in mind and body to make contact with other humans. In describing the behavior of neurons, Cozolino explains that they are similarly predisposed to connect to one another: "Just as we survive and thrive through our relationships with others, neurons survive and grow as a function of how 'well connected' they are" (Cozolino, 2010, p.67). When these connections are used, neurons synthesize new proteins that strengthen them—a process cogently captured in the well-known phrase "neurons that fire together wire together" (Keysers & Perrett, 2004, p.504). In the first few years of life, it is the nonverbal communication between child and caregiver— "right brain to right brain"—that supports this process of neural development (A. N. Schore, 2003b, 2009). An essential feature of this process is the mother's capacity to empathically attune to the infant's inner state, and to convey this attunement to the infant through her actions, her nonverbal communication (tone of voice, eye gaze, etc.), and eventually, through her spoken words. Repeated interactions of the experience by the child of "empathic accuracy" allow the child to begin to have the experience of "feeling felt" (D. J. Siegel, 2010, p.11). This caretaking ability, part of what Siegel refers to as "mindsight" (D. J. Siegel, 2010), also actively fosters the mentalizing capacity in the growing child (Fonagy et al., 2014). It is also what is meant by the creation of an "intersubjective field," a term used in the psychodynamic psychotherapy literature to refer to the synchronization of two embodied consciousnesses into one transactional therapeutic field during the course of psychotherapy (Ammaniti & Gallese, 2014). The concept of an intersubjective field also has direct relevance to the contingent and marked responsiveness between caregiver and child in the early parent–child dyad. Attunement enhances empathy by providing the mother with a felt sense of the child's emotions, which in turn enhances her sensitivity and responsiveness. The net effect is a strengthening of the attachment bond and of the security that the child develops as a result of consistent and responsive caregiving. As elaborated in Part III, this relational attunement is also the foundation of effective grief therapy.

Mirror Neurons: What Are They, and What Do They Do?

The concept of mirror neurons was first described by researchers conducting studies of monkeys, when they made the incidental discovery that when they (the researchers) performed certain actions (picking up a peanut, putting the peanut in their mouth), parts of the monkeys' brains lit up that were the same as the regions of their brain that were engaged when the monkey itself was picking up or eating the peanut (Rizzolatti et al., 1996). This discovery was received with considerable excitement in the scientific community and led to a number of theories about the role of mirror neurons in communication, learning, and social interaction (Ammaniti & Gallese, 2014). Questions about the existence of mirror neurons in human beings remain a matter of debate within the scientific community (Cozolino, 2010), but their discovery has provided one exciting, if hypothetical, explanation for the remarkable capacity for empathy in human beings.

Before discussing the quality of caregiving and its impact on brain development in greater detail, a comment is in order regarding the emphasis in this chapter (and elsewhere in this book) on maternal care. This emphasis reflects the fact that most attachment research has focused on the bond between mothers and infants. Recently, researchers have reported that fathers, as well as mothers, undergo neurological and hormonal changes when they are involved in caregiving (Grossmann et al., 2005; Swain et al., 2014). Based on an analysis of MRI data, Swain and his colleagues have reported that these changes, which appear to begin about four months after the birth of the child, are more pronounced in fathers who stay home to care for their children (Swain et al., 2007). More research is needed on the role of fathers in the attachment process and the neurobiological development of their offspring.

Positive Attuned Caregiving

As Schore and other researchers have reported, attuned interactions between mother and child trigger the release of endogenous opioids that have an important role in sculpting the developing architecture of the infant's brain and producing subjective feelings of pleasure and well-being in both parent and child (A. N. Schore, 2003a, 2012). One of these endogenous opioids is oxytocin, a hormone and neurotransmitter that induces a sense of well-being. When a mother holds and comforts her child, oxytocin is released in both the infant and the mother, producing pleasurable sensations that promote further contact, which releases more oxytocin, and so on. And since neurons that fire together wire together, the result is the growth of areas of the brain associated with social recognition and bonding. At the same time, the experience of responsive maternal care and the resulting neuronal growth lay the foundation for internal working models that have a lasting impact on attachment orientation.

Abuse or Neglect: The Neurobiology of Insecure Attachment, and Vulnerability to Stress

In contrast to the scenario described in the previous section concerning the developmental influence of attuned care and a secure bond, non-optimal care (ranging from non-responsiveness, to neglect, to outright abuse) negatively impacts the development of the brain, and inescapably, the development of a range of brain functions such as self-regulatory capacity. Like the attachment behavior of the secure infant, the dysregulation of anxiously and avoidantly attached infants that can be observed at a behavioral level can also be understood at a neurological level. The long term effects of chronic childhood stress are evident in this comment from a client, now in his forties, as he attempts to describe the insecurity and fear he experienced as a child.

> "My mother wasn't just an alcoholic, she was a rageaholic. When you're a kid and your mother is a really scary person, you just *freeze* . . . I mean . . . I . . . wouldn't you . . . and I'm still that way, I realize I still do that."
>
> *Vince*

Findings from neuroscience correlate with psychological research and clinical observation concerning the long term impact of environmental stressors, particularly parental neglect and abuse, on brain development in infancy (Hart & Rubia, 2012; Lanius et al., 2010; Van der Kolk, 2014). These effects can be found in brain regions related to managing the response to threat. For example, elevated levels of cortisol, a stress related hormone associated with abnormal development of the HPA axis system, have been found in infants who received dysfunctional care (Bureau et al., 2010). The HPA is a brain and hormonal circuit that helps to maintain internal equilibrium and manage response to threats. Additional links have been identified between a dysregulated HPA axis and insecure attachment classification in infancy (Cassidy & Shaver, 2008). For example, infants classified as insecure have higher levels of cortisol during separation and a slower return to baseline cortisol levels following the Strange Situation (Loman & Gunnar, 2010). These findings are consistent with Main's observations concerning the adverse effects of maternal abuse on response to stress (Main & Hesse, 1990). Main observed that infants classified as disorganized generally had mothers who exhibited difficulty in regulating their own affective responses, a deficit that correlated with the mothers' reports of their own abuse as children. These mothers tended to ignore or actively reject their distressed infant's bids for attention, probably because distress in the child prompted distress in the mother. In disorganized dyads, no one is in charge of tending to painful feelings and restoring emotional equilibrium, and the result is an escalating exchange of dysregulated affect (Hesse, 2008).

Another way of understanding how adverse early experience compromises function is through the process of "neuronal pruning" (Cozolino, 2010, p.67). As we have said, neurons must be connected to one another to survive. Neurons that are not wired to other neurons lose their inactive branches or die completely. In the absence of opportunities to be reregulated with the help of the mother's mature nervous system, the neural networks that would build self-regulatory capacity in the infant's brain are not activated, do not connect with other neurons, and fail to develop. This means that important opportunities for learning are lost, critical areas of the brain do not develop fully or well, incentives for bonding are diminished, and what could be a process of expanding social engagement and growth is short-circuited. In light of what neuroscience has revealed about the role of early attachment in shaping the brain, Schore and Schore have proposed that attachment behavior, which Bowlby saw as being prompted by the infant's need for safety and a secure base, can now better be understood as "the essential matrix for creating a right brain self that can regulate its own internal states and relationships" (J. R. Schore & Schore, 2008, p.44).

We know that trauma experienced in adulthood affects adults on many levels—cognitive, emotional, and physical. These effects of adult trauma are magnified in the case of early developmental trauma (Allen, 2001; Lanius et al., 2010). It has become increasingly clear that the effects of early trauma are the most damaging and difficult to undo, a finding that is not unexpected given the pervasive vulnerability of young children, including their immature neurological development. Early relational trauma is a "double whammy" of painful experience and impaired capacity to regulate the emotions elicited by those experiences. Schore, Van der Kolk, and others have described the impact of chronic deprivation of contingent, attuned care on neurological development, and the tendency toward dissociative states that is observed in many children subjected to these conditions (Hart & Rubia, 2012; Kagan, 2004; Luecken, 2008; A. N. Schore, 2003a; E. P. Solomon & Heide, 2005; Van der Hart et al., 2006; Van der Kolk, 2014). When a child feels unsettled, she looks to her caregivers for comfort and reassurance. If the caregiver cannot manage his or her response to this expressed need, then instead of providing comfort, the parent may become angry or rejecting. This response from the caregiver leads first to hyperarousal in the child on physiological, psychological, and behavioral levels. That is, the child initially tries harder to get her parent's attention. During this phase, the child's heart rate, blood pressure, and respiration all speed up. If the needed response is repeatedly not elicited, however, the child will eventually enter a state of psychological hopelessness and neurological hypoarousal or down-regulation, at which point a second cascade of internal events will be triggered. In this phase the child appears to shut down or freeze, almost as though she is trying to avoid attention and become "unseen." This is viewed as a strategy of last resort, employed when the child feels terrified and helpless, and can only hope to survive by avoiding notice. As previously discussed, this pattern of freezing and psychological numbing when confronted with distressing feelings can become a lifelong strategy for managing unbearable affect. As an adult, such an individual is more likely to freeze, shut down, and dissociate when confronted with painful feelings. Dissociation becomes the *primary way a person learns to regulate their emotion*, or as Schore concludes, in these cases the "dissociative metabolic shutdown state is a primary regulatory process used throughout the lifespan" (A. N. Schore, 2009, p.120). This, in turn, lays the foundation of many young adult and adult psychiatric disorders that involve difficulty with affect management and a maladaptive coping style that centers on dissociation as a psycho-biological defense (A. N. Schore, 2003a).

Marta

Marta, 42, has come for therapy following the death of her father. She cannot remember much of her childhood. When the therapist gently asks a series of questions about what her family was like when she was growing up, Marta becomes quiet and her gaze drifts over the therapist's shoulder to the opposite wall. Within moments she has dissociated, and it takes several minutes to reestablish contact with her. Even then, she appears stunned, avoids eye contact, and is unable to speak.

No matter how attuned and compassionate the therapist is, recalling early abuse is painful and frightening. Given that grief is also painful and frightening, it is not surprising that bereaved clients who have experienced early abuse, neglect, or loss may become overwhelmed, emotionally numb, and psychologically dissociated. This kind of response seems to be related both to a client's limited recall of painful events and his or her limited capacity to tolerate the affective arousal that remembering these events provokes. We now understand that both of these responses are more likely to affect people whose early environment did not support brain development that would facilitate affect regulation, cognitive control, and memory recall.

Adult Development

Neuroplasticity and Neurogenesis

Contrary to what was earlier thought to be the unchanging nature of the brain past childhood, we now know that the brain continues to morph in structure and capacity throughout the life cycle. Well into adulthood, new neurons grow in areas of the brain involved with learning and memory, including the hippocampus, the amygdala, and the cerebral cortex. Synaptic connections between neurons also increase with age. As in infancy, what promotes continued development in adulthood is a level of arousal that stimulates but does not overwhelm the brain. New learning builds the brain, while excessive stress or trauma inhibits growth and interferes with the integration of experience.

Maturation and Neural Integration

As adults, we generally have more control than we did as children over the circumstances of our lives. As a result, we usually have more ability to directly influence what becomes wired into our brains (Hanson, 2013). Nevertheless, it remains true that much of what happens in life is unpredictable and beyond our control. Certain events, like the kinds of traumatic losses that are discussed in Chapter 6, can disable even the strongest and most resilient among us. Still, we know that some people seem more capable than others of integrating the effects of adverse experience into their identity and moving on with their lives.

We might suppose that these people are among the lucky ones who were raised in a good environment, by caregivers who supported their emotional and physical growth, and to a significant degree, we would be right. But as we have seen, adverse experience early in life is not a definitive predictor of compromised functioning. According to attachment theory, and in line with studies using the AAI, the effect of early experience, particularly early traumatic experiences, is mediated by the extent to which a person has been able to process and make sense of those experiences (Bakermans-Kranenburg & van IJzendoorn, 2009). If our emotional foundation has been subject to assaults that have not been addressed and repaired, whatever we build on it may be fragile. But if, with the support of others, we have identified and attended to our emotional injuries, and integrated our experiences into a coherent life narrative, then this need not be the case (Cozolino, 2010; Hesse, 2008; Holmes, 2010). Integration has two separate meanings that can both be used in discussions of how experience shapes the brain. In infancy, interaction with an attuned caregiver promotes the development of neural networks and the integration of functional areas of the brain, resulting in increased self-regulatory capacity. Over the course of a person's life, the integration of experience on a neuronal/psychological level occurs when a person has been able to address the experiences rather than dissociate from them, make sense of the feelings, memories, and thoughts associated with those experiences, and ideally grow from them. Sense-making allows the individual to integrate his experiences into a larger and more adaptive worldview. In cases of traumatic experiences, integration becomes a more challenging enterprise, since people typically develop unconscious protective stances toward those experiences (i.e., psychological defenses) that serve to dissociate them from the distressing emotional and physiological arousal triggered by the events.

Viewed this way, many of the problems that cause people to seek therapy, including grief therapy, can be understood as a lack of integration. This lack of integration can also be understood as a fragmentation or dissociation of the psychological self into different parts (in extreme cases, this can result in psychiatric disorders such as Dissociative Identity Disorder) (A. N. Schore, 2003a; Van der Hart et al., 2006). This brings us back to the quote from Cozolino that opened this chapter. Cozolino asserts that many complaints and symptoms are related to sub-optimal functioning of neural networks that are underdeveloped, under-regulated, over-taxed, or poorly integrated (Cozolino, 2010). "Applying this model," he writes, "therapy is a means of creating or restoring coordination among various neural networks" (Cozolino, 2010, p.24). The therapeutic environment is a learning environment "designed to enhance the growth of neurons and the integration of neural networks. I propose here that all forms of therapy, regardless of theoretical orientation, will be successful to the degree to which they foster appropriate neuroplasticity" (Cozolino, 2010, p.25).

Cozolino's prescription for a therapeutic environment that supports these goals is worth noting here. As we will see, his recommendations have much in common with what Wallin, Holmes, and others have described as an attachment-informed approach to psychotherapy (Holmes, 2013; Wallin, 2007). Cozolino cites the following as the characteristics of an environment that enhances neural plasticity, growth, and integration in psychotherapy:

- the establishment of a safe and trusting relationship
- arousal of mild to moderate levels of stress
- activating both emotion and cognition in the service of integration
- the co-construction of new personal narratives through the encounter between therapist and client (Cozolino, 2010, p.26).

Goals of Psychotherapy

When emotions and thoughts cannot be tolerated, the mind finds ways to circumvent or suppress them, a point elaborated by Vaillant in his classic work *The Wisdom of the Ego*

(Vaillant, 1993). The defensive coping strategies that are mounted distort reality to varying degrees, but the goal is always the same: to reduce the painful anxiety that accompanies the underlying affect. As Cozolino tells us, once the neural connections that make up these defensive strategies are wired in, they shape our lives, influencing what we approach and what we avoid. The work of therapy, in this regard, is to help clients become curious about what causes them distress, and in a controlled way, to move toward rather than away from this distress. By bringing up the source of the anxiety in a safe context (i.e., in the presence of a caring therapist), and by allowing the person to experience the anxiety in a titrated fashion (i.e., to dose exposure so that the person's defensive strategies are not excessively triggered), the person gradually builds up his ability to tolerate the seemingly intolerable, to confront her thoughts and feelings, and ultimately to reexamine and put into perspective the experiences that engendered these feelings. The result is that therapist and client work together to create a narrative of the person's life that is both honest and balanced, at once emotionally resonant and tolerable.

The direct applicability of this perspective to bereavement therapy becomes clear when we consider how frequently clients' narratives of relationships or losses feel incomplete or distorted. An adult child who cannot understand why he grieves for a parent who abused him; a spouse who cannot let go of the belief that she "should have known" that her husband was going to take his life—these come to mind as examples of narratives that omit or distort factual details, and that fall far short of capturing the complexity of attachment or of grief.

When a person has latched onto a perspective that is unfair or illogical, and which the clinician's efforts (as well as those of family and friends) have done nothing to modify, it is time to give the language based left brain a rest and try a different way. By attending to the client's facial expressions, posture, and other nonverbal cues, and by identifying the emotional correlates of experience, the therapist can help a client to develop a narrative of the relationship and the loss that is more inclusive, balanced, reality based, and often times, forgiving of self and others. This kind of therapeutic process has much in common with the repeated positive interactions that ideally occur between parents and children, particularly those that take place when a child is upset, and the parent helps them regain emotional balance (Cozolino, 2010).

Thus, Cozolino, and many others whose work we have mentioned, concludes that the work of psychotherapy is to change the brain through sustained empathic and directed interaction (Cozolino, 2010). The process by which change occurs in the adult brain is both similar to and different from the kind of brain sculpting that occurs in childhood. In both cases, learning is a process of making new neural connections, particularly in areas of the brain that support emotional processing and meaning-making. However, while parenting is mostly about construction, psychotherapy is more about reconstruction and revision. Children are at a disadvantage with regard to making sense of experience, because their brains are still developing. They do the best they can to process incoming data, but distortions inevitably creep in: they feel responsible for things that are not their fault, and draw conclusions about themselves based on the sometimes unfair and harsh words they hear from others. The remnants of these lessons from childhood carry on into adulthood, and may constitute much of the material that people end up addressing in therapy.

Whatever childhood fears and feelings linger beneath the surface of an apparently well-functioning adult, they are most likely to emerge when the person is under stress (Van der Hart et al., 2006). Faced with the stress that accompanies significant loss, many people find themselves flooded with memories about old hurts, imagined failures, and fears about their ability to function as adults. Thus, the loss of a significant person is an event that for many people triggers a painful re-experiencing of old and unprocessed hurts, and also one that offers an opportunity for new learning and growth.

Rebuilding the Brain in Work with the Bereaved

When people are afraid, when they have reached a point where they feel they cannot possibly manage one more emotional hurdle, the idea of shutting down or running away can hold great appeal. What grief therapy can provide in these circumstances is the support a person needs to stay put, psychologically speaking, so that they can develop the capacity to tolerate their feelings, make sense of their thoughts, and accommodate to the changed reality of their lives.

One way of understanding complicated grief is that it represents a breakdown in the processing of information related to the loss (Shear & Shair, 2005). According to this view, such a breakdown occurs when the reality of the loss cannot be tolerated, as in the case of sudden violent death, or when the bereaved was highly dependent on the person who died. Under these circumstances, defenses can be triggered that allow the mourner to delay confrontation with reality, but which can also interfere with the integration of the loss. An important aspect of therapy in these cases is to provide an environment in which the bereaved can learn to tolerate feelings associated with the loss, as well as gain perspective on the meaning of the relationship and its absence for the individual. This occurs through a process of support, skill development, activation and integration of memories, and the co-construction of new personal narratives (Shear et al., 2011). As with all new learning, this psychological strengthening process is associated with enriched synaptic connections between existing neuronal networks, and even the creation of new neural networks in the brain (D. J. Siegel, 2012a, 2012b).

Summary

Interest in the neurobiology of the developing brain and the differential impact of secure vs. insecure attachment experiences has expanded exponentially over the past 20 years, and will undoubtedly continue well into the future. A great deal has been learned about how the brain processes information and the role that temperament and experience play in people's capacity to integrate the situations that they encounter. The investigation of the neurological basis of thought and behavior is in its early stages to be sure, but it has already generated findings that help us understand what environmental factors support normal development, and how development is adversely affected when these supportive factors are unavailable or severely deficient. We know enough about the brain and about how healthy brains develop to say that knowledge of the quality of caregiving people received in early childhood allows us to make reasonably sound inferences about how they process information about themselves, their general orientation and openness to interpersonal relationships, and their capacity to regulate affect and cope with stress. The "decade of the brain" can be seen now as the beginning of what will undoubtedly be a long and fruitful period of inquiry into the study of how our brains develop, what enables us to manage difficult emotions and heal from loss, and how we are all shaped by our interactions with others (O'Connor, 2005, 2013; Steele & Steele, 2008). In the next chapter, we will look at how these insights about the brain, along with insights from attachment theory, can enrich our understanding of bereavement and the process of healing after loss.

Part II

Bereavement through the Lens of Attachment: Advances in Research, Theory, and Practice

Research on the nature and course of grief over the past 20 years has consistently identified people's attachment orientation as a significant factor in their adaptation to loss (Burke & Neimeyer, 2013). Contemporary models of bereavement draw heavily on attachment theory, particularly Bowlby's views regarding the association between insecure attachment and complications in grief (Mikulincer & Shaver, 2013). Also in the past two decades, concepts from attachment theory have been integrated into a growing number of models of general psychotherapy practice (Costello, 2013; Holmes, 2013; Obegi & Berant, 2010; Wallin, 2007). Much of the literature detailing attachment-informed approaches has direct applicability to work with the bereaved (Zech & Arnold, 2011). What is missing from the discussion of attachment and bereavement is a model of grief therapy that is based on an integration of insights from attachment theory and research, and contemporary theory and research in bereavement. Our purpose in the following three chapters is to advance this project. In Chapter 4 we review contemporary models of bereavement, highlight the ways in which attachment orientation interacts with and expands upon these models, and illustrate the application of these expanded models in clinical work with the bereaved. The specific contribution of attachment theory to our understanding of loss in different kinship relationships will be examined in Chapter 5, and Chapter 6 will focus on how attachment history and mode of death intersect, with an emphasis on traumatic loss.

4 Insecure Attachment and Problematic Grief

Contemporary Models and Their Implications for Practice

"Poor Fanny! she would not have forgotten him so soon!"
"No," replied Anne, in a low, feeling voice, "that, I can easily believe."
"It was not in her nature. She doted on him."
"It would not be the nature of any woman who truly loved."

Jane Austen, Persuasion 1816

Why love if losing hurts so much? I have no answers any more . . .
Twice in (my) life I've been given the choice: as a boy and as a man.
The boy chose safety, the man chooses suffering. The pain now is
part of the happiness then. That's the deal.

William Nicholson, Shadowlands 1993

To be creatures who love, we must be creatures who can despair at what we lose.

Andrew Solomon, The Noonday Demon: An Atlas of Depression 2000

There is a reason that the words "love and loss" are so frequently linked in literature, and in writing about bereavement. Love and loss are part of the same experience; in choosing one, we invite the possibility of the other. Nor is it unexpected to find that certain parallels arise in how we attach, and how we react to separation. The quote from Austen reflects what many would consider the inescapable connection between deep love and deep grief. But although someone who has loved deeply may feel a similar depth of pain, one is not a measure of the other and there is more to understanding the connection between love and loss than the intensity of the attachment. How, then, do we make sense of the variations in people's response to loss? What factors play a part in influencing the duration and intensity of grief? Researchers and clinicians have their own ways of evaluating relationships, and their own methods for predicting how someone will react and cope in the aftermath of significant loss. What has emerged as a common theme in the research and clinical literature concerning bereavement is the recognition that understanding the nature of a person's orientation to attachment—in particular, the extent to which they can trust and depend on others, and their willingness to be depended upon, within healthy limits—provides a good deal of insight into how they will grieve. It seems that many of the same aspects of our emotional makeup that contribute to the way that we form attachments also come into play when we lose someone to whom we are attached.

We begin this chapter by briefly reviewing the evolution of models of the grieving process, with a focus on two current, and complementary models: the Two Track Model of Bereavement (TTM) (Rubin, 1981), and the Dual Process Model of Bereavement (DPM) (M. S. Stroebe & Schut, 1999).

Models of Grief and Grief Resolution

Stage, Phase, and Task Models

The literature on death and dying remained of little interest outside of a small cadre of professionals until 1970, the first appearance of *On Death and Dying* (Kübler-Ross, 1997). Although she intended it to be a description of the psychological adjustment to dying, Kübler-Ross's model was popularized as a description of the course of grief (Hall, 2014). With the publication of the hugely influential *Grief Counseling and Grief Therapy*, William Worden introduced an alternative model in which healing from loss involves the completion of a series of tasks, including accepting the reality of the loss, processing the pain of the loss, and adapting to the new life circumstances imposed by the loss (Worden, 1983/2008, 2009). In a similar manner, Rando described grief as a series of six processes (Rando, 1993). Both Rando and Worden emphasized the active work of grieving, a view described as the "grief work hypothesis" (M. S. Stroebe, 1992), and both models have achieved a wide level of influence and utilization among practicing grief therapists.

Newer Models of Grief and Mourning

In the late 1980s, several reports were released that raised questions about the efficacy of grief interventions and, by extension, the models of grief and grief resolution on which they were based (Allumbaugh & Hoyt, 1999; Jordan & Neimeyer, 2003; Kato & Mann, 1999). Much of what was written in the aftermath of these reports challenged the assumption that all bereaved people need to engage in "grief work" in order to work through the "stages" of grief. Research by Bonanno and colleagues, for example, identified substantial variation in how people respond to loss (Bonanno et al., 2004). At the same time, the literature on grief therapy came to reflect a consensus that to increase their effectiveness, interventions for grieving people needed to be tailored to the particular needs and concerns of the bereaved, their readiness for treatment, and the specific nature of the loss (Neimeyer & Jordan, 2013; Zech et al., 2010).

In short, while stage models and the grief work approach are appealingly straightforward, the idea that people recover from loss by completing a set of tasks or progressing through a series of stages has been the subject of continuing challenge within the professional community, and increasingly, the broader public (Bonanno, 2009; Neimeyer & Jordan, 2013). Another challenge to traditional grief models concerns the shift from an emphasis on decathexis as the desired end point of mourning, to an assumption that many grievers will maintain a "continuing bond" with the deceased (Klass et al., 1996; Rubin, 1999). While initial accounts of continuing bonds theory emphasized the advantages of continuing bonds with respect to adaptation to loss, subsequent research has shown that the bonds people maintain with the deceased, like the relationships they have with the living, are sometimes healthy and adaptive, and sometimes self-destructive and problematic (Field & Friedrichs, 2004). Chapter 5 includes a fuller discussion of continuing bonds in bereavement.

To summarize, the current thinking within the field is that there is no one way that people respond to loss, no one way to cope with grief, and no one way to help people who are grieving (Rubin et al., 2012). This emphasis on recognizing the diversity of factors that influence grief response, and in particular, the significance of the griever's continuing bond with the deceased, is reflected in the Two Track Model of Bereavement.

The Two Track Model (TTM)

The TTM (Rubin et al., 2012) represents bereavement as an adaptive process mediated by two distinct but interactive sets of variables. The first set consists of factors that impact the bereaved's biopsychosocial functioning, such as their employment status and their physical and mental health, and the second concerns the nature of the bereaved's ongoing emotional attachment and relationship to the person who has died (Rubin, 1981). For example, how often does the bereaved think of the deceased, and are these memories a source of distress, comfort, or both? The TTM was the first model of the bereavement process to propose a version of continuing bonds theory, and Rubin and his colleagues have used the model to explain how and why an unresolved or problematic bond with the deceased can complicate a mourner's adaptation to loss.

> First and foremost, loss occurs at the interface of the individual and his or her relationship with another . . . In the case of understanding bereavement, once the significance of the interpersonal has been grasped, the nature of the relationship to the deceased rightfully takes its place as a major domain of interest.
>
> (Rubin et al., 2012, p.23)

According to the authors, once we recognize bereavement as the response to a relational loss, we find that the questions that arise about how to account for variations in grief are much the same as the questions that Bowlby posed in his studies of how people form attachment bonds. What are the characteristic features of a healthy bond? How do people manage short and long term separation from attachment figures? How do we account for the differences in how people respond to separation?

An example of the relational aspect of the TTM is the bereavement experienced by parents who have lost a child. As will be discussed in Chapter 5, the nature of a parent's role as caregiver influences their response to the loss, and the way they deal with it. Parents who lose a child frequently experience persistent feelings of failure and guilt, as well as a powerful desire to reconnect with their deceased child (M. S. Stroebe et al., 2013).

The TTM focuses less on the *process* of bereavement and more on the *factors* that affect it. A second model, the Dual Process Model, has more to say about the dynamic process of normal and problematic bereavement.

The Dual Process Model (DPM)

The DPM (M. S. Stroebe & Schut, 1999, 2010) posits that healthy grief involves a process of *oscillation of attention* on the part of the bereaved, such that crying, yearning, and other

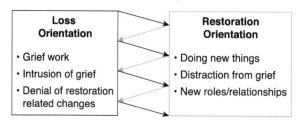

Figure 4.1 The Dual Process Model: Flexible attention. Adapted from M. S. Stroebe and Schut (1999).

feelings and behaviors related to the loss (the *Loss Orientation*) alternate with periods in which attention is directed to changing roles and responsibilities (the *Restoration Orientation*) (Figure 4.1). The DPM incorporates Bowlby's assertions regarding the importance of "flexible attention" in healthy adult bereavement, as well as his hypotheses concerning the patterns of adaptation associated with various types of insecure attachment (M. S. Stroebe et al., 2005).

We can recall Bowlby's suggestion (see Chapter 2) that anxiously attached individuals, whose emotional dependence would have been evident when their loved one was alive, would be expected to have an extended and highly disruptive response to the person's death. Avoidantly attached individuals, those who were resistant to forming close attachments and generally downplayed the importance of emotions and their own need for emotional support, would tend to suppress conscious grief. In their continuing elaboration of the DPM, Strobe and Schut demonstrate how the patterns described by Bowlby complement the DPM, establishing it not only as a general model of oscillation, but a more specific and predictive model of how oscillation breaks down as a result of the coping strategies employed by people who are insecurely attached. In their introduction to what they term "the extended DPM," Stroebe and Schut propose that anxious, avoidant, and disorganized attachment patterns contribute to specific types of disturbances in oscillation, which are in turn associated with predictable problems in adaptation to loss (M. S. Stroebe et al., 2005). Research support for this model has been summarized by Mikulincer and Shaver (Mikulincer & Shaver, 2008b) and is discussed in the next section.

In contrast to traditional models of the grieving process, the DPM incorporates the assumption that learning over time to "compartmentalize" and intermittently turn away from grief is as much a necessary part of the mourning process as moving toward, and through, the grief. According to the DPM, an individual who is overly focused on the loss side of the loss/restoration process would not be helped by interventions that actively and consistently direct their attention to the details of the loss (M. S. Stroebe et al., 2005; M. S. Stroebe et al., 2006; Wijngaards-de Meij et al., 2007b). Clinicians who use these strategies with loss-focused clients run the risk of deepening the bereaved's feelings of distress and amplifying their tendency to ruminate about the deceased, with the potential result being a downward spiral of decreased energy, increasing isolation, and hopelessness. Techniques that move the individual toward a Restoration Orientation will be more important in these cases. For example, if an individual has become socially isolated, reconnecting with friends may become a major focus of grief therapy. Conversely, for a client who avoids any confrontation with the loss, the clinical task becomes one of helping the bereaved person to gradually expose themselves to the reality of the death, with all of its attendant thoughts and feelings. In summary, as the name of the model suggests, bereavement is a two pronged process of alternately moving "toward" and "away from" the loss, and the role of a grief therapist is to help the client engage in that part of the process she seems unwilling or unable to engage in herself.

In the following discussion we will look at research related to the DPM, starting with the work of Mikulincer and Shaver, who have made major contributions to the development of an attachment perspective on grief, and whose research has been a source of substantial empirical validation for the role of insecure attachment in problematic responses to bereavement.

An Attachment Perspective on Disordered Grief: Mikulincer and Shaver

Anyone who reviews the literature on contemporary applications of attachment theory will find much to absorb in the work of Mario Mikulincer and Philip Shaver (Cassidy & Shaver, 2008; Mikulincer & Shaver, 2007, 2014; Shaver & Mikulincer, 2011), whose model of attachment system functioning in adults focuses on the dynamics of the attachment behavioral system in adolescence and adulthood and its relation to other behavioral systems, including exploration and caregiving. According to this model, which the authors describe as an "extension and refinement of previous control systems models of attachment dynamics" (Mikulincer & Shaver, 2007, p.30), once a person's attachment system is activated, he or she will initiate strategies to regain a sense of felt security, and will not engage in activities governed by other behavioral systems, such as exploration, until this goal is attained. The behavioral patterns proposed by Bowlby as insecure/anxious and insecure/avoidant, and incorporated into the DPM by Stroebe and Schut, parallel the *hyperactivating* and *deactivating* strategies described by Shaver and Mikulincer (Shaver & Mikulincer, 2009, p.23).

Research by Mikulincer and Shaver and others supports the proposition that attachment style moderates the choice of proximity or support seeking as an emotion regulation strategy (Kim et al., 2014; Mikulincer & Shaver, 2008a, 2008b; M. S. Stroebe & Schut, 2010). Children who are secure in their attachment style are more likely to seek contact when they feel separation distress, a response that reflects expectations that their attachment figures will be available and responsive to their needs. Insecurely attached children, having different expectations, will tend to employ one of two *secondary attachment strategies*: hyperactivation (for the preoccupied/anxious) or deactivation (for the fearful/avoidant). The child adopts these strategies as a way of managing her relationship with an unavailable, unreliable, or rejecting attachment figure. As previously noted, these attachment strategies may be functional for the child in the context of her caregiving environment, but they can become problematic in adulthood. Anxiously attached adults risk alienating potential friends and partners with their excessive neediness and clinging behavior (hyperactivation of the attachment system). Avoidantly attached adults may alienate potential friends and partners with their excessive independence and apparent lack of interest in intimacy (deactivation of the attachment system). Research suggests that the problems in relationships caused by overdependence or avoidance also affect the trajectory of bereavement in the insecurely attached (Mikulincer & Shaver, 2013).

While secure attachment confers an advantage in managing separation distress (Mikulincer & Shaver, 2013), it does not prevent people from experiencing emotional pain when a loved one dies. When the separation from a loved one is irreversible, primary strategies for seeking comfort—which heretofore may have been focused largely on the deceased—are no longer relevant, and secondary strategies must come into play. In the months following significant loss, securely as well as insecurely attached people are likely to experience days in which they cannot think of anything but the person who has died, and days in which their energy and attention are unaccountably taken up with other things. *This is the nature of grief.* Thus, Mikulincer and Shaver acknowledge that even healthy grief involves alternation between confrontation of the loss and periods of avoidance and respite.

> By driving people to experience the deep pain of loss, repeatedly reactivate memories of the deceased alongside the realization that the person is gone, and yearn for his or her proximity and love, attachment system hyperactivation allows mourners to explore the meaning and significance of their lost relationships, and find ways of maintaining reorganized, mainly symbolic bonds with loved partners. Deactivating strategies can also contribute productively to the reorganization process by enabling momentary detachment from the deceased and inhibition or suppression of painful feelings and thoughts.
>
> (Mikulincer & Shaver, 2008b, p.95)

In cases where this oscillation has broken down, intervention may be necessary, in which case the grief therapist's role is to help bereaved people "oscillate within normal bounds," thus enabling them to "reorganize their attachment hierarchy" and gradually integrate the loss (Mikulincer & Shaver, 2007, p.76). Mikulincer and Shaver have commented on the need for more research concerning the hypothesis that oscillation, as represented in the DPM, is what promotes healthy adaptation to loss. However, they suggest that clinical reports provide evidence of the need to support the bereaved in alternating between attention to the emotional reality of the loss and periods of respite and reengagement (Mikulincer & Shaver, 2007). Because bereavement is an irreversible loss of connection, Mikulincer and Shaver assert that "mourning provides an excellent, if saddening, research laboratory in which to study secondary attachment strategies" (Mikulincer & Shaver, 2007, p.72). Clinicians who work with the bereaved have ample opportunity to observe the use of these strategies.

Attachment and Loss: Research on the Role of Attachment Orientation in Response to Loss

Attachment orientation has consistently been identified as a significant factor in response to loss (Burke & Neimeyer, 2013; Meij et al., 2007; Parkes & Prigerson, 2010; M. S. Stroebe et al., 2005; Thomson, 2010; Wijngaards-de Meij et al., 2007b; Zech & Arnold, 2011). In a study of the role of attachment style in bereavement at one year following the death of a spouse, a family member, or a close friend, Wayment and

Vierthaler found that anxiously attached individuals showed higher levels of grief and depression, and avoidant individuals higher levels of somatic symptoms (Wayment & Vierthaler, 2002). Other researchers have reported similar findings, and have interpreted them as indicating that avoidance as a defense can collapse under the weight of high stress, including the stress associated with traumatic bereavement (Wijngaards-de Meij et al., 2007a).

In a study based on the DPM, Delespaux and colleagues investigated the mediating impact of negative vs. positive appraisal of bereavement stressors on a subject's flexible coping, that is, their use of both loss oriented (LO) and restoration oriented (RO) coping strategies (Delespaux et al., 2013). They predicted that individuals with anxious attachment would exhibit more negative appraisals of stressors, would use primarily LO coping strategies, and would show more intense grief reactions, while individuals with higher attachment avoidance would have lower negative appraisal of stressors, use primarily RO strategies, and have less pronounced grief responses. Their findings confirmed these assumptions, and would seem to suggest that avoidant individuals, despite their use of only one type of coping strategy, manage their grief more successfully than those who are anxiously attached. The authors urge caution in this interpretation of their findings, most importantly, because none of their subjects made exclusive use of either RO or LO strategies.

Overall, findings related to the grief of anxiously attached people support the assumption that their grief is both more intense and persistent than that of securely attached people (see Mikulincer & Shaver, 2013 for a review). The role of avoidant attachment in bereavement has been less clear, but recent studies suggest that avoidance is associated with problematic bereavement, particularly in cases of traumatic loss, and should not be confused with resilience (Meier et al., 2013).

Fraley and Bonanno (Fraley & Bonanno, 2004) studied attachment style in 59 participants, who were assessed for grief, anxiety, and depression 4 and 18 months after the first measurement. The authors used the categorization introduced by Bartholomew and Horowitz (Bartholomew & Horowitz, 1991), which differentiates "fearful avoidance," characterized by a fear of being hurt or rejected, from "dismissing avoidance," characterized by the minimization of emotion and an emphasis on self-reliance and independence. Fraley and Bonanno hypothesized that fearfully avoidantly attached individuals would have a significantly more problematic response to bereavement than dismissively avoidantly attached individuals. The results of their study substantiated this hypothesis, leading them to suggest that in assessing the impact of avoidant strategies, researchers and clinicians need to take into account the underlying dynamic driving the individual's avoidance. In a subsequent study, researchers assessed the psychological adjustment of people who were close to the World Trade Center in New York City at the time of the terrorist attacks in 2001 (Fraley et al., 2006). This study confirmed the researchers' hypotheses regarding the response of anxiously avoidant individuals, but findings with regard to dismissively avoidant individuals were mixed. While reports from friends and family regarding the adaptation of these individuals indicated that they were doing well, the respondents themselves reported a high level of PTSD symptoms and depression. These findings make sense when we consider the tendency of avoidantly attached individuals to downplay their need for support from others, a denial that stems both from the desire not to draw attention to their distress, and from their belief that there is little to be gained from reaching out to others, as there is nothing that anyone can do to help them (Parkes, 2013; Parkes & Prigerson, 2010). In short, despite external evidence suggesting that they are doing well, people with an avoidant coping style may continue to experience considerable internal distress.

In an effort to clarify the role of attachment anxiety and avoidance in coping with bereavement, Meier and colleagues (Meier et al., 2013) collected data on 656 recently bereaved young adults. In the first of two studies using this data, the authors looked at the differing impact of anxious and avoidant attachment, and found that higher levels of attachment related anxiety, but not avoidance, were associated with more problematic bereavement. The second study focused on the response of anxiously and avoidantly attached individuals to violent loss (accident, suicide, homicide). Results from this study showed that avoidance was associated with problems in physical and mental health, a finding that is consistent with the study of World Trade Center survivors previously discussed (Fraley et al., 2006). Also consistent with that earlier study, the authors emphasize the role of trauma in the collapse of avoidant defenses and argue that this finding challenges the "illusion of coping in avoidant attachment":

> This study highlighted the illusion of coping in avoidant attachment, as grief appears to manifest in general health symptoms and even poorer mental health functioning . . . Those violent loss survivors attempting to cope with the loss through avoidance may have been unable to integrate the loss as part of their life narrative, rendering them more susceptible to Prolonged Grief Disorder.
>
> (Meier et al., 2013, p.331)

Researchers have also looked at variables that may mediate the effects of attachment orientation on bereavement. In their study of bereavement after pregnancy loss, Scheidt and his colleagues found that social support correlated inversely with grief, symptoms of anxiety and depression, and overall psychological distress and PTSD symptoms (Scheidt et al., 2012). This finding is consistent with findings from studies demonstrating the importance of social support in coping with bereavement (Dyregrov & Dyregrov, 2008; Mancini & Bonanno, 2009; Mikulincer & Shaver, 2009; W. Stroebe et al., 2005). Whatever benefits accrue from the availability of social support, these are less likely to be available to anxiously and avoidantly attached individuals, who, in comparison to those who are securely attached, tend to have lower numbers of individuals they can turn to for support (Collins & Feeney, 2004), and are less satisfied with whatever support they do receive (Collins & Feeney, 2004; Dykas & Cassidy, 2011). The role of attachment in the decision to seek professional counseling has also been studied, although not specifically with respect to grief therapy. As predicted by attachment theory, the available evidence suggests that avoidantly attached individuals are less likely than anxiously attached individuals to seek counseling (Cheng et al., 2015; Shaffer et al., 2006). They are less likely to believe in the value of therapy relative to the potential risks of self-disclosure as compared to anxiously attached individuals, who, consistent with the observation that anxiously attached individuals devalue their ability to manage without the help of others, are more inclined to seek help from a therapist, more willing to self-disclose, and more positive in their appraisal of the potential benefits of therapy (Shaffer et al., 2006; Vogel et al., 2008).

Neurological Evidence of the Role of Attachment in Coping with Attachment Related Stress

While most studies of the role of attachment in coping with emotionally stressful events rely on self-report measures or interviews, recent inquiries into how people manage emotion have taken advantage of advances in brain imaging to address questions about how people manage emotion at a neurological level. In one of the first such studies, Gillath et al. used fMRI to identify differences in the neural processes underlying the emotion regulation strategies of avoidantly and anxiously attached individuals (Gillath et al., 2005). Given the instruction to think about negative relationship scenarios (conflict, breakups, or death of a partner), subjects with an anxious attachment orientation showed more activation in areas of the brain related to emotion and less activation in areas related to the down-regulation of emotion than non-anxious people, suggesting they "react more strongly to thoughts of loss while under-recruiting brain regions normally used to down-regulate negative emotions" (Gillath et al., 2005, p.835).

In another study using fMRI, Vrtička and colleagues identified distinct patterns in brain activation as a function of attachment anxiety or avoidance (Vrtička et al., 2012). For example, when exposed to strongly negative emotional scenes, avoidantly attached individuals were found to have less activation in areas of the brain associated with the reappraisal of negative stimuli and higher activation in areas of the brain associated with the suppression of emotion. These findings "reveal that reappraisal may not work for these individuals, leading to impaired down regulation of amygdal reactivity" (Vrtička et al., 2012, p.473). This pattern may help explain "why avoidantly attached individuals become highly emotional when their preferred regulation strategies fail or cannot be employed" (Vrtička & Vuilleumier, 2012, p.12). While further research is needed before firm conclusions about the neurological correlates of emotion regulation strategies can be reached, available scientific data supports theoretical assumptions about the association between attachment insecurity and altered or less efficient cognitive capacities (Vrtička & Vuilleumier, 2012).

Bridging Research and Practice

Along with the research presented in Chapter 3 concerning the impact of early attachment on development, and in particular the negative effects of early relational trauma, the findings reported in the previous section have implications for every aspect of service delivery for problematic grief, from program development to diagnosis and treatment. Shaffer and colleagues assert that the most important limitation of counseling is that it can only help people who seek treatment (Shaffer et al., 2006). The research cited here suggests that many people who are bereaved are lacking in social support, and that within this group, the subgroup of avoidantly attached individuals is among the least likely to seek the help of a professional counselor (Shaffer et al., 2006; Vogel et al., 2008). If a bereaved person does make it into a grief therapist's office, research suggests that the therapist will be more likely to build a strong alliance and to develop an appropriate strategy for treatment if the client's attachment orientation is taken into account (Levy et al., 2011). Levy and colleagues recommend that clinicians "titrate their interpersonal styles so as not to overwhelm dismissing patients or to appear disengaged, aloof or uninterested" to patients who have a preoccupied/anxious attachment style (Levy et al., 2011, p.396).

The loss of someone who is loved and trusted is a wrenching blow, but it is all the more difficult for people who are lacking in internal resources and external support. These resource deficits are among the factors that complicate the grief of people who are insecurely attached. The defensive strategies that insecurely attached individuals employ are, in addition, frequently obstacles to treatment. Establishing a strong therapeutic bond with a bereaved person who is insecurely attached is both essential and challenging, and depends very much on the clinician's ability to gain the client's trust. Trust is what allows the avoidant client to risk an encounter with feelings that are usually avoided or denied. Trust is what makes the anxious client willing to try to do things that they don't want to do, whether it is to go more deeply into their experience of their grief, or conversely, to let go of it and to begin to adapt to the new and changed world. As we will discuss more fully in Chapter 8, *trust in the therapist* promotes behavioral flexibility, enabling the bereaved individual to engage in the oscillation between loss and restoration that characterizes healthy grief. It also fosters a willingness to engage in exploratory behavior around examining their own internal experience and trying out a broader range of coping behaviors.

In the following section we provide examples from our own work and from the clinical literature on the integration of an attachment perspective into work with the bereaved. Several of the clients introduced here will reappear in Chapter 9, where we will focus on how to help people develop the resources they need to integrate significant loss.

Insecure Attachment and Complicated Grief

The Anxious Client

Ruth

Ruth, 48, admits that she always worried about something happening to her mother or father. An only child, she stayed close to her parents after graduation from college and saw them regularly. Now that her parents have both died she talks about having "lost her footing." Unmarried and with only one close friend, Ruth admits that she has never felt entirely comfortable being on her own. She depended on her parents for help in making all life decisions, and does not know how she will go on without them. Asked to speak about her childhood, Ruth describes a father who continually accused her of being too provocative in her dress and too free in stating her opinions. Although they were frequently in conflict about Ruth's choice of friends, career, and views, she never gave up on the idea that she could "win his love" by being a dutiful daughter.

Gloria

Gloria, 52, is a wife and mother of two teenage children. Her own mother is in a nursing home, and is not expected to live for more than six months. Gloria visits her several times a week. Her mother is extremely critical of Gloria, complains her daughter does not spend more time with her, and is never pleased with Gloria's efforts to bring her things she thinks her mother would like. Gloria feels tormented by the need to visit her mother and by her persistent feeling that she is a failure as a daughter. She weeps throughout the session, stopping only briefly when the therapist asks her a question or encourages her to pause and breathe. With all this, what terrifies Gloria the most is that her mother will die, and that without her, she will not be able to live. She sees her future as a period of torment while her mother lives, to be followed by a collapse into complete desperation when she dies.

Many people experience the fear and dislocation described by Gloria in the early stages of grief, but for the anxiously attached person, this fear is pervasive and unrelenting. What is different about the grief of a person who is anxiously attached, and why is it so often difficult for them to believe that they are capable of going on with their lives?

In the parlance of the DPM and TTM, the anxiously attached client has become entrenched in a Loss Orientation, and her biopsychosocial functioning is compromised. She is afraid of how she will manage without the deceased, or soon to be deceased, and her fear is amplified by a tendency toward negative expectations concerning the future, and a lack of faith in her capacity to deal with the uncertainties and stresses of everyday life on her own.

Trudy

Trudy, a 55 year old widow, has been in a support group for five years, but continues to feel that her life is out of control. Trudy describes her husband as a caring and responsible husband and father who earned a steady income, paid all the bills, and generally managed all the details of their lives. Prior to her husband's death Trudy had never worked or lived on her own; she moved in with her husband directly from her parents' home at the time of her marriage. Trudy recalls her parents as having been very loving. She was an only child and they treated her, in her words, "like a china doll." There was never any question when Trudy was growing up that her future would be in a marriage exactly like the one she eventually found, with a husband who would take care of her in much the same way that she had been cared for by her parents.

Not surprisingly, the illness and death of her husband threw Trudy into a panic. In addition to having to take on all domestic and financial responsibilities, she was faced with the need to find a placement for her adolescent son, who was diagnosed with autism, and whose periodic outbursts were disruptive and frightening. She despaired of being able to make plans for her son without her husband's help.

Trudy was extremely tearful in our sessions and frequently expressed the fear that she would never be able to get her life back on track. She felt alone and overwhelmed. Her sadness about her husband's death was layered with anger for his having deserted her by dying.

Anxiously attached clients are some of the easiest people with whom to establish a therapeutic bond, because they are desperate for connection. Their desperation is fueled by the need to identify and stay close to someone who will supply the strength and insight they find lacking within themselves, and they typically look to the therapist to fill this role. These clients also tend to have a pervasive fear of being criticized, rejected, or abandoned by the clinician. Their already shaky sense of self-esteem and self-efficacy has been compromised by the loss, and they find the world without the deceased to be mostly devoid of pleasure, meaning, or hope. They are pessimistic about their ability to survive the loss, and many report that others around them do not understand the extent of their grief and despair. Their memories of the deceased are often idealized, and they report significant distress at the thought of losing those memories of and connection with their loved one. The individual who is anxiously attached will generally be relieved to have someone really listen to them, and may seek extra contact with the therapist, either by trying to prolong a session, or by requesting more frequent sessions or additional contact (phone or e-mail) between sessions. Anxiously attached clients usually have ready access to their feelings about the loss, themselves, and their future, particularly their negative feelings. They will be open to suggestions that the therapist makes that involve self-care, but will often insist that they have no energy for exercise or social activities.

An important consideration in understanding the dynamic of bereavement in people who are anxiously attached, and one with important implications for their treatment, is that these individuals tend to operate on the assumption that sadness, yearning, and other painful emotions are "congruent with attachment goals, and they may seek to sustain and even exaggerate them" (Mikulincer & Shaver, 2014, p.241). In other words, anxiously attached individuals have learned that holding onto painful feeling states, and making their distress known to others, increases the likelihood that they will have their attachment needs met. They sustain this state of hyperactivation through an appraisal process in which the threatening aspects of events are magnified, their inability to manage their distress is exaggerated, and attention is focused on recalling past painful experiences and anticipating those that may occur in the future (Mikulincer et al., 2010; Shaver & Mikulincer, 2010). While anxiously attached clients may have some insight into their distress, their ability to reflect on the loss, reflect on its meaning, and construct a coherent narrative will often be compromised by the intensity of their affect.

The Avoidant Client

Margaret

Recalling the deaths of her mother and then her father in the preceding two years, Margaret sat on the edge of her chair, expressionless, her checkbook in one hand and her keys in the other. She looked around the room and her eyes settled on the office clock. With a tentative smile, the clinician said, "You look like you're going to bolt at any minute. The feeling I'm getting is that you think this is a waste of your time." "Oh, no," Margaret replied. "It's not that you're wasting my time; it's that I don't want to waste your time. Me talking about my feelings—why would anyone want to listen to that?"

The therapist said, "Hmm, well that's an interesting question—it makes me wonder where you got the idea that no one could possibly be interested in hearing about your feelings. Have you always felt that way? What about when you were a child? What did you do when you were, say, 5 or 6 and you were upset, crying?"

Margaret replied, "I don't remember ever crying as a child. I guess I was a very stoic child."

The nature and course of bereavement among avoidantly attached people, who do not present what is typically considered the "picture" of a grief stricken individual, have been a source of ongoing disagreement among researchers and clinicians (Parkes, 2013). The question that has consistently been raised about people who profess no particular emotional distress following a loss is whether these people are coping effectively with the loss, or are employing a strategy of suppressing uncomfortable or intolerable feelings. Clinical experience suggests that what brings avoidantly attached individuals into treatment is the breakdown of this strategy, signaled by the emergence of feelings that they are not equipped to manage, and often accompanied by a range of physical symptoms or dysfunctional behaviors, such as substance abuse or irritability in relationships. An additional motivation for treatment can be social pressure, typically from family members or friends, to seek professional help for their problems, and sometimes for their apparent lack of any response to the loss. As the following narrative suggests, these clients can be quite straightforward when it comes to their personal boundaries and the rules by which they want the clinician to abide.

Hannah

Hannah sought grief counseling six months after the death of her husband, who had been living with chronic heart disease for six years. Hannah made it clear from the outset that she had only come for counseling because her husband's hospice nurse told her that she should. When Hannah seemed about to tear up and the clinician made her usual gesture of offering her a tissue, Hannah balked, assuring her that she would not be crying, that she did not "cry in front of anyone, and what's the point of crying anyway." Asked about where she had learned that crying is pointless, Hannah waved away the question, adding that she was "not here to talk about my family, and don't expect me to do that." Hannah was determined to get through her bereavement as she had gotten through life until that point—with fierce determination and the resolute forward movement of a soldier in battle.

Despite her skepticism, Hannah continued to come to therapy, and after two months began to talk about the guilt she felt about not having taken better care of her husband. She also consented to disclose some details of her childhood. Hannah's parents ran their own business and traveled a great deal, during which time Hannah was left in the care of a series of nannies. She dismissed the idea that this was a problem for her in any way because she was "very independent."

After two months and six sessions, Hannah canceled several appointments, eventually leaving a brief message saying that she was doing much better and that she was very busy and would call to reschedule when she had more time. She returned three months later at the urging of a friend who was aware that Hannah was not sleeping, had lost a great deal of weight, and had suffered several minor physical injuries. When she arrived, Hannah reported that in addition to her physical symptoms, which were beginning to concern her, she had little interest in doing anything or seeing anyone and little hope that things would get better for her in the future.

Avoidantly attached clients, particularly those who, as Muller (Muller, 2010) has suggested, developed this orientation in response to early experiences of abuse or neglect, are likely to be guarded in relation to the grief therapist. They often display a reluctance to self-disclose, and their tone may at times become hostile. The avoidantly attached client will frequently minimize any need for help with their grief. Within the sessions, they will appear wary of losing control of their emotions, or making themselves vulnerable in the clinical encounter. Moreover, they often appear to be out of touch with or dissociated from their own thoughts and feelings about their loss, tending to minimize its impact on themselves and their life or showing an inability to articulate their feelings (Deno et al., 2013).

Avoidant clients may show little interest in cultivating ongoing psychological connection with the deceased, since they will see this as either not possible, or not necessary. The clinician may find themselves wondering "Is this all you feel?" or "Why don't you seem upset about this?" In response to questions about past losses or early experiences with caregivers, avoidant clients will typically state that "everything was fine," or "it was no big deal," or they may say that they are unable to recall memories and associated feelings about childhood. They may have an initially impressive ability to intellectualize about their experience, but their story will often lack a sense of the deep feeling that loss usually elicits in people. They will usually want practical answers, advice, and tools for coping—particularly about quickly restoring their functioning and "getting on" with their lives. In terms of the DPM, these clients often present with a premature and exclusionary RO, one that allows them to avoid going deeply into an LO.

The likelihood of ruptures in the therapeutic relationship with avoidant clients will be reduced if the clinician is respectful of the boundaries that the avoidant client has so assiduously constructed, both in respect to their response to the loss, and their engagement in the therapeutic process itself. The overarching goal in working with an avoidant client is to help them, gradually and at their own pace, develop access to and tolerance for their negative emotions about the loss, while supporting their ability to explore, and then extract themselves from, the depths of their grief.

Finally, while early trauma is most often associated with disorganized attachment, Muller proposes that it is also a factor in the development of an avoidant attachment orientation (Muller, 2010). Avoidantly attached individuals, he writes, remember and report traumatic events, but tend to minimize their meaning or negative impact. Referencing Bowlby's concept of *defensive exclusion*, Muller describes avoidant attachment as a strategy developed to keep hurtful attachment experiences out of awareness:

> Having developed a worldview that others cannot be depended on, the individual tends toward a pattern of self-reliance and a view of self as independent, strong, and normal. Along with this pattern, there is a tendency to dismiss and devalue experiences of closeness, intimacy and vulnerability.
>
> (Muller, 2010, p.2)

The Disorganized Client

Vince

Vince first sought help following the death of his best friend in a house fire. In the course of his sessions with the therapist it became apparent that Vince had significant problems with anxiety. He used alcohol to self-medicate, mostly on weekends, and was able to function at work. In gathering information about Vince's history before the loss, it emerged that his mother had died two years earlier. He did not at first have much to say about his mother, but what soon became clear to both the therapist and client was that Vince's anxiety had begun in childhood, a time in his life when he often felt alone and afraid. Vince also admitted that he, doubted his capacity for intimacy, and feared that now that his friend was gone he would be completely alone.

As a fuller picture of Vince's early life emerged, the traumatic nature of his child-hood and the extent of unresolved feelings about his mother came more clearly into focus. Speaking of her, Vince became quite agitated and his sentences became disjointed and contradictory, reflecting the nature of the relationship with a woman who was alternately nurturing and (usually after several cocktails) terrifying. Vince described his mother as "two people . . . and you never knew which person you were going to get. Even now, I can't tell you if she was a good mother or a bad mother, a sober, responsible person or just a raging alcoholic."

In our experience, many people who seek help in dealing with complications in their bereavement have the kind of early relational trauma reported by Vince. The observation that early trauma is prevalent in people who present in treatment with bereavement issues has been reported elsewhere (Zech & Arnold, 2011). In Vince's case, problems with emotion regulation that could be traced back to a chaotic and frightening childhood became overwhelming in the aftermath of his friend's death. The flood of feelings, and the sudden traumatic loss of the one person he had been able to turn to for support, set off a secondary wave of painful memories about his childhood, many of which involved a similar sense of being alone and unsafe.

Vince's description of his mother as "two people," one safe and comforting, and the other frightening and hurtful, brings to mind Main's accounts of the mothers of infants classified as disorganized with respect to attachment (Main & Solomon, 1986). Main observed that the behavior of infants whose mothers exhibited this kind of erratic and unpredictable behavior was likewise, unpredictable and contradictory, as though the infants were never sure about whether they should approach, or avoid, their caregiver. In the most extreme cases, these infants lapsed into a state of dissociation, immobilization, and feigned death (Main & Hesse, 1990). These responses can persist into adulthood, and are often evident in the behavior of bereaved adults who, in the language of the AAI, have unresolved losses or trauma (Thomson, 2010). In the following example, a bereaved client exhibits the shutdown and dissociation described by Main, a response that, as discussed in Chapter 3, may be a reprise of her first and best strategy for coping with emotional pain.

Marta

Marta, 42, sought grief counseling after the death of her father. It seemed difficult for Marta to "settle" in the therapist's office, and she spoke of her father in a halting manner, stopping often to look down at the floor until she was prompted by the therapist to continue. Marta had no long term relationships and few friends. Her relationship with her mother and siblings was strained, and she spent much of her time alone. Marta reported a number of health issues that she felt prevented her from living a fuller life, although she was not able to describe clearly what the source of these symptoms was or why she had not been able to find any relief from them.

In discussing Marta's history, it emerged that her father had been a "difficult" man, and that her mother frequently had angry outbursts that included physically attacking her children. Questions about the extent of the abuse, and her father's involvement in it, were met either with silence or with fragmented accounts of violence between various family members, some of it directed at Marta.

Soon after beginning treatment Marta indicated that she wanted to understand more about her childhood and why she was so reluctant to go anywhere near the neighborhood where she had grown up. Several attempts were made to help Marta assemble memories of her childhood, but on each occasion, her narrative would become fragmented and dreamlike, until she stopped talking and sat staring into space. On some occasions these episodes were preceded by Marta reporting that she felt a tingling in her legs, followed by loss of feeling in her lower extremities.

Retelling the story of a painful and frightening childhood is a difficult, but critical component of treatment for many survivors of early attachment trauma (Allen, 2001, 2013), but when this memory work produces a dissociative, shutdown response, it is not our practice to continue on this course (Rothschild, 2000). This type of response in a client signals the need for work on building internal resources and external sources of support, as detailed in Part III. Once these resources are in place it may be possible to resume building the narrative and to move the client, one step at a time, toward a reconstitution of memory that helps them to make sense of their current functioning. For example, a client who goes through life convinced that other people cannot be trusted, and who looks for the insult in every comment directed their way, may not relate these attitudes to early relational trauma. By providing an explanation of the effects of early trauma, the clinician can help the client begin to modify their appraisal of the intentions of others, which may be the first step in helping the client reduce interpersonal conflict and build social support.

Audrey

Although her father had died two years before, Audrey, 51, still felt his presence every day. The emotional abuse that she and her siblings had suffered as children continued to affect all of them, but in different ways, and it was hard for her to talk to either of them about what they had been through. Her relationship with her mother was even more problematic, largely because of her mother's refusal to acknowledge that theirs had been anything but a "perfect" family.

In the two years since her father's death Audrey's life had "collapsed"; she had lost her (good) job and had a series of brief, unsuccessful relationships. Her poor health was also a matter of serious concern, and she did not have the energy to look for a new job. She was about to lose her condo, and felt that she would then have no alternative but to move in with her mother.

The intensity of Audrey's account of her relationship with her father and her tendency to periodically lapse into the present tense in talking about him were evidence of the lack of resolution concerning Audrey's early trauma and her father's death. She felt that the residual effects of her father's violent outbursts and unrelenting verbal attacks had left her crippled, depriving her of the energy, direction, and will needed to establish a "normal relationship and a normal life."

Audrey was able to access many memories of her childhood, but they only served to fuel her anger, frustration, and sense of powerlessness. Financial difficulties that arose while Audrey was being seen in therapy led to her moving in with her elderly mother, with whom Audrey had a relationship precariously balanced between love and hate. Within a few weeks of moving in with her mother, Audrey reported that she was "mad all the time." Her anger was fueled by comments from her mother, which she interpreted as expressions of her mother's belief that Audrey was incompetent and would never be able to live independently, despite the fact that she had been doing so for more than two decades. Perhaps the hardest to bear, Audrey heard in her mother's criticism the voice of her father, who could emotionally flatten any member of the family with his furious contempt.

As these examples illustrate, survivors of abusive and/or neglectful early caregiving, many of whom have features of disorganized attachment, face a number of difficulties in dealing with grief, including impaired emotion regulation, mistrust of others, a loss of cognitive and executive functioning, and low self-esteem (Allen, 2013). The reluctance to let down their guard reflects the experience of being mistreated by, and consequently afraid of, their caregiver. The negative view of self is a holdover from childhood, when most of what they heard and internalized was criticism and accusation. Given the deeply embedded nature of their low self-regard, these clients tend to reject positive comments regarding their strengths or competencies. The more hopeful and positive the clinician, the greater the likelihood that the clinician's opinions will be dismissed, resulting, paradoxically, in an empathic failure in the therapeutic relationship.

In keeping with their need to protect themselves from others, people with an attachment orientation shaped by early trauma tend to attribute hostile or critical intent to others, and the speed and intensity with which they rise to their own defense makes it difficult for them to establish or sustain healthy relationships, even though they may yearn for such attachments. Like Marta, they may not have a clear memory of specific incidents of abuse, but over time, a sense of the danger and dysfunction of their early family life may come into focus. When the memories do come back, the person is then confronted with a whole new set of questions, the biggest one being, why? This is a question that Vince confronted again and again as he tried to make sense of his mother's frighteningly erratic behavior. Like Audrey, he despaired of ever being able to understand the behavior and intentions of other people well enough to risk letting them get close.

The Restoration of Mentalizing: A Common Factor in Attachment-Informed Grief Therapy

We propose boldly that mentalizing – attending to mental states in oneself and others – is the most fundamental common factor among psychotherapeutic treatments . . . To be effective – in establishing a therapeutic alliance, for example – we clinicians must mentalize skillfully; concomitantly, we must engage our patients in mentalizing.

(Allen et al., 2008, p.1)

Jon Allen has devoted much of his career to understanding how early relational trauma affects mental health and more recently, to explaining how psychotherapy works to restore healthy functioning (Allen, 2001, 2013). Young children have emotional and physical needs that they cannot fulfill on their own, and they become distressed if an attuned caregiver is not present to satisfy them. An attuned caregiver understands the child's thoughts and feelings, mirrors back these aspects of the child's experience, and responds to the child's needs on the basis of that understanding. Part of what Fonagy refers to as mentalizing, this process is at the heart of healthy emotional development, a premise we have examined in previous chapters. The engaged presence of a caregiver who can mentalize accurately about the child's experience and reflect that back to the child is what enables a child to become aware of himself as an independent being who has the capacity to understand himself and to expect that others will understand him. Put differently, the empathic attunement involved in mentalizing on the part of the caregiver supports the development of mentalizing in the child. In Allen's view, mentalizing is the "psychological glue that bonds attachment relationships" as well as the foundation of emotion regulation (Allen, 2013, p.31). In the absence of mentalizing on the part of the parent, the child is "left psychologically alone in unbearable emotional states repeatedly" (Allen, 2013, p.31). Allen proposes that treatment in these cases begins with the creation of a safe therapeutic environment that promotes the development of mentalizing, and with it, increased capacity for emotion regulation. The therapist, in other words, performs the fundamental function of an attachment figure in a secure bond, supporting reregulation in the short term and promoting the growth of internal self-regulation over the longer term, by virtue of strengthening the individual's capacity for mentalization.

In childhood, secure attachment enables a child to move flexibly between seeking safety and exploration. In adulthood, the goal is much the same. In grief therapy, this flexibility is what enables the bereaved person to move between a Loss and Restoration Orientation, between abject grief and emotional equanimity. Supporting emotional and behavioral flexibility is, as we have seen, a goal not just for grief therapy with survivors of early relational trauma, but for grief therapy as a whole.

Vince

Over the course of a year, Vince began to identify the roots of his anxiety in the frightening and unpredictable conditions of his childhood environment. It was difficult for Vince to acknowledge just how out of control his mother had been on many occasions, because he felt that talking about these memories was a kind of betrayal. He eventually came to realize that what was at issue was not a need to blame his mother, but to assign responsibility for events in his life that had resulted in a negative sense of himself, a view bound up with shame about his own drinking. It was important for Vince to realize that he did not have to blame his mother, but neither did he have to forgive her. Instead, what he needed was to be able to see her behavior for what it was, and then to understand some of the factors in her own life that had led her to behave as she had—in other words, to mentalize about his mother. As the intensity of Vince's feelings about his mother decreased, he was able to talk about her, and ultimately about the loss of his friend, without becoming overwhelmed. While he continued to periodically refer back to his childhood experience, Vince became increasingly interested in talking about his present life and his goals for the future.

These cases illustrate the connection between attachment experience and bereavement, and accord with research that has identified attachment as a significant factor in a range of life transitions and stressors, including significant loss (Burke & Neimeyer, 2013). In the remainder of this chapter, we will expand upon the role of attachment status as a factor in response to loss. Specifically, we will consider the implications of viewing attachment as a neurobiological system helping to maintain physical and psychological homeostasis, and the dysregulation that inevitably results from the death of a loved one—an event that permanently removes from a person's life someone who was critical to system functioning.

Attachment, Loss, and Dysregulation: Insights from Neuroscience and Related Research

As discussed in Chapter 3, neuroscience research has provided an additional body of evidence for the lasting impact of early caregiving and the persistence of regulatory deficits in children and adults who do not receive adequate physical and emotional nurturance (J. R. Schore & Schore, 2008). These deficits are associated with a range of emotional problems and with difficulties in coping with a variety of life stressors (Lobb et al., 2010). While many life events can impact a person's psychological functioning and physical well-being, several writers have suggested that significant interpersonal loss imposes a uniquely significant strain on coping capacity and biological regulation (Sbarra & Hazan, 2008; Shear & Shair, 2005). Shear and Shair offer a model of the mourning process that is informed both by attachment theory and by Hofer's (Hofer, 1996) animal research on the role of attachment relationships as "biobehavioral regulators." According to Hofer, in mature adults, many of the mutual regulatory functions of relationships are maintained by an internal representation of the relationship when the attachment figure is not available. Thus, adults do not need the continual physical presence of an attachment figure to feel secure and to keep their attachment system deactivated. Instead, the internal representation of the person largely serves that function, as long as the psychological availability of the attachment figure is not threatened. However, as Shear and Shair observe, and as we have noted, the death of a loved one is a different matter. By definition, responding to this kind of loss requires the mourner to confront the *permanent absence* of someone who has played a role both as a real and present attachment figure (or recipient of caregiving in the case of parents), and as a representational figure in the individual's internal working model of the relationship.

Another important contribution to our understanding of interpersonal loss as a uniquely significant stressor is Sbarra and Hazan's analysis of research concerning the physiological and emotional impact of bereavement (Sbarra & Hazan, 2008). Consistent with the position taken by Shear and Shair (2005), as well as by Mikulincer and Shaver (2008b), Sbarra and Hazan argue that the grief triggered by the loss of an attachment figure is fundamentally different from the response to other types of (non-relational) loss.

When long term mate relationships end, many adults lose the person who helps them maintain psychological and physiological homeostasis . . . Accordingly, when relationships dissolve, it is this state of security that must be regained as individuals recover from separation and loss experiences.

(Sbarra & Hazan, 2008, p.142)

This understanding of the impact of partner loss, which is supported by research concerning the neurobiology of adult attachment, the functional elements of human co-regulation, and the particulars of biobehavioral response to attachment figure loss (Mikulincer & Shaver, 2008b; Pietromonaco et al., 2006; Shear & Shair, 2005), accords with Schore and Schore's assertion that the primary function of attachment relationships is to *interpersonally regulate multiple biological and psychological systems within the individuals involved in the relationship* (J. R. Schore & Schore, 2008, 2014). It is also consistent with Mikulincer and Shaver's discussion of grief as a *dysregulation of these systems* (Mikulincer & Shaver, 2008a). Citing Mikulincer and Shaver, Sbarra and Hazan explain that the loss of a significant attachment figure deprives us of the felt sense of safety that enables us to engage in exploratory activity. Sbarra and Hazan integrate this view of dysregulation into a two stage model of grief in response to relational loss. The first stage is dysregulation, a consequence of the disruption of homeostasis previously discussed. The transition from dysregulation to the "organized stress response," represented by the DPM, comes second. The authors suggest that we can better understand how the DPM process of oscillation breaks down in complicated grief by understanding *the role of attachment relationships in regulation of biological systems*, and the dysregulation that results from loss of the attachment figure.

In Sbarra and Hazan's model, the sleep disruption, loss of appetite, and decreased energy associated with acute grief result from the loss of a person who served a "homeostasis maintaining function" (Sbarra & Hazan, 2008, p.149). In the immediate aftermath of loss, these admittedly distressing symptoms can have an adaptive function. Like the weakness and fatigue that accompany physical illness, these symptoms are arguably "part of a state that aids in physiological reorganization and recuperation during times of stress" (Sbarra & Hazan, 2008, p.153). In other words, grief depletes our energy and makes it hard for us to focus on the things that usually occupy our attention, facilitating increased attention to the reality of the loss and the feelings associated with it. Grief forces us to slow down, so that we can adjust to the changes presented by the loss. However, when this acute phase of mourning results in a continued flow of stress hormones and compromised immune functioning, along with a number of other negative biological events that adversely affect mental and physical health (Kiecolt-Glaser et al., 2002; Thoits, 2010), the individual is likely developing complicated grief.

Having thus made a case for the central role of biobehavioral dysregulation in bereavement, Sbarra and Hazan ask the question that so many others have posed: how do we account for differences in adaptation to loss? Their answers bring them back to evidence of the role of attachment orientation in mediating the individual's response to loss. Secure attachment comes into play first in the movement from dysregulation to organized oscillation, and second in maintaining the balance between hyperactivating and deactivating strategies for coping with loss. The DPM represents bereavement as a process of oscillation between loss and restoration, and complicated or prolonged grief as a breakdown in oscillation. Sbarra and Hazan emphasize the role of physiological systems in this process. The DPM relates problematic grief to the *overuse of secondary strategies* associated with insecure attachment. Intervention models based on the DPM are therefore designed to promote the oscillation process. Sbarra and Hazan emphasize the *biological dysregulation* associated with loss of an attachment figure, and conclude that managing this dysregulation is "the chief task in coping with loss" (Sbarra & Hazan, 2008, p.161). Reregulation is a necessary precondition for healing from the loss of an attachment figure, or in the case of parents, of a caregiving recipient (see Chapter 5). This theme—of dysregulation in response to loss, and the role of attachment figures, including the grief therapist, in facilitating reregulation—is one that will recur throughout the remaining chapters of this book.

From Reregulation to Integration

> When all is well and we are in a state of calm, there is no reason to learn anything new. At the other extreme, states of high arousal and danger are not the time to learn anything new.
>
> (Cozolino, 2010, p.231)

> We need to always keep in mind that as primates, attachment equals survival and abandonment equals death.
>
> (Cozolino, 2010, p.285)

Taken together, these two quotations make an interesting point about recovery from bereavement. First, Cozolino tells us that human beings tend to learn new things when there is a *need* for them to learn, when there is a disconnect between what we know, and the knowledge we need to survive and succeed in a changing world. In this sense, a certain amount of discomfort is good. But too much arousal, too much discomfort, and we are not able to learn. And if, as Cozolino succinctly puts it, the loss of a key relationship triggers terror in a person, then as long as that state continues, it is unlikely that the person will be able to learn anything new. With respect to grief therapy, this would suggest that the dysregulation brought on by acute grief must be brought within manageable limits before the integration of experience can occur. Before the therapist can help a grieving client to explore their relationship with the deceased, and with the new world they face in the absence of their loved one, the immediate, acute physical and psychological impact of the loss must be addressed. Once a certain amount of reregulation and system "settling" has taken place, then the client can begin to learn, and to rebuild an internal and external world in congruence with their changed circumstance.

Even mourners with a secure attachment orientation will for a time be dysregulated by the loss of a loved one. For these individuals, intervention may be more on the order of grief counseling than grief therapy (Worden, 1983/2008, 2009). While dysregulated by their loss, helping mourners to reregulate and begin to adjust to life without their loved one may primarily be a matter of being a good listener, helping to normalize what they are going through, and offering a cognitive scaffolding for understanding their reactions to the loss. For individuals with insecure attachment, the process is likely to be more complicated, and treatment more nuanced and tailored to the client's specific attachment orientation. Yet even in these cases, as we already have seen, the attuned therapist can help a client reregulate and begin to focus flexibly, openly, and honestly on the work of establishing a continuing bond with the deceased, while attending to the demands of their new life, and the relationships that remain a part of it.

For many bereaved people, living with grief is a daily hardship that feels unbearable, until they bear it, and discover that there are still things in life that can surprise and delight them. The opportunity to bear witness as people discover their own strengths, to be there when the flicker of light in their eyes signals the beginning of renewed hope for a future in which happiness is once again a possibility, is part of what makes counseling the bereaved such fulfilling work. In Part III we will address in detail how this process unfolds.

Summary

We will leave discussion of the details of the treatment strategies introduced here for Part III, and conclude this chapter with some final observations about the value of attachment theory in bereavement research, theory, and practice. We began by looking at models of the grief process, and observed that as our understanding of grief has evolved, these models have increasingly emphasized variability in the course of grief as opposed to a fixed trajectory. Both the TTM and the DPM draw attention to the variations in how people respond to loss and the multiple factors that affect the course of their bereavement. The DPM, in particular, draws upon Bowlby's views regarding the role of attachment security in enabling a person to respond to loss in a manner that promotes healthy adaptation. Mikulincer and Shaver make explicit use of Bowlby's ideas in their explanation of how insecure attachment compromises the ability to flexibly attend to thoughts and feelings related to the loss, and those that are related to accommodating the changes brought about by the loss and attending to ongoing relationships and responsibilities. We have also reviewed research that supports the theoretical assumptions of Bowlby and contemporary theorists, including neurological research that helps us understand how insecure attachment impacts people's ability to manage stress and recover from events that disrupt and dysregulate their emotional equilibrium. Together with models of the grief process, this research suggests the importance of attachment experience and attachment orientation in how people respond to significant loss. Through the use of case studies from our own practices, we then began to address some of the implications for practitioners of an attachment-informed approach to bereavement therapy. We concluded with a brief examination of attachment relationships as a co-regulated biobehavioral system that becomes dysregulated by loss, bringing attention to the imperative for the therapist to bring the system back within tolerable bounds before the real work of reintegration and restoration can begin.

Bereavement is a response to the loss of a relationship, and all grief therapies have in common the provision of a particular kind of skilled social support designed to help the individual acknowledge and tolerate loss related feelings and thoughts. In an environment that encourages honest appraisal of the relationship with the deceased and realistic assessment of the challenges imposed by the loss, bereaved individuals become better able to acknowledge and tolerate loss related feelings and thoughts, and at the same time to recognize that there are people and pursuits that continue to be of value and make life without the deceased still worth living.

Our goal in this chapter has been to demonstrate how understanding a client's attachment orientation can help identify the link between attachment and bereavement, and to illustrate a variety of ways in which factors related to attachment can contribute to complications in grief. A further goal has been to suggest that sensitivity to attachment orientation or style can help the therapist avoid errors that may compromise the therapeutic bond over the course of treatment. In the next two chapters we will direct our attention to variations in bereavement response and bereavement treatment that are attributable to two related sets of factors: those having to do with the kinship relationship with the deceased, and with trauma in the mode of death.

5   The Impact of the Relationship with the Deceased

In this chapter, we will examine the impact of a variety of relational factors on adjustment to loss, including kinship relationship to the deceased, the nature of the relationship with respect to dependency, emotional distance, or proximity, and other psychological factors. We will also look at findings concerning how these factors affect the quality of the attachment bond with the deceased *after* the death has occurred, a relationship that has been described as the continuing bond with the dead (Klass et al., 1996). We will then explore the implications of these findings when viewed through the lens of modern attachment theory.

Kinship Relationship with the Deceased

Different relationships serve different functions and fulfill different needs in people, and these differences manifest themselves in the diversity of responses to loss. The impact of different kinds of kinship losses has been studied extensively, and we begin with a brief review of some of the findings from this research.

Death of a Spouse/Partner

Researchers in thanatology have focused a great deal of attention on the impact of partner loss, with many of these studies concentrated on the loss of a married spouse among the elderly (Carr & Jeffreys, 2011; Carr et al., 2006). These studies have identified a number of negative sequelae of partner loss, including elevated rates of depression, anxiety, complicated grief, financial difficulties (particularly for women), loss of social connections, and excess mortality (including suicidality, particularly for elderly males) (Byrne & Raphael, 1997; Innamorati et al., 2011; McIntosh, 1992). However, these negative outcomes are by no means universal or inevitable after the death of a long term partner. Instead, researchers have identified several different "loss trajectories" after the death of a partner, which range in intensity and duration from a relatively minor and short-lived disturbance in the surviving partner's functioning, to chronic depression and/or complicated grief in other mourners (Mancini et al., 2006). Thus, partner loss, particularly in later life, does not automatically lead to long term problematic outcomes. In comparison, younger spouses generally experience more psychological distress, a finding that is probably due to the increased difficulties of single-parenting and economic hardship that may accompany the loss of a partner in the child-rearing years (Carr et al., 2006).

Most of the challenges that accompany partner loss are related to the long term nature of the relationship, and the functional and emotional interdependency that marriage and other long term intimate relationships entail. Life partners provide economic benefits, sexual and psychological companionship, emotional support for coping with stressful events, the opportunity for shared parenting if children are involved, labor sharing around domestic responsibilities, and mutual caregiving in times of illness. Loss of a person who is relied upon to fill these role functions amplifies the responses that are characteristic of partner loss: yearning, loneliness, anxiety about coping in the world without the partner, and a sense of disorientation about how to proceed in life. Among the elderly, the emotional burden of loss often comes at the end of an extended period in which the survivor has cared for their partner through a long and debilitating illness, and is already stressed and exhausted (Carr & Jeffreys, 2011; Carr et al., 2006). In short, the loss of a partner, although not universally debilitating, produces significant distress, whether it occurs earlier or later in life.

Attachment and Partner Loss

In most Western cultures adulthood is a time when, sooner or later, a person's primary attachment relationship is transferred from parents to a spouse or partner (Jordan et al., 1993; Walsh & McGoldrick, 2004). Indeed, the failure to make this transition can produce major conflict and dysfunction within marital and family relationships (Jordan et al., 1993). Ideally, the relationship a person builds with their life partner provides an emotional safe haven in times of distress, and a secure base for dealing with the larger worlds of work and social relationships. Partners also play a crucial role in reciprocal affect regulation and adult identity development and maintenance (Mikulincer & Shaver, 2007; Sbarra & Hazan, 2008). The loss of a partner who provides emotional grounding, particularly in times of distress, can be highly destabilizing for the surviving partner.

This perspective is supported by the growing body of research demonstrating that one of the most robust predictors of complicated grief following partner loss is the attachment style of the bereaved partner (Parkes, 2013). This includes both the bereaved individual's attachment style in the relationship with the deceased partner, as well as the attachment style developed by the individual in their family of origin. For example, numerous studies have shown that high levels of dependency in the marital relationship are usually associated with poorer bereavement outcomes following the death of the spouse (Denckla et al., 2011; Mancini et al., 2009; Ott et al., 2007). Dependency appears to be a marker for an anxious or a preoccupied attachment style in both the relationship with the deceased, and in the mourner's general attachment style (Johnson et al., 2008). In these instances, the marriage may have helped the spouse by offsetting earlier attachment deficits, including difficulties with emotional self-regulation. Without the partner's support, these difficulties may reemerge, and can result in a marked impairment of self-regulation and other attachment related functions. Lowered self-esteem, and a higher incidence of depression, have also been identified in this group of bereaved spouses (Johnson et al., 2008). There is also evidence that the quality of the prior marital relationship moderates attachment style and bereavement outcome, with an avoidant attachment style being most helpful in bereavement situations where marital quality was high (Mancini et al., 2009), and the partner has a dismissively avoidant attachment style, rather than a fearfully avoidant attachment style (Fraley & Bonanno, 2004) (again suggesting the role of anxiety in contributing to complicated grief outcomes). To summarize, long term partners serve as significant attachment figures, and their loss is often associated with the distress and activation of the attachment system that such a loss entails.

Death of a Child

> Mothers express intense feelings of pleasure and satisfaction when they are able to protect and comfort their children; they experience heightened anger, sadness, anxiety, or despair when they are separated from the children, or when their ability to protect and comfort the child is threatened or blocked.
>
> (George & Solomon, 2008, p.835)

One of the most consistent findings in bereavement research is that the death of a child has a significant and sometimes very long-lasting impact on most parents—especially on mothers (Buckle & Fleming, 2011; Tedeschi & Calhoun, 2003). The literature suggests that the death of a child (including adult children) is experienced as an event that is out of the developmental order of life and one that may engender profound feelings of helplessness and failure on the part of the parents. This is true regardless of the cause of death; however, parents who see the death as being one that they could have prevented (e.g., SIDS deaths, suicide, drug overdoses) seem particularly vulnerable to feelings of guilt and failure (Feigelman et al., 2012; Keesee et al., 2008; Lichtenthal et al., 2013; Rando, 1991; Rubin, 1993; Rubin & Malkinson, 2001).

Empirical studies have demonstrated that bereaved parents can experience high levels of problematic reactions, including intense sadness, guilt, depression, and yearning for the child, increased levels of marital tension or estrangement from the other parent (although increased divorce rates have not always been found), and longer lasting effects than after other forms of kinship loss (Feigelman et al., 2012; Rubin, 1993; Rubin et al., 2001). In addition, not only marital but also parental functioning may be seriously disrupted by the death of a child. While day to day functioning does usually recover, many bereaved parents report a more or less permanent state of yearning for their child that is relatively immune to diminution over time.

Attachment and Child Loss

To understand bereavement, Bowlby (and most subsequent attachment theorists) have largely focused on the model of a distressed child seeking reunion with a caregiver/ attachment figure. However, Bowlby also discussed an additional and crucial behavioral system: *the caregiving system* (George & Solomon, 2008; Mikulincer & Shaver, 2007; J. Solomon & George, 1996). Other neurologically based researchers and theorists have likewise described the biological basis of the caregiving system and its manifestation in adult intimate relationships (Coan, 2008; Nelson & Panksepp, 1998; Panksepp & Biven, 2012). As with attachment behaviors, caregiving behaviors are biologically rooted in the vital need to protect the helpless human offspring, and as such, confer an evolutionary advantage on the infant who is the recipient of such behaviors (Archer, 1999). Also like attachment behaviors, the caregiving behavioral system can be understood as having a set-point goal: nurturance, protection, and ultimately, survival of the child (George & Solomon, 2008; Mikulincer & Shaver, 2007). As such, an extremely diverse range of behaviors can be seen as falling into the category of caregiving behaviors. Anything from a mother nursing her infant, to a parent earning an income to support the family or put a child through college, can be broadly understood as caregiving behaviors. And lastly, like attachment behaviors, the caregiving bond reflects an intense affective bond between the caregiver and the child, and tends to be particularly activated by separation and threat. *In short, the caregiving behavioral system is the reciprocal of the attachment behavioral system, but it has a different goal—the protection of another person (usually a dependent child), rather than protection of the self.*

Simply put, parents serve as a secure base and a safe haven in times of distress for their offspring, but in healthy family functioning, the reverse is *not* true, at least with young children. Parents seek proximity with their distressed child, not to assure their own physical survival, but that of their children. Of course, successfully protecting and nurturing a child can engender powerful feelings of gratification and accomplishment in a parent—key elements of the psychological identity of parents. It has also been postulated that parents are "wired" by evolutionary forces to try to ensure the survival of their genetic legacy (Simpson & Belsky, 2008). In this very broad sense, caregiving does involve a parent's attempt to survive, psychologically and genetically. It is also true that the role of caregiver and the role of care-recipient can and often do reverse. This can be observed when adult children assume the role of caregiver and attachment figure for their aging and more dependent parents (Field & Wogrin, 2011). Additionally, it has long been noted that in dysfunctional family systems, younger children often take on the role of a psychological (or even physical) protector of their parents, a premature reversal of these roles sometimes referred to as a "parental child." But this is generally viewed as a pathological deviation from the normal positioning of parent and child in healthy family development (Walsh & McGoldrick, 2004).

We believe that in order to appreciate the impact of child loss on bereaved parents, it is crucial to understand this fundamental difference in the goal or set-point of caregiving behavior. Unlike the common attachment theory formulation that grief in adults is similar to separation distress in a child who has been separated from an attachment figure, when a parent loses a child, much of the emotional pain endured by a bereaved parent has to do with the perceived failure to protect and nurture the child—ultimately, to keep the child from death. In a very real sense, the feelings that bereaved parents report after the death of their child are the mirror image of the attachment based feelings that a child may experience upon separation from their parent(s). Perhaps most prominent of these are the intense feelings of yearning for reunion with the child, a kind of *caregiver proximity seeking* that reflects the deep feelings of purpose and pleasure that nurturing and protecting a child may provide. Likewise there may be protest at the separation from the child through death, although most commonly this anger is directed at the self and manifests as guilt over the child's death, not anger at the child for abandoning the parent (the suicide of a child may be an exception to this). Bereaved parents can also display a tremendous amount of attachment related anxiety about the child's well-being that is accompanied by an urge to search for their child. All of this occurs despite the parents' cognitive understanding that their child is biologically dead. In short, parents display attachment type behaviors and emotions after the death of their child, but they are the result of bonding with their child as the recipient of their caregiving efforts, not of the loss of an attachment figure. The primary aim of the behavior, rather than providing safety and security for the parent, is to provide this for the child—a persistent response, even when the child is deceased. Put differently, the caregiving behavioral system stays activated for a considerable period of time after the death of a child, and the gradual deactivation of it is a central component of the grieving process for grieving parents.

Death of a Sibling

Compared to the death of a spouse or a child, there is a relative dearth of research and clinical literature on the impact of the death of a sibling. That which does exist is focused primarily on the effects of the loss of a sibling in childhood, rather than in adulthood (Marshall & Davies, 2011). Still, clinical experience suggests that for some people, the death of a sibling may be a significant loss with a lasting effect on the surviving sibling(s). As with the other losses being described in this chapter, it is useful to examine the function that siblings play in each other's lives in order to understand the impact of this type of kinship loss.

For many adults, the sibling relationship is the longest continuous relationship in their life, spanning childhood, adolescence, adulthood, and on into later life. Siblings provide continuity to an individual's identity and sense of personal history in a way that is unmatched by other relationships. Depending on the nature of the sibling relationship, their birth order, and the family dynamics surrounding their childhood, siblings may serve as important additional adjunct attachment figures during childhood development, providing psychological security, support, and an important intimate relationship. They may help to counteract some of the negative effects of dysfunctional attachment dynamics between children and parents in the family, mitigating the effects of neglectful or abusive parenting. Of course, sibling relationships can also be a source of significant conflict and competitiveness during childhood, and can sometimes have a major impact on the development of emotional insecurity and low self-esteem, particularly when parents selectively favor one sibling over another. The reciprocal of this family dynamic for the favored child is a sense of guilt, unworthiness, and sometimes hyper-responsibility for a sibling who is openly out of favor with the parents. Lastly, siblings (usually older siblings) may also serve as role models for how to deal with parents, other authority figures (e.g., teachers), and peers. They thus can be an important source of learning and new information about the world for younger brothers or sisters, particularly around differentiation from the family of origin.

For some siblings these functions may continue into adulthood and even old age. They include serving as a foundation of emotional support and identity, as well as later functions of financial support or practical help in childcare, management of aging parents, etc. This can have obvious benefits when the adult sibling relationship is close and more or less egalitarian. However, it can also have predictable disadvantages when the siblings continue to act as rivals or antagonists toward one another. The emotional gravitational pull of family of origin dynamics between siblings, even among otherwise well-functioning and autonomous adults, is a common clinical problem (Jordan et al., 1993). When considering the impact of the death of a sibling, then, these various attachment functions and roles, both childhood and adult, will need to be identified and mourned when they are lost.

Death of a Parent

The death of an older parent is the most common form of bereavement in the developed world, even more universal than the death of a spouse (Balk, 2013). Perhaps because of this, the research literature suggests that it is also typically the least disruptive of losses for adults (Jordan & Ware, 1997). The death of an older parent is also the least likely to produce a complicated grief response. For most people, the normal developmental course of life involves a diminution of parents as important attachment figures (Moss et al., 2001). Note that this is different from parents continuing as a source of affection, shared history, reciprocal obligation, and sometimes, practical and financial assistance.

Attachment theory suggests that by the time adulthood is reached, the relationship between the child and their parent has been internalized as a working model of both interpersonal connection, and emotional security. In addition, the need for attachment figures has been largely transferred to other important persons in the individual's life, including their spouse, siblings, and close friends (Jordan et al., 1993). The death of an older parent is likely to produce sadness and nostalgia over the loss of a key figure from one's past, and perhaps someone who continues to play an important role in the family as a grandparent. But it typically does not produce the intensity of attachment related feelings of insecurity, anxiety, and yearning in adults who had developed a secure attachment with their parent during childhood, and have subsequently transferred that attachment to a partner and other adults (Moss et al., 2001).

All of this presumes, however, the growth of a secure attachment between child and caregiver during the developmental years of childhood. When the relationship between a parent/caretaker and child has resulted in either an anxious or avoidant attachment style, the reaction to the death of the parent may be very different. In these cases, the process of differentiation from the parents has been only partially completed, and the transformation of the relationship into one of mutual respect among equals may have important lacunae that become apparent in bereavement. For example, winning a parent's approval may continue to be a strong motivation for contact between parent and child, and the failure to win the parent's esteem a major source of concern for the anxiously attached adult child. Or, for an avoidantly attached offspring, interaction with their parent may continue to be filled with resentment and conflict that is managed by emotional and geographical distancing. Still another variation involves substantial financial and emotional dependency on the parent by the child. This is frequently accompanied by a failure to make successful connections with a life partner outside the family of origin and/or a failure to create a successful work/career trajectory without the help of the parent. In summary, when there has been a truncated process of differentiation between parent and child, and something other than a secure attachment style has evolved between them, there is likely going to be an upsurge of attachment related emotions and complicated grief reactions upon the death of that parent(s).

Janice

A middle aged woman named Janice and her husband, Albert, sought couples therapy for ongoing marital conflict and unhappiness. It quickly became apparent to the therapist that the husband had a very hostile and unresolved relationship with his self-absorbed, abusive, and alcoholic father, with whom Albert had developed a very avoidant attachment style. He continued this pattern with Janice, so that her angry demands that he provide more intimacy and support in the marriage were usually met with a defensive withdrawal on Albert's part. In contrast, Janice was an only child, and she was heavily involved in a mutually co-dependent relationship with her widowed mother—her father having died when Janice was 5 years of age. Janice and her mother had thus been mutual caretakers for one another for most of Janice's life. They had multiple daily contacts by telephone and in person. This level of contact was fueled by her mother's 20 year battle with cancer and Janice's need to protect her mother. This need to provide help to her mother was accompanied by significant anxiety about how Janice would cope without her only parent. Janice had worried for years about the well-being of her mother, essentially since the death of her father. Albert, in turn, was resentful and critical of what he perceived as his wife's over-involvement with her mother, and what he believed was his mother-in-law's manipulative use of her illness to keep Janice closely enmeshed. Perhaps predictably, as the mother finally moved closer to actually dying, Janice experienced a tremendous upsurge of anxiety about the loss of her "only friend," and an even greater amount of caregiving involvement on her part. After her mother died, Janice went into a significant depression, reacting not only with sadness about her mother, but with deep feelings of being alone in a world where she felt unable to fend for herself—reminiscent of what a 5 year old child might feel if her parent had died.

This case vignette illustrates some of the dynamics when attachment related problems are transmitted intergenerationally (Jordan et al., 1993). The loss of the father for a young mother and her 5 year old daughter sets up a deep and fixed pattern of dependency and mutually anxious attachment between the pair. The normal close involvement between a 5 year old child and her parent became filled with anxiety about feared separation that warped the developmental processes of healthy separation between the two, so that Janice, although demanding more intimacy with her husband, did not feel psychologically free to engage emotionally with him. The husband, although he resented his wife's enmeshment with her mother, also was mystified about how to provide the emotional security that his wife craved, and that might have allowed her to have a more balanced and differentiated relationship with her mother. This difficulty on the part of the husband could be directly traced to the avoidant attachment style that he developed in his family of origin, where closeness to a parent was emotionally (and sometimes physically) dangerous—and distance was the only safe refuge from the risks of intimacy.

Continuing Bonds with the Deceased

The death of a loved one ends a life, but not a relationship.

(Albom, 2002)

Until relatively recently, mental health professionals have operated under the assumption that the normal work of grief necessarily involves confronting the reality of the physical death and relinquishing the emotional attachment to the deceased, sometimes called the grief work hypothesis (M. S. Stroebe, 1992). Note that this was not Bowlby's assumption (Bowlby, 1980), nor is it the view represented in some long-standing models of the mourning process, among them the Two Track Model of Bereavement (TTM) (Rubin et al., 2012). However, the fullest expression of this perspective came with the publication in 1996 of the groundbreaking book *Continuing Bonds* (Klass et al., 1996).

In essence, Klass and his colleagues proposed that most bereaved people around the world and throughout recorded history have maintained some type of psychological connection with their deceased loved ones, despite their physical absence. This important shift in our understanding of the mourning process has led to a considerable amount of theoretical and research activity over the last 15 years, including by attachment theorists (Boelen et al., 2006; Epstein et al., 2006; Field, 2006; Field & Filanosky, 2010; Field et al., 2005; Field et al., 2013; Klass, 2006; Schut et al., 2006; Wood et al., 2012). In the remainder of this chapter, we will explore the concept of continuing bonds with the deceased, and its implications for an attachment-informed approach to grief therapy.

The concept of continuing bonds with the deceased as a positive outcome of bereavement has gained widespread clinical acceptance, and a number of techniques have been proposed that seek to enhance the continuing bonds relationship (Neimeyer, 2012f). Despite this change in practitioner views, however, the research evidence has been mixed and complicated as to the role continuing bonds has in facilitating bereavement recovery (Boelen et al., 2006; Schut et al., 2006; M. S. Stroebe et al., 2012). For example, Field suggests that not all continuing bonds are necessarily adaptive or helpful, and that the usefulness of maintaining a continuing bond with the deceased (particularly in partner loss) is dependent on the form it takes (Field & Filanosky, 2010; Field et al., 1999; Field et al., 2003), and the amount of time since the death (Field & Friedrichs, 2004).

Field has also offered an empirically based framework for understanding and distinguishing between adaptive and maladaptive continuing bonds between the mourner and the deceased (Field, 2006, 2008; Field et al., 2005). Building on the theoretical work of Bowlby, Field posits that healthy bereavement adaptation requires acknowledgment of and accommodation to the fact of the death, i.e., recognition that the deceased has physically died and cannot ever be available again in this fashion. For some mourners, this unalterable reality is unbearable. It produces what Bowlby called a mentally "segregated system" (Bowlby, 1980), which could also be described as a dissociated state of mind. In the literature of traumatology, dissociation is a primary human response to unbearable trauma of all kinds from which there is no escape (A. N. Schore, 2002b, 2002c, 2013). Thus, death results in a permanent and unfixable trauma for the bereaved. In essence, the mourner operates with two separated states of consciousness: one in which the reality of the death is acknowledged, and the other in which the death is not recognized. Note that this is not the same as believing that the loved one is in heaven—a conviction that acknowledges the physical reality of the person's death on earth. Instead, Field describes this as the mourner continuing to behave *as if* the deceased has not died— and in extreme cases, to consciously believe this to be the case. Signs of this process can include great distress at making changes to the deceased's belongings, active avoidance of triggers associated with the death (e.g., refusal to attend the funeral or visit the grave), and speaking of the deceased in the present, rather than past tense. Field notes that these types of continuing bonds, which involve holding onto external aspects of the relationship with the deceased, are common in the early days and weeks of mourning, particularly after sudden and unexpected death. However, they gradually give way to an acknowledgment and acceptance of the fact that the loved one is dead, and in uncomplicated grief, they lead to a transformation of the form of the connection with the deceased. This revised bond is characterized by an acceptance of the reality of the biological death (with its attendant emotional grief responses), and a newly reorganized psychological and/or spiritual connection with the deceased (Field, 2006, 2008; Field & Wogrin, 2011; Pearlman et al., 2014). This revised, internalized connection entails cultivating memories of the deceased, along with identification with their values and goals and potentially, a continuation of the deceased as an attachment figure for the mourner. To summarize, Field argues that adaptive continuing bonds can be distinguished from maladaptive continuing bonds by the extent to which the mourner has transformed the attachment to the deceased from one of an external relationship with a living person to an internal psychological connection to a deceased person—a transformation that acknowledges the reality of the physical death. Field and others have provided empirical support for this model, demonstrating that people who manifest an external connection have significantly poorer bereavement outcomes, while those with a transformed and internalized connection show better outcomes (Field & Filanosky, 2010; Field et al., 2013).

Implications for an Attachment Approach

What are the implications of the continuing bonds perspective for attachment-informed grief therapy? A number of authors have addressed this topic (Field, 2006; Field et al., 1999; Field et al., 2005; Ho et al., 2012). As originally conceptualized by Bowlby, attachment theory emphasized the important role of internalization of attachment relationships as the basis for healthy developmental separation. Thus, what allows the developing child to tolerate separation from his or her attachment caregivers is the internalization of a secure relationship with them. Analogously, continuing bonds theory and research suggest that the internalization of the relationship with the deceased allows the mourner to tolerate the permanent separation created by death. It follows from this that, psychologically speaking, *the deceased may continue to serve as an attachment figure for the mourner.* The form and function of this attachment may serve a number of different purposes that are worth enumerating. Most prominently, as the following case illustrates, the mourner may continue to use the deceased as an important source of felt security and a safe haven, particularly in times of distress.

Susan

Susan was a middle aged widow with a very anxious attachment style who sought grief therapy after the sudden death of her husband of many years. Susan's attachment history included being raised by a mother who herself was raised in foster homes after the early death of her own mother. Susan was subjected to neglect, empathic failure, and devaluing verbal abuse from her mother. Susan's relationship with her husband (also raised in an abusive family environment) included genuine aspects of affection and intimacy, coupled with considerable conflict and hostile dependency. When her husband died, Susan was deeply saddened, but also tremendously frightened about her ability to cope in the world without her partner. She expressed an intense yearning for her husband's return, and a similarly desperate need for the therapist's sustained attention and care. With the help of the clinician, Susan was gradually able to step back from and observe the dynamics of her dependency on her husband, and to begin to manage her affairs without him. But the clinician also encouraged Susan to maintain a continuing bond with her deceased husband as a supportive attachment figure. For example, the clinician suggested that Susan trust what she believed were signs of her husband's watchful presence over her (e.g., the appearance of rainbows or jet contrails at just the time when she was feeling distressed). The therapist also actively supported Susan's efforts to consult with her husband by asking for his guidance in prayer, and contemplating what support and advice he would offer her if he were alive.

This vignette illustrates not only that the perceived availability of the deceased can serve as a general source of comfort and reassurance for the mourner, but also that the relationship may be used in ways that are similar to the period when the deceased was alive. In the case of Susan, her fears about making decisions and taking risks (such as buying a new car) were made easier by her use of her husband as a resource for making important decisions that were difficult for her to make on her own—a function that is a direct continuation of the role that he played in the marriage before his death.

Beyond serving as a safe haven during periods of distress, the deceased may also function as a secure base for exploration. For example, in cases of spousal loss where the dying partner offered their blessing for adaptation to a changed world, including remarriage after the death, the mourner may use this symbolic support from the dead partner to counteract feelings of disloyalty to the deceased, and to make necessary changes in carrying on without them.

Saul

Saul, who was widowed after the death from an illness of his beloved wife, rather quickly became involved with a single woman who had been close friends with his wife. Shortly after this new relationship began, while shopping for clothing in the same department store that he and his deceased wife had visited many times, he ran into a doctor who had taken care of his wife at the end of her life. The two men chatted fondly about Saul's wife. Without knowing about the new relationship, the doctor concluded the conversation with a firm statement that "I know that she would want you to be happy and find someone else." Saul found this conversation to be much more than just a chance occurrence. Rather, he had a powerful sense that his deceased wife was watching over him, and had sent the doctor to him as a messenger with her wishes for how he should go forward. This encounter helped to resolve Saul's conflicting feelings about whether he should be getting involved with someone else after his wife's death. In addition, one of the effects of the new relationship was that Saul began exploring new activities and developing new interests outside of his work life—activities that "my wife always encouraged me to do."

The deceased may also continue as the recipient of the mourner's caregiving behavior. This is most clearly seen in the response of bereaved parents, who may continue to engage in symbolic caregiving behaviors such as tending to their child's grave or keeping their memory alive by consolidating and sharing stories about their child with others. Klass notes that this is one crucial function for parents of bereavement support groups such as Compassionate Friends, i.e., collectively holding and keeping alive the memory of the deceased child, thus allowing the continuing bond to develop (Klass, 1997, 1999). All of these behaviors can be viewed as a continuation of the parental role with the child, and a reinforcement of the continuing bond between parent and child.

Allison

Allison was deeply bereaved by the death of her adolescent daughter in a motor vehicle accident. They had experienced a close relationship, despite the strains that adolescent development had introduced in their lives. Caregiving for her daughter had always been Allison's first priority. After the death, Allison felt exceedingly lost, without a sense of purpose beyond caring for her other, younger child. At one point, when she was talking about this void and the pressure that she felt from her husband to "move on" by making changes in her daughter's bedroom, the therapist suggested that Allison consider taking a part of the room and converting it into a "shrine"—a dedicated memorial to her daughter. He noted that the creation of family shrines for deceased loved ones, particularly children, was a common cultural tradition in many societies. Allison went home and immediately went to work on developing the shrine. She found great comfort in selecting photographs of her daughter and some of her jewelry and other objects for the space. She also found that the ritual of keeping fresh flowers at the shrine, which required ongoing attention from Allison, was a source of devotion to her daughter that allowed Allison to feel closer to her child. She reported that when the yearning for her daughter was particularly intense, she could go and sit before the shrine and talk with her daughter in a way that allowed her to remember the happy moments they had together, rather than the sadness about her absence. Allison has also been able to begin changing and discarding some of the other objects in the room, so that it can be used for other purposes.

A continuing bond with the deceased may also entail more abstract functions that may or may not have been a part of the living relationship. For example, bereaved parents and siblings will sometimes report that the death of their child/sibling has provided a new sense of purpose and inspiration for their life (Lichtenthal et al., 2013).

Maria

Maria was devastated by the suicide of her 24 year old son. This event was profoundly transformative for Maria, whose role up until her son's death was primarily as a housewife and mother to her children. After a period of time spent healing from her loss,

Maria became a dedicated activist on behalf of other people bereaved by suicide in the U.S. Maria has organized survivor bereavement support groups in her state and has become a vocal proponent of the need for suicide prevention and postvention. Maria came to see this work as a living memorial for her son, as well as a way of restoring to her own life a sense of meaning and purpose that had been shattered by the suicide of her son.

It is important to understand that, as with attachment relationships with a living person, a continuing bond with the deceased may also change and grow over time (Malkinson et al., 2006; Rubin et al., 2012). Rubin and his colleagues note that this bond may have all of the characteristics of a relationship with a living person—affection, dependency, hostility, etc.—and that it is possible for the relationship to transform over time from a disturbed and disturbing one into one of affection and support within the mourner.

Summary

In this chapter, we have considered a number of relational factors related to bereavement, with particular attention to differences in bereavement associated with the kinship relationship to the deceased. Our relationships with parents, siblings, partners, and children serve many different purposes, fill many different needs, and are subject to many different kinds of expectations. These needs and expectations have a significant impact on people's grief responses. The violation of the expectation that their children will outlive them affects the intensity of parents' grief; the same may be true for a wife who did not expect that her husband would leave her to face life alone. Another important variable considered in this chapter is the nature of the continuing bond with the deceased. With respect to both of these variables, attachment theory provides a framework for understanding differences in grief response, and sensitivity to these aspects of people's grief is integral to attachment-informed grief therapy.

In the next chapter, we examine another very important element of the response to bereavement—the mode of death—and focus on the profound ways in which homicide, suicide, and other forms of traumatic death affect bereavement. Attachment theory will again serve as our organizing principle for understanding how this factor affects bereavement, and how to provide effective therapy to the bereaved.

6 Trauma and the Mode of Death

When someone we love dies, we feel the pain of separation, and yearn for their return. Yearning and separation distress are the hallmarks of mourning. But some deaths engender an extra burden of suffering for the mourner. In these instances, the *mode* of death—the manner in which the actual dying process occurred—tends by itself to invoke reactions of shock, horror, rage, fear, guilt, and vicarious suffering in the mourner. These reactions can come in response to what the mourner actually saw, heard, touched, or smelled at the death scene. Or, they can emerge simply from what the bereaved imagines the death scene looked like, and what they believe their loved one may have suffered as they died. The response of the bereaved in these cases involves a fusion of the grief and trauma responses that has been described as *traumatic bereavement* (De Leo et al., 2014; Pearlman et al., 2014).

Sarah

Sarah sought grief therapy for her self-described complicated grief, three years after the suicide of her young adult son. The son had been depressed, living at home, and in considerable conflict with his parents. Sarah found his body hanging in the young man's living quarters in the basement of their house. He had been dead for several hours, and his mother realized with utter horror that she had slept through the night with her son's lifeless body hanging in the room below her own bedroom. Sarah recalls vividly every detail of the morning when she made that terrible discovery: how her son's face looked, how his body felt, and how the police and emergency medical responders acted. In addition to intense yearning for her son and self-blame for not preventing his death, Sarah was tormented by the memories of that morning, which have barely subsided in the three years since her son's suicide.

Sudden, unexpected, and violent deaths often result in traumatic bereavement. Examples of traumatizing deaths include homicides, suicides, accidental and natural disaster related deaths, and war or terrorist related casualties. Depending on the experience of the mourner, other types of sudden deaths may also be traumatizing. Deaths resulting from stroke, cardiac arrest, or seizure, for example, can also be terrifying, and the after effects of fear and helplessness can be felt for a considerable length of time. Similarly, prolonged illnesses such as cancer can sometimes precipitate a trauma reaction that includes intrusive and disturbing memories of the loved one's agonizing decline and death.

Traumatic grief responses seem to occur relatively independently of the quality of the prior relationship with the deceased. They may, however, be related to the *mourner's* previous experience with traumatic losses or other traumatizing experiences. Early relational trauma in particular is a risk factor for a complicated grief response (Lobb et al., 2010). This association is consistent with the well-established empirical finding from traumatology that a significant risk factor for developing post-traumatic stress disorder (PTSD) after adult exposure to a traumatic event is a history of traumatic abuse as a child (Van der Kolk, 2014). In this chapter, we will examine the nature of traumatic losses and the grief they engender, and offer some observations on different types of traumatic deaths. We will review the neurobiology of the trauma response, and briefly survey the empirical literature on the impact of exposure to a traumatic death. We will also outline the role of attachment relationships, both early and current, in ameliorating or exacerbating the effects of a traumatic mode of death. Finally, we will set the stage for Chapters 7 and 8, which explore the role of a secure attachment relationship with the clinician in helping mourners to cope with all types of bereavement—traumatic or non-traumatic.

The Nature of Traumatic Deaths

What is it about certain deaths, such as suicides, homicides, and accidental deaths that evokes the trauma response? In an excellent new volume on traumatic bereavement, Pearlman and her colleagues offer the following description of traumatic death:

> Sudden, traumatic death is abrupt and occurs without warning. . . . a death is more likely to be traumatic if it is untimely; if it involves violence or mutilation; if the survivor regards it as preventable; if the survivor believes that the loved one suffered; or if the survivor regards the death, or manner of death, as unfair and unjust.
>
> (Pearlman et al., 2014, p.18)

In addition to grief, traumatic deaths elicit profound feelings of shock, confusion, and above all, helplessness in the survivors. Since they are frequently perceived by the mourner as involving human volition, and therefore human error or malevolence, traumatic deaths are also more likely to provoke rage at others (e.g., a perpetrator or God), as well as intense feelings of guilt for not having prevented the death. These feelings accompany diminished self-worth, and a loss of the assumptive world in the traumatically bereaved (Currier, Holland et al., 2008; Kauffman, 2002; Neimeyer & Sands, 2011; Sands et al., 2011). The latter refers to a shattering of the mourner's sense of efficacy, justice, benevolence, and coherence in the world. Traumatic deaths, then, compound the pain of loss, and produce symptoms that are often frightening in their severity and persistence. Research on the neurobiology of trauma helps us understand the prevalence of traumatic grief among survivors of traumatic loss.

The Neurobiology of Trauma

The neurobiology of the trauma response has been studied extensively in the last three decades (Putnam et al., 2005; A. N. Schore, 2002c, 2012). Mammals (including human beings) have evolved a complex neurobiology that allows the animal to detect and protect itself from threats in the environment, such as predators, that could pose a danger. This emergency response system also involves the rapid recognition of risk and subsequent behavioral response by the animal to deal with the danger. The amygdala, a crucial part of the limbic system of the brain that is associated with emotional memory, decoding of the emotions in facial expression, and appraisal of danger, produces an extremely rapid appraisal of the threatening stimuli (see Chapter 3). This is followed by activation of a neuro-hormonal cascade that runs from the hypothalamus to the pituitary gland to the adrenal glands (HPA axis), and results in the body being flooded with stress hormones (e.g., cortisol). Simultaneously, the perception of a threat produces a swift activation of the autonomic nervous system (ANS). Specifically, there is a response by the sympathetic nervous system (SNS—the metaphorical "gas pedal" of the ANS). These two reactions (activation of the HPA axis and the SNS) produce a sudden arousal in the organs and systems needed for action—an increase in heart rate and blood flow to the large muscles of the arms and legs, and a shutting down of unnecessary processes such as digestion in the gastro-intestinal (GI) system. Visual and auditory attention is also greatly narrowed to focus on the specific source of the threat. All of this prepares the animal to either rapidly flee or to attack the threat—the so-called "fight or flight" response. Subjectively, this hyperarousal of the SNS is experienced as tremendous rage or fear.

In situations where domination or escape is not possible, there is a third response, which involves the opposite of this hyperarousal of the SNS. This is the "freeze" response, which involves hyperactivation of the parasympathetic nervous system (PNS—the metaphorical "brakes" of the ANS). This is a shutting down of the body's intense push to attack or escape, and a replacing of it with passivity and constriction—an energy conservation strategy that Porges has noted involves activation of the dorsal vagal nerve (Porges, 2011). In human beings, this response is accompanied by the subjective experience of emotional numbing and psychological dissociation—depersonalization, derealization, and amnesia for events. This dissociative response is the "escape when no escape is possible," a psychological way of fleeing from a situation that cannot be physically controlled or evaded (A. N. Schore, 2002a, 2003a).

To summarize, we can think of mammals as having a normal baseline range of emotional arousal—not too high or intense, and not too low or constricted. When traumatized, the animal is knocked out of this emotional comfort zone by the traumatic event, and moves into a hyperaroused bodily state, dominated by the SNS, and sometimes followed by a hypoaroused state, dominated by the PNS.

The Trauma Response in Human Beings

In most mammals, this adaptive emergency response dissipates quickly once the threat is gone, and the animal's physiology returns to baseline. Learning also occurs, as the animal's brain associates the danger with the particular stimuli linked to this encounter (sights, sounds, smells, specific locations, etc.). Human beings, however, can become "stuck" in either a hyperaroused or hypoaroused state—or oscillate between the two. We call this condition PTSD, and what appears to happen is that the neurophysiology of the individual does not reset itself back to its normal oscillatory range (Foa et al., 2009; Herman, 1992, 1995; E. P. Solomon & Heide, 2005).

Another factor that makes an emergency more complicated in human beings is the fact that the trauma reaction can be evoked when a person is confronted with a situation that is massively *psychologically* threatening, even if it presents no physical danger. This is true because human beings live in a world of socially and intra-psychically constructed meanings (Neimeyer & Raskin, 2000). As noted in the beginning of this chapter, this assumptive world of the individual reflects the person's identity, their expectations about the fairness, safety, orderliness, and controllability of the world, and their beliefs about the value or risks of relatedness to other people. The experience of traumatic death can challenge, even destroy, an individual's assumptive world (Currier et al., 2006; Currier, Holland et al., 2008; Kauffman, 2002; Neimeyer et al., 2002).

Don and Janice

Don and Janice sought therapy after the murder of their young adult son in a convenience store robbery. The young man was working as a clerk at the store when two masked and armed men entered the store and demanded money. Their son complied with the robbers, but another clerk in the store pressed a button in the store that set off an alarm to summon the police. The couple's son was shot as the startled and panicked robbers fled the store. The son died on the way to the hospital in an ambulance.

Imagine the experience of these parents as they try to make sense of what has just happened. While understanding that murder happens to some people, Don and Janice have heretofore found their world to be safe for themselves and their children. They may even believe that their moral actions and careful adherence to the teachings of their religion ensure that they and their loved ones will be protected by God. Don and Janice may also believe that as conscientious and cautious parents, they can protect their offspring from danger. They may operate on the conscious or unconscious assumption that as long as they anticipate and plan for the future, they can prevent bad things from happening to their family. As a result of their past experiences, Don and Janice may also assume that human beings are basically good, and that if they live a moral life and stay away from bad people, they will not be harmed. All of these basic assumptions about oneself and the world are likely to be violated for Don and Janice by the apparently random murder of their son.

Understanding this key aspect of traumatic deaths helps us to understand and respond in a more helpful way to the needs of a traumatically bereaved person. Consider, for example, what might occur after Don and Janice arrive at the Emergency Department of their local hospital. The parents are permitted to view their child's body, and insist on seeing his face, which has been damaged by a gunshot wound to his head. The death of a child does not usually present a risk to a parent's immediate physical safety, but it can be immensely threatening to their sense of identity, self-esteem, and well-being. As we described in Chapter 5, their caregiving/protective responses are likely to be powerfully activated by the news that their son has been shot, along with profound shock and grief when they arrive at the hospital to find him already dead.

The reactions of these newly bereaved parents are very likely to include responses that are the equivalent of the fight, flight, or freeze responses of animals that are in the grip of intense danger. For instance, Don, a normally peaceful and mild-mannered person, may fly into a rage upon getting the news of his son's death and then viewing his body—wanting to find and attack the perpetrator, or perhaps even attacking the doctor who brings the unbearable news (fight response). In contrast, his wife may scream and attempt to bolt from the room—a sign of an instinctive need to flee from the enormous threat to her psychological well-being posed by this terrible news (flight response). Perhaps Janice may then become profoundly withdrawn over the next few days and weeks, refusing to leave her bedroom or interact with anyone (freeze response). All of these reactions are rooted in the same physiological process experienced by an animal fighting with, fleeing from, or trying to hide from a predator—only in this case, they serve as a desperate protective response for the survivor's psychological self from a reality that is so radically different from the world they have known that it is experienced as incomprehensible, unreal, and unbearable.

A third important aspect of traumatic bereavement is that, unlike most other traumatic events, the "danger" to which the individual is reacting persists. In most other traumatic events (e.g., involvement in an automobile crash), the danger is real but temporary, and a continuing emergency response is no longer necessary or appropriate. Much of our understanding of trauma has emerged from the experience of soldiers facing such real, but temporary life-threatening combat situations. Veterans with PTSD are having their nervous system continue to react as if they were still in a war zone, even if they are now safe and at home (Van der Kolk, 2014). Remember, however, that the trauma response can be elicited by psychological danger, not just physical danger. *In traumatic bereavement the psychological threat includes separation, the permanent absence of the deceased.* In this sense, all losses through death may include some degree of trauma, since the individual can never "escape" the threat of separation from their loved one. This is why an important aspect of grief therapy involves the facilitation of a psychological continuing bond with the deceased (see Chapters 5 and 10)—probably because this bond helps reduce the perceived threat involved in separation from the loved one through death. It is also why helping clients who are traumatically bereaved almost always involves helping them with affect regulation and meaning reconstruction as part of the work (see Chapters 9 and 10) (Landsman, 2002; Neimeyer et al., 2006).

In summary, we can say that traumatic deaths are ones in which the mode or circumstance of the death evokes a powerful emergency response in the mourner—the trauma response. This response is neurophysiological, and can add greatly to the complications in the overall mourning process. It is evoked both by the threat of perpetual separation from the loved one, and in the case of unexpected, violent, and sudden deaths, the horror of the way in which the loved one died.

Attachment and Traumatic Bereavement

As we have suggested in previous chapters, the human personality is shaped by relational experience, with early relationships being the most impactful. In the context of repeated interactions with our early caregivers, we learn many things. These include a foundational view of the world as safe, and ourselves as both competent and esteemed by others. We learn how to be a separate individual with our own distinct feelings, thoughts, and ideas, while also being connected to, understanding of, and being understood by others. We also learn how to manage our internal states, including our bodily experiences (sexual arousal, pain, fatigue, etc.), our distressing thoughts ("I've made a big mistake," "Nobody likes me," etc.), and perhaps most importantly, our strong emotions (fear, joy, jealousy, attraction, anger, sadness, etc.) (D. J. Siegel, 2010, 2012a). Lastly, depending on the security of our attachment style, we develop expectations about whether being close to another person is likely to bring us comfort or distress when we are threatened.

These skills may or may not, however, be up to the challenges embedded in a traumatic loss. There is now considerable evidence that children who are raised in environments that are impoverished in terms of positive affect and empathic attunement from caregivers, and instead are inundated with abusive, frightening, and affectively overwhelming interactions with their caretakers, are likely to develop distinct vulnerabilities to subsequent stressful events in later life (Lanius et al., 2010). They also are subject to the emergence of psychiatric disorders that reflect these vulnerabilities. For example, recent studies have demonstrated that a potent risk factor for the development of complicated grief disorders is a history of insecure attachment relationships in childhood (Meert et al., 2010; Meier et al., 2013).

Affect Regulation

Perhaps the most crucial factor in traumatic bereavement is one that we have already identified, i.e., affect regulation. By definition, trauma pushes people outside of their emotional comfort zone, producing intense emotional dysregulation (rage, panic, and dissociation/numbing) and ANS arousal. People who have poor foundational skills at reregulating their emotional arousal are likely to have even greater problematic responses when faced with the traumatic death of a loved one. Alternatively, they may have developed a relatively stable set of psychological survival skills that are nonetheless self-defeating, even damaging in their consequences for dealing with this type of loss. The use of these habitual but dysfunctional tools for coping is likely to be greatly intensified by the traumatic death of a loved one.

In addition, the level of security of an individual's attachment style may produce problems when it interacts with the nature of the loss. For example, consider a person whose avoidant attachment style means that they generally shun intimacy and rarely disclose their inner thoughts and feelings to other people. This tendency to withdraw may become more pronounced when the individual is very distressed and their attachment system has been activated. Recall that attachment style is reflective of how emotion was originally co-regulated interpersonally between the individual and their early caregivers. Most losses typically produce some degree of regression in an individual's defensive style. If an individual has learned that seeking emotional proximity with others results only in disappointment, frustration, or further psychological injury, they will be faced with a significant challenge when confronted with a sudden, unexpected, and violent death. Likewise, if their experience has been that being in touch with deep emotions within themselves represents a frightening loss of control, then the intensity of their grief after the traumatic loss of a loved one will be actively avoided or minimized. Rather, an avoidantly attached individual is likely to seek the "safety" of isolation when they are upset, and to try to reduce their internal arousal through techniques such as "keeping busy" or the use of psychoactive substances (alcohol, drugs, etc.). Moreover, as Shear and Shair point out, if the deceased played a mutual co-regulation function for the mourner (e.g., they were spouses), the bereaved person may experience major dysregulation of their physical, psychological, and social functioning (Shear & Shair, 2005). Considerable empirical evidence backs the finding that social support is a key factor in both bereavement and trauma outcome, helping to buffer people from the worst effects of these difficult life experiences (Dyregrov, 2005; Dyregrov & Dyregrov, 2008; Reed, 1998; Vanderwerker & Prigerson, 2004).

In contrast, consider a mourner with an anxious attachment style. This individual's early experiences with caregivers have taught them that attachment figures are unreliable and unpredictable in their availability, so that desperately maintaining proximity to attachment figures is the only way to assure their accessibility. In the initial surge of support that usually accompanies a traumatic loss, this person may feel helped by their social network. However, the intense need for the continual presence of others, coupled with the typical withdrawal of social support over time, may create a spiral of ever-increasing neediness in the mourner and corresponding frustration and burnout among people supporting that individual. As the social network begins to withdraw, the anxiety of the mourner increases and becomes overwhelming for others around the individual. This can then lead to feelings of abandonment, unworthiness, and depression. In addition, recall that traumatic deaths are also frequently perceived as being preventable, meaning that someone is at fault for the death. The anxious mourner may be overcome by ruminative guilt over the circumstances of the death and painful feelings of unworthiness for failing to prevent it. This combination of a great internal need for reassurance and comfort, coupled with poor skills at self-soothing, may lead to a very complicated grief reaction. The existing literature on risk factors for complicated grief generally supports the observation that an anxious attachment style is a clear risk factor for the development of complicated grief, particularly after the sudden, unexpected, and violent death of a loved one (Ho et al., 2012; Meier et al., 2013; M. S. Stroebe et al., 2005; Thomson, 2010).

Meaning-Making after Traumatic Bereavement

The principles that we are outlining here around affect dysregulation as a result of traumatization apply equally well to other domains of functioning that may be impacted by a traumatic death. These include physiological dysregulation (e.g., sleeplessness, loss of appetite), cognitive dysregulation (e.g., difficulty with concentration, absentmindedness), and interpersonal dysregulation (e.g., becoming irritable or confrontational with a marital partner). And, as we have suggested earlier in this chapter, the survivor of a traumatic death is very likely to have their assumptive world damaged by the loss as well.

Harriet

Harriet, a 49 year old mother of two, sought grief therapy after the death of her young adult son in a hiking accident. While hiking in the southwestern region of the U.S. in exceptionally hot weather and rugged trail conditions, her son became separated from his hiking companion and lost on the trail. After an extensive search, his body was found by a rescue team three days later. He had fallen and injured his leg, and had died of exposure and dehydration. Harriet had many complex reactions to the death of her oldest child and only son, including guilt, regrets about problems in their relationship, and disturbing images of what her son's final hours were like (see Chapter 10).

In addition to the traumatic nature of the death, there was another trauma related factor that complicated Harriet's mourning process, and made the task of providing assistance to her more difficult. Harriet seemed to feel an inordinate sense of guilt about her son's death, given that it was the result of an accident that no one could have foreseen, and for which no one could reasonably have been held accountable. She ruminated about her perceived failures as a mother, and at times questioned whether her son's death was a punishment from God for her inadequacies. Over the course of the treatment, the therapist began to explore these feelings of guilt and responsibility in more depth. What emerged was a revelation in one session that Harriet had been sexually abused by both her grandfather and her father from the ages of about 6 through to 10. The abuse stopped when Harriet was finally able to tell her mother, who confronted Harriet's father about the abuse. However, Harriet's mother provided almost no support for her daughter or help in putting the abuse in some kind of perspective and neither of her parents ever talked with Harriet again about this issue.

What became clearer through the therapeutic dialogue was that the abuse had left Harriet with a profound sense of shame, unworthiness, and a chronic thought of self-blame ("When bad things happen, it's my fault"). Although she carried a tremendous amount of anger about her abuse and the lack of protection from her parents, for the most part Harriet was excessively concerned with avoiding conflict with other people, and maintaining their positive regard for her. She was quick to take responsibility for any problems that occurred in her relationships, but when she did so, often ended up feeling resentful toward the other person. This pattern showed up in both her marriage, and at times in the relationship with the therapist.

This vignette illustrates the dynamics that can be evoked when a traumatic death befalls someone with an earlier trauma history, particularly developmental or relational trauma resulting from abuse and neglect by early caregivers (Herman, 1992, 1995; Van der Kolk, 2014). Harriet's difficulties were complicated by the loss of a child, by the nature of her son's death (sudden, unexpected, and involving a painful dying process), and by her early life experiences with attachment figures. In such situations, the therapist needs to be aware of, and with appropriate timing and client cooperation, attend to the synergism between the vulnerabilities created by the earlier traumatic experiences and the emotional injuries created by the traumatic circumstances of the current loss. For Harriet, the probable nature of her son's death had left her with deeply disturbing feelings of anguish at the suffering of her child as he died. These were addressed by a technique of going over her fantasies about what the dying process had been like, and at one point helping her retell the death in a different and more bearable way (see Chapter 10). In addition, the death of her son had reactivated and greatly intensified all of the painful and debilitating feelings that Harriet originally experienced in her earlier relationships with her caregivers. These included strong feelings of self-blame, along with resentment that she had no choice but to accept this blame. These confusing feelings became an additional major focus of her grief therapy.

All of this essential therapeutic work could not have been accomplished without the establishment of a relationship of trust, openness, and sensitive attunement on the part of the grief therapist to the complicated feelings involved for this client. As a sexual abuse survivor, creating a sense of psychological safety in the therapeutic relationship was a crucial but slow and delicate process for the clinician. Emphasizing the collaborative nature of their work together, and carefully respecting Harriet's autonomy about the content and speed of the therapeutic process, were paramount in creating a venue in which she could feel understood rather than judged, and supported rather than coerced. Once the abuse was revealed, and with Harriet's permission, the therapist began a gentle exploration of the impact of the abuse on Harriet's assumptive world and feelings, and their relation to her feelings about her son's death. By "tacking" back and forth between her past experiences and her current grief, Harriet and the therapist were together able to gain perspective on the meaning of the loss of her son for her. Gradually, Harriet was able to sort out which feelings were coming from which events, and also to understand better the role that her earlier abuse had played in her current grief. By the end of the treatment, she was better able to experience her son's death for what it was: a tragic accident, but one for which no one was at fault, and for which she had a right to grieve deeply. It also helped her to understand and process the feelings of shame and unworthiness generated by her early abuse.

Summary

Many things influence the response that an individual makes to the death of a loved one. In this chapter, we have focused on one of the most important of these factors, the mode or circumstances surrounding the death. When a death is sudden, unexpected, and violent, and particularly if it is viewed by the mourner as being the result of human error or malevolence, then it is also usually experienced as "preventable and unacceptable" in nature. Traumatic deaths are likely to add extra burdens of guilt, blame (self or other), and angry protest to the already painful feelings of sorrow and yearning for the deceased. Likewise, a mourner's early experiences with key attachment figures, and the resulting attachment style that emerges from such experiences, often play a central role in producing complicated grief reactions in survivors of traumatic loss. The capacity to address the complex and layered mourning processes in a mourner who has experienced multiple traumas in their life requires a solid understanding of attachment dynamics, attachment styles, and the crucial role of the therapeutic relationship in fostering change in bereaved persons. These are all themes to which we will return in later chapters.

Part III

Clinical Implications: Toward Attachment-Informed Grief Therapy

Bowlby hoped that his work on the role of attachment in infancy, and its impact throughout a person's life, would provide an impetus for changes in public policy and the development of clinical approaches incorporating his concepts. He was disappointed by the initial lack of interest in his ideas outside a narrow band of academics (Holmes, 2013). In recent years, however, Bowlby's ideas, particularly those having to do with the importance of secure attachment in infancy and childhood, have been integrated into public and privately funded health, education, and welfare programs in the U.S. and elsewhere (Juffer et al., 2012; Slade, 2007). Likewise, the task of translating attachment theory into practice has been taken up by an ever increasing number of clinicians and researchers (Holmes, 2009; Obegi & Berant, 2010; Slade, 2008; Wallin, 2007).

Danquah and Berry, in their introduction to a recent collection of essays exploring the applicability of attachment theory to clinical practice with adults, express the hope that the material presented will provide readers with a new perspective on how to identify and treat a range of clinical problems for which people seek help (Danquah & Berry, 2013). Our purpose here is similar with respect to grief therapy. In this chapter, after briefly reviewing our assumptions about the value of bringing an attachment perspective to grief therapy, we present an overview of our clinical model. We then elaborate on elements of this model in the chapters that follow. Chapter 8 addresses how the therapeutic relationship is used in attachment-informed grief therapy. In Chapter 9 we focus on how to strengthen self-capacities, particularly emotion regulation, in order to allow clients to better tolerate and integrate difficult feelings. In Chapter 10 we discuss the reconstruction of meaning in adaptation to loss and illustrate the application of an attachment-informed approach to facilitating this process.

7 A Model of Attachment-Informed Grief Therapy

I never know how I'm going to feel from one minute to the next. It's like there's a gremlin inside me who gives me all this pain, and then just at the moment when I can't stand it anymore, he stops, and then just when I start to feel a little better, he starts it up again. I feel like two people. One person who can have a good day, and can go out and do things. And another person who doesn't want to do anything or see anyone. I just can't imagine how those two people are ever going to be one person.

Bereaved parent

An important feature of the basic attachment dynamic is that threat-triggered attachment behavior and exploration are mutually exclusive.

(Holmes, 2013, p.17)

At some point in life, most people will experience the death of someone they love and will struggle with a range of feelings, among them an intense feeling of longing for the person to return. Depending on the nature of the relationship and a person's capacity for independent survival, this longing may be overlaid with the fear that they will not be able to withstand the emotional and physical impact of grief. Faced with the prospect of an indeterminate future filled with painful longing, bereaved people sometimes express a desire for their own death. The recently bereaved often have little interest in going anywhere or seeing anyone. There is a sense that they are carrying something very heavy, and there is no way for them to put it down.

In Bowlby's view, these emotional and physical features of grief are the adult equivalent of the response shown by many young children when they are separated from their attachment figures, a combination of protest, despair, and collapse. In adults as in children, the distress caused by separation is a deterrent to engagement and exploration. Once the attachment behavioral system is triggered, it will remain engaged until the connection to the loved one, and with it, a sense of safety and emotional balance, are restored, or until the individual adapts to living in the world without the deceased. The mind may know that reunion is impossible, but the desire and the need for it remain. This internal conflict between wanting physical reunion, and knowing that it is impossible, and the disorientation that this conflict produces, resolves for most people over time. However, a substantial percentage of the bereaved will continue to experience symptoms associated with acute grief for an extended period, and it is with these people that the support offered by grief therapy can be most helpful (Currier, Neimeyer et al.,

2008; Neimeyer & Jordan, 2013). This support can take many different forms, and can include a variety of techniques depending on the needs of the client, the skills of the clinician, and the setting in which the therapy is provided (Neimeyer, 2012f). While techniques may vary, the attuned presence of a therapist who validates, clarifies, and helps the client explore feelings and needs brought on by a significant loss is fundamental to most forms of grief therapy (Neimeyer & Jordan, 2013). In this sense, grief therapy is essentially a collaborative effort in which client and clinician work together to identify and address obstacles to integration of the loss. These obstacles can include unresolved conflicts in the relationship with the deceased, problems related to the nature of the death, or difficulties that result from changes in life circumstances, among many others (Rubin et al., 2012).

We propose the following as a general definition of grief therapy—one that reflects our own view regarding the importance of attachment in understanding the process of bereavement and the role of the grief therapist.

A Definition of Grief Therapy

Grief therapy is a concentrated form of empathically attuned and skillfully applied social support, in which the therapist helps the bereaved person reregulate after a significant loss by serving as a transitional attachment figure. This includes addressing deficits in affect regulation and mentalizing related to both the loss at hand, and early neglect or trauma, as needed. In an environment that encourages exploration and growth, the bereavement therapist supports the bereaved in experiencing and tolerating feelings relating to grief, integrating new information and skills, and developing a new self-narrative that incorporates the impact of the loss. The goal of grief therapy is integration of the loss on a psychological and neurological level. Successful grief therapy encourages a state of flexible attention to the loss, and to the relationships, roles, and experiences that are still available to the bereaved individual, in order that they may reengage in life, without relinquishing their attachment to the deceased.

This definition directs attention to attachment as a factor in adaptation to bereavement and as a factor in the design and delivery of grief interventions. It does not change the goal of grief therapy (Worden, 2009), but it does reflect our understanding of the therapeutic process by which that goal is reached. This understanding is consistent with the emergent shift in the paradigm of psychotherapeutic change described by many clinicians/researchers (Cozolino, 2010; Cozolino & Santos, 2014; A. N. Schore, 2012; J. R. Schore & Schore, 2014; D. J. Siegel, 2010, 2012a). These writers argue that what transpires in psychotherapy happens not only through cognitive, language based interventions, but also through the emotion rich, right brain to right brain communication between therapist and client, a connection that serves an affect regulating function not unlike that served by the secure connection between parent and child (A. N. Schore, 2009; J. R. Schore & Schore, 2014). The regulatory function of the therapeutic relationship is particularly important in grief therapy, where the painful feelings that bring clients into treatment are often a consequence of the loss of a significant attachment figure. The grief therapist's role in helping clients reregulate, and teaching them how to manage emotions and to make sense of their experience, will be particularly relevant when working with clients whose development was compromised by the adverse circumstances of their early environment and the quality of caregiving they received.

Assumptions Guiding Attachment-Informed Grief Therapy

In line with the many researchers and clinicians whose work has been cited in earlier chapters, we regard variations in attachment experience and orientation as critical factors in understanding how people form relationships with others, how they respond to the death of a loved one, and how they utilize the resources they bring to the tasks of adapting to significant loss. This analysis, along with contributing to our understanding of the roots and trajectory of normal and problematic bereavement, has implications for the practice of grief therapy, and it is to these that we now turn.

The assumptions on which our approach is based are summarized here:

Concerning attachment:

- Early attachment experience impacts neural development and lays down a template for relationships with other people.
- Early attachment experience has a formative and lasting impact on the development of an individual's attachment orientation, their set of expectations about subsequent close interpersonal relationships.
- Early attachment experience has a formative and lasting impact on core self-capacities and self-identity, in particular capacities related to mentalizing and self-regulation.
- Attachment orientation is a factor in how people cope with adverse life events in general and with the death of a significant attachment or caregiving recipient figure in particular.

Concerning grief:

- Loss of an attachment relationship is dysregulating and destabilizing: separation distress in childhood is mirrored in the distress that accompanies the death of an attachment figure or a caregiving recipient in adulthood.
- Reregulation in the aftermath of loss, like the recovery of emotional balance in infancy, is a dyadic and transactional process that is facilitated by, if not dependent on, the engaged, attuned presence of one or more other people.

Concerning problematic grief:

- Attachment related problems that persist into adulthood are often present in complicated grief.
- Difficulties related to affect management and self-regulation are present in many survivors of early abuse or neglect, and often interfere with their adaptation to later losses. Self-regulation involves capacities for both the tolerance of strong affect that may be associated with loss, and maintenance of the coherence of the mourner's self and world narratives.

- Traumatic loss is a risk factor for problematic grief independent of attachment orientation. However, previous trauma, including early relational trauma, amplifies the effect of adult traumatic loss and compounds the likelihood of protracted dysregulation.

In what follows, we will briefly elaborate on the components of this definition of grief therapy, taking into account these assumptions. We will describe the roles of the therapeutic relationship, the increase in the ability to tolerate distressing affect, the acquisition of new information and skills, and the role of meaning-making and narrative revision in grief therapy. Just as all of these are functions that attachment figures serve for a growing child, they are all important components of grief therapy. Our discussion of each of these highlighted functions will then be expanded in the remaining chapters.

The Therapeutic Relationship

Because it involves the loss of attachment, Bowlby regarded bereavement as a period in which attachment related needs are likely to be intense, making the quality of the therapeutic relationship particularly important. In counseling the bereaved, Bowlby emphasized, "the patient's experience of the therapist's behavior and tone of voice and how he approaches a topic are at least as important as anything he says" (Bowlby, 2005, p.180). Based on our clinical experience and our reading of the literature, we believe that the foundation of all successful grief therapy (indeed all psychotherapy) is the development of a trusting, emotionally safe, and psychologically nurturing therapeutic relationship. While virtually all approaches to psychotherapy acknowledge the importance of the therapeutic alliance, only some of them see it as the primary "active ingredient" in treatment, even though a robust body of empirical research supports this proposition (Duncan et al., 2010; Norcross, 2011). Even within the field of grief therapy, relatively little attention has been paid to this fundamental element of interventions (Zech & Arnold, 2011). This emphasis on the primacy of the therapeutic relationship is a distinguishing feature of attachment-informed therapy (Holmes, 2013; Wallin, 2007, 2010).

As illustrated in Chapter 4, and elaborated on in Chapter 8, empathic attunement depends on the clinician's ability to maintain a stance of flexible accommodation to client attachment needs, which vary from person to person and from session to session over the course of the mourning process (Wallin, 2007; Zech et al., 2010). The warm and nurturing approach that is comforting to some clients will trigger defenses in others. Some clients will be hungry for soothing words while others will insist that what they need are tools to help them work through their grief and get on with their lives.

Strengthening the Capacity to Tolerate Emotion

Attachment theory draws many parallels between the role of attachment security in childhood and in adulthood. In childhood, relational security is associated with flexibility in emotional expression and behavior. In other words, securely attached children are able to experience a range of emotions, and to express them in a spontaneous and non-conflicted manner. In contrast, the emotional awareness and expression of insecurely attached children is subject to what they have learned are the preferences of unreliable or rejecting caregivers (Holmes, 2001; Wallin, 2007). In adulthood, relational security confers comparable benefits with regard to social and emotional functioning. The ability to experience, acknowledge, and manage emotion is a singularly important indicator of mental health (Gross & Muñoz, 1995; Mikulincer & Shaver, 2008a). Difficulties in emotion regulation are a defining feature of many psychiatric diagnoses (Berking et al., 2012; A. N. Schore, 2003a, 2003b) and remediation of these difficulties has become a major focus of the treatment of these disorders (Mennin & Fresco, 2009, 2014). In the context of bereavement therapy, it can reasonably be assumed that addressing deficits in emotion regulation can positively affect the course of bereavement in clients who are struggling to cope with sadness, yearning, and other grief related feelings.

In keeping with what we have learned about the impact of insecure attachment on the development of emotion tolerance and self-regulation, we must expect that many clients with problematic grief will need help building these skills, either because they come to the therapeutic encounter with a basic deficit in these skills from early relational experiences, or because the loss itself has been sufficiently traumatizing that even a securely attached person may be significantly dysregulated by the death (see Chapter 6). Compounding the difficulties caused by a lack of internal resources, these mourners may also be lacking in social support and other external resources (Neimeyer & Jordan, 2013). As discussed in Chapter 4, depending on their characteristic manner of response to painful emotion, these mourners will tend to overuse one of two secondary regulatory strategies, either becoming immersed in the loss (hyperactivating) or suppressing awareness and behaviors related to the loss (deactivating) (Mikulincer & Shaver, 2013).

Whether in childhood or adulthood, we grow through experiences that challenge but do not overwhelm us. As Ogden (Ogden, 2009; Ogden et al., 2006) explains, the ideal therapeutic environment provides a level of arousal that is comfortable but not *too* comfortable. An attuned grief therapist works with clients to create a balance between too much and too little engagement with their emotional reactions to the death. Through moment to moment awareness of a client's physical and emotional state, the therapist continually seeks to expand the client's affective flexibility.

In a similar vein, Holmes describes the ideal therapeutic balance between nurturing and confronting the client. Successful therapy requires that the therapist initially accommodates to the role "allocated by the patient's unconscious expectations" (Holmes, 2013, p.18). With avoidant, deactivating clients, this might mean that the therapist starts with an analytical approach, engaging the client intellectually before making the move to engage them emotionally. With anxious, hyperactivating clients, it might involve a degree of "boundary flexibility," such as an exchange of messages between sessions. Over time, the therapist modifies their approach in order to move the client in the direction of an expanded pattern of interaction, one that increases the client's interactional repertoire.

Beth

A highly anxious client sought treatment following the death of her mother. The day after their initial session, the therapist received a request from the client for an *appointment over the weekend. The therapist responded by reminding the client that she did not offer weekend appointments. The therapist received, and responded to, several additional communications from the client. Feeling increasingly agitated by the client's intrusions, she decided that she would have to have a conversation about boundaries with the client, a prospect she dreaded. But on further reflection, she decided on a different approach. At their scheduled appointment the following week, the therapist commented: "Well, I want you to know that you were very successful in communicating to me **just how anxious** you are. In fact, when I was thinking about seeing you today I became a bit anxious myself, and I thought, **this is how she feels all the time.**"*

This exchange was important for several reasons. It established, once again, that there were limits to the clinician's availability, but at the same time conveyed that she was very conscious of the level of the client's distress. Client and therapist were able to share a moment of levity, which diffused any lingering resentment that might have remained on either side, and from that point forward a strong therapeutic bond developed. Secure in the knowledge that this relationship was in place and that she could fall back on it if needed, the client was able to begin to allow some distance from the clinician. The clinician also taught her a number of self-soothing techniques, and as she became more confident about her internal resources for self-regulation, the client was able to address ongoing conflicts with members of her family that were compounding the distress related to her mother's death.

Of course, some clients will resist any move on the clinician's part to promote the client's independence, including suggestions about how they might learn to manage their emotions more effectively. They may regard such efforts as yet another example of someone telling them that they should get a hold of themselves and get back to the business of living. In counseling the bereaved, it is important for clinicians to be careful to not make premature attempts to get clients to move toward a resolution of their grief.

A clinician's ability to sense when and how to give clients a gentle nudge in order to broaden their emotional and behavioral range is one of the pillars of clinical wisdom in grief therapy described more fully in Chapter 8. In the following exchange, the clinician suggested to Robert, 44, whose father had died eight months prior, that he begin thinking about looking for work:

Robert: "I don't want to hear this. All I really wanted today was to be soothed. I feel like you're sticking pins in me."
Clinician: "I'm sorry you feel that way. My instinct, you know, is to soothe you. My impulse is to soothe you. But if all I do is soothe you, nothing will ever change."

This response was met with a nod from the client, who jokingly concluded the session by announcing that he was never coming back (he did).

The ability to gradually accommodate to a loss occurs through repeated interactions of this sort, always within the context of a secure bond. To maintain that sense of security the clinician must be sensitive to the client's state of mind and their tolerance for emotion and closeness within the therapeutic relationship (Muller, 2010).

Restoring Mentalizing

> Mentalizing is the key to self-regulation and self-direction . . . By integrating *a sense of self and a sense of connections with others*, mentalizing enables us to manage losses and trauma, as well as distressing feelings such as frustration, anger, sadness, anxiety, shame and guilt. (emphasis added). Mentalizing, we manage these feelings *without* resorting to automatic fight or flight responses or efforts to cope that are ultimately self-destructive or maladaptive.
>
> (Allen, 2003, p.93)

Described in Chapter 2 as the ability to understand what is happening in one's own mind, as well as in the minds of others, the capacity to mentalize develops in infancy within the security of an attuned, nurturing relationship, and as Allen explains, is an essential component of healthy self-regulation of emotion (Allen, 2013). In the context of grief therapy, impaired mentalizing and emotion regulation become targets of treatment when these impairments complicate grief and amplify the difficulties associated with integrating loss. Problems in mentalizing are most often apparent in people with a history of early attachment trauma, many of whom exhibit characteristics of disorganized attachment (Hesse, 2008; Main & Hesse, 1990). Learning to mentalize can help a person make sense of their past, including the past relationship with an abusive parent. Being able to look back on a confusing and frightening time from a place of safety, the adult who survived can take his place next to the child who could not escape.

Integrating New Information and Developing New Skills

We believe that working with people who are grieving involves not only helping them come to terms with their loss, but also helping them build, or rebuild, connected, productive lives. For many people, this will require learning new skills. Broadly speaking, we can identify three categories of skills that mourners acquire as they heal from their losses. The first are the skills involved in emotional and cognitive self-regulation.

Sam

Sam was disturbed by his bouts of weeping at work after the death of his beloved daughter in a boating accident. He worked in a mostly male work setting, where his periodic weepiness was viewed as being at best a socially awkward lapse in self-control, and at worst as a dangerous distraction from his responsibilities on the job, which required vigilant attention. Over time, Sam settled on a strategy of allowing himself to cry on his way to and from work while driving in his car, but actively suppressing his tears while he was at work. With appropriate cautions about the risks of "driving while crying," the therapist supported Sam's acquisition of this adaptive skill in self-regulation, given the realities of his work environment.

The second category of skills includes self-care skills that may have deteriorated since the death, or may never have been well developed by the individual. These skills include care of the physical, emotional, and spiritual self. For example, recent evidence suggests that exercise can be a potent antidote for depression, including the depressive symptoms that accompany bereavement (Stanton & Reaburn, 2014). It is common for us to inquire about the exercise history of the bereaved clients with whom we work, and after taking into account the health and age of the individual, to encourage them to begin some kind of regular physical activity—ranging from simply going for regular walks to starting exercise programs at a gym or health club. In a similar fashion, we may encourage an individual whose religious practice has lapsed to resume their involvement with their faith community, as well as their solitary practice of prayer.

The third group of skills often needed by mourners includes the ability to manage their relationships with other people, particularly the changes in relationships that have come about as a result of the death:

Patricia

Patricia found that many people treated her differently after the death of her daughter to suicide. Some people who related to her were intrusive, often asking questions about the details of the death and demanding an explanation for something that Patricia could barely understand herself. In contrast, other friends and work colleagues avoided any mention of the death when they were with Patricia, or simply avoided having contact with Patricia at all (for example, crossing to another aisle when they saw her in the grocery store). The death of her daughter had placed Patricia in the very unfamiliar social position of having to actively manage her boundaries, and protect herself in relationships with other people in ways that she had never needed to do before. This became a focus of her work with her grief therapist, as she decided how she wanted to handle the complex reactions of other people to her new status as the "Mom of a child who killed herself." She also considered suggestions offered by her therapist about ways that other suicide survivors have learned to deal with people's insensitive intrusions or hurtful avoidance.

These examples illustrate the new repertoires of skills and knowledge that bereaved persons will need help with developing. Also evident in these examples is the social nature of grief and the role of a bereaved person's environment in either facilitating or complicating their integration of loss. Part of a grief therapist's role is to encourage clients to identify and connect with people in their lives who are supportive, and, as much as possible, to limit contact with people who make them feel worse than they already do (Burke et al., 2010).

Meaning-Making after Loss: The Development of a Revised Self-Narrative

The relationship with an attuned support person helps the bereaved client to stay present with painful emotions and to gain perspective about the changed self and world created by the death. Some of this information may become the nucleus of a new life narrative, one that replaces a storyline built on negative beliefs about the self, an exaggerated sense of responsibility for problems in a relationship, or a general expectation that relationships with others will be hurtful or disappointing. In the case of traumatic bereavement, the mourner's beliefs about their ability to control what happens to them and to the people they care about may be shattered by the death. In such cases, meaning-making will involve the reconstruction of these beliefs to take into account existential realities that can no longer be denied.

Kanesha

Kanesha, a married woman in her late twenties, sought grief therapy after the sudden death of her younger brother to a cerebral hemorrhage. Exploration of her history revealed an extremely abusive history with both of her parents, with her father being unpredictably and terrifyingly violent toward his children, and her mother being extremely manipulative in keeping her daughter attached to her as a support person. This latter behavior included feigning heart attacks and blaming her daughter for them when, as an adolescent, Kanesha wanted to begin dating. In many ways, Kanesha and her brother formed a kind of "Hansel and Gretel" alliance with each other in order to survive the abuse from both parents. She had taken a lead role in trying to protect her younger brother from the malevolent interactions with their parents. When her brother died as a young adult, Kanesha became depressed and suicidal, developing a kind of magical thinking about her responsibility for keeping her brother alive, and her unworthiness for having failed to do so. The therapy focused on helping Kanesha examine the roots in her abusive childhood of the narrative that she had constructed about her brother's death and her role in it. With the therapist's support Kanesha was also able to confront the reality that random, but terrible things can happen to anyone without their being a judgment about that person's worth.

The development of an expanded self-narrative is also an important element of recovery for people who believe, figuratively and sometimes literally, that they will not be able to survive without the person who has died. The loss of a spouse is painful for many people, but it can be disabling for a woman whose core self-narrative, learned in the context of her early relationships with caregivers (as well as societal expectations about the gender roles of women), is that she does not have the strength or skill to manage on her own. Similarly, a widower who believes himself inept at dealing with emotion may feel overwhelmed by the prospect of caring for his bereaved children. In these situations, the therapist can often help a bereaved person find evidence of aptitudes they claim not to have and skills that may have been underutilized or even devalued in the past. Helping bereaved people realize that they are stronger, kinder, more resourceful, and more resilient than they believe themselves to be can provide a powerful infusion of hope for people who doubt their ability to function in the world without the deceased.

Revising the Narrative of the Relationship with the Deceased

According to the Two Track Model of Bereavement (TTM) (see Chapter 4), the factors that influence how a person adapts to relational loss can be grouped into two domains: their day to day functioning, and the emotional valence and intensity of their ongoing relationship with the deceased (Rubin et al., 2012). Like many parents who lose a child, Sylvia struggled with the feeling that she should have done more to save her daughter, who died after an extended illness. In Sylvia's case, however, this feeling was amplified by Sylvia's lingering sense that her daughter had not loved her.

Sylvia

Sylvia was referred by her physician and friend, who reported that she seemed "very down, maybe depressed." Sylvia confirmed that she was not feeling herself, and noted that since her 23 year old daughter's death she had not been able to forgive herself for failing to be more available to her during her illness. Based on information collected in the first and second sessions, it became clear that Sylvia had endeavored to be more of a presence in her daughter's life, but that her daughter had in fact resisted Sylvia's intervention. Subsequent sessions focused on identifying Sylvia's interpretation of her daughter's response, and what became clear was that to Sylvia, her daughter's refusal to accept her help "proves that she didn't love me."

This discussion helped pave the way to Sylvia's understanding that her pain was a composite, not only of grief and guilt, but also of resentment and a feeling of rejection. She mourned the lost opportunity to build a better relationship with her daughter, one that would have allowed her to be closer to her daughter during the final stages of her illness. Sylvia was invited to "introduce" her daughter, and in the course of doing so, she talked about her daughter's fierce independence and her refusal to be "pitied or babied" by friends and family. As she talked about her daughter, Sylvia came to realize that her daughter's behavior was not a personal rejection, but a reflection of a lifelong pattern of wanting to take responsibility for herself and not depend on others. Sylvia was able to see that in backing off in response to requests from her daughter, she was honoring her daughter's wishes.

Following this work, Sylvia was able to imagine having a conversation with her daughter, articulating her own concerns and expressing what she thought would be her daughter's explanation for her steadfast refusal to accept help. During this conversation Sylvia found that she was able, for the first time since her daughter's death, to recall many instances in which her daughter had communicated clearly her love and gratitude for Sylvia's support and care. After two months Sylvia reported feeling "much more at peace" about her daughter, having realized that "a lot of what was hurting so much was the feeling that my daughter didn't love me, and now I realize that that just isn't true."

The Reconstruction of Meaning and Purpose in Life

The central role of meaning-making in recovery from loss has been elaborated by Neimeyer and his colleagues, both in terms of theory and empirically supported clinical practice. In this view, bereavement is fundamentally a process of meaning reconstruction, through which the mourner must find a way to accommodate not only the loss of the person who has died, but also aspects of their personal identity that were linked to that person (Gillies & Neimeyer, 2006; Neimeyer & Sands, 2011). Someone whose role as caregiver provided a sense of purpose, or whose relationship with a spouse or child was central to his or her identity, will have to reconfigure their sense of self, and will benefit from guidance in establishing a new basis for their identity. In such cases the first task of therapy is often to help the bereaved client understand their sense of dislocation.

Jennifer

Jennifer, 56, moved in with her father after her mother's death and took care of him until he died several years later. Although she had often felt resentful about having to spend most of her free time taking him to the doctors and cooking him special meals, she now felt let down, lethargic, and unsure about what she would do with the rest of her life.

The therapist engaged Jennifer in a discussion of what had been most fulfilling to her about caring for her father, and of what the loss of her identity as a caregiver meant to her. Jennifer came to understand that her lethargy was mostly caused by the sudden vacuum of purpose and meaning in her life. This was a powerful realization for her because, unlike the loss of her father, it was something over which she had control. Jennifer now saw her emotional state as a problem that she could attack as she had attacked her father's medical problems.

In the months that followed, Jennifer began to expand her base of social support and to pursue interests that had been sidelined during the period of her father's illness. Through a process that has been described as "mapping the terrain of loss" (Kosminsky, 2012), Jennifer was able to differentiate her yearning for her father from the secondary effects of losing her identity as a caregiver. The shift from hopelessness to purposefulness and from isolation to engagement that Jennifer was able to make was the end result of changes in her thinking, her emotions, and her behavior. This kind of reorganization of the self is what we hope to see in our bereaved clients.

Summary

Psychotherapy, like parenting, is neither mechanical nor generic.

(Cozolino, 2010, p.30)

A good therapist, like a good parent, does any number of things, and usually multiple things at the same time. A therapist provides a secure base from which clients can explore thoughts, feelings, and environments that they would otherwise avoid, and also helps them to reflect on the behavior and feelings of others (i.e., to mentalize). A therapist encourages a hopeful, realistic view of the client's potential for healing and growth, and this positive regard promotes a more positive sense of self in the client. Grief therapists do many of these same things in the course of helping clients cope, adapt, and come to terms with loss.

Advocates for the use of attachment theory in psychotherapy have generally argued that it is best viewed not as a particular "brand" of psychotherapy, but rather as a framework that supports all forms of psychotherapy. Insights from attachment theory, which have been supported by neuroscience research, have direct application to the development of treatment strategies for the bereaved, particularly in cases where bereavement is complicated by problems that are related to early trauma.

Attachment theory also provides a rationale for the importance of the therapeutic relationship, which we have argued is particularly critical in working with the bereaved. Attachment-informed approaches to psychotherapy, including our own, put particular emphasis on the procedural aspects of therapy that contribute to the creation of this bond. The loss of a significant person is a uniquely stressful event, one that is qualitatively different from other types of stressful events, including other types of losses (Sbarra & Hazan, 2008; Shear & Shair, 2005). The reassurance and sense of safety that a strong therapeutic bond provides are thus particularly important for someone who has recently suffered a significant loss. We trust that the case examples we have included throughout this book convey our belief that the therapeutic relationship is central to work with the bereaved and a sense of what this commitment to the primacy of the relationship looks like in practice.

In the following chapter we offer a more systematic discussion of what we regard as the core capacities that support the development of a strong therapeutic alliance in attachment-informed grief therapy.

8   The Therapeutic Relationship

Core Capacities of the Attachment-Informed Grief Therapist

What is it about the experience of feeling understood that is so valuable to someone who is bereaved? How is it that one human being can provide comfort and facilitate healing for another, even in the worst of times? Why does the failure to receive this support compound the suffering a loss may entail? And, what does this most basic of human needs teach us about our role in providing grief therapy?

Carol

Carol entered grief therapy shortly after the suicide of her son. The first session was extremely sad for client and therapist alike, as Carol recounted the details of her son's death, and her shock, confusion, and profound sorrow at the loss of him. Her despair was palpable, and she wept for much of the session. At the end of the meeting as they were about to part, the therapist followed a human impulse to somehow offer comfort in the face of this wrenching sorrow. He said, "Do you need a hug?" Carol said, "Yes," and they embraced for a moment as the therapist simply said, "I'm so sorry."

Unaccustomed to hugging new female clients at the end of first sessions, the therapist later wondered "What's going on here? Why did I do that?" Early in their next session, he said to Carol, "I don't usually end first sessions that way—what was your experience of that?" Without a moment's hesitation Carol replied, "It was fine. I felt like you understood."

In this chapter, we seek to answer these foundational questions about what grief therapists offer by examining the relational aspects of grief therapy—that is, the pivotal role of the therapeutic relationship in fostering recovery from loss. Decades of research have established that the therapeutic alliance is a critical variable in the effectiveness of psychotherapy (Allen, 2013; Duncan et al., 2010; Norcross, 2011). Although there have been recent discussions of the role of the therapeutic relationship in the field of thanatology (Neimeyer, 2012d; Pearlman et al., 2014; Winokuer & Harris, 2012), historically very little attention has been paid to this central aspect of grief therapy. In an effort to address this gap, we begin this chapter with a brief review of the theory and robust body of research on the therapeutic relationship as it impacts general psychotherapy outcomes. We will then look at the linkage between this literature and the insights from attachment theory and neurobiology that we have discussed previously. More specifically, we will offer a formulation that recognizes the grief therapist as a *transitional attachment figure* for the bereaved individual, one who provides a safe haven and a secure base from which reregulation of the self becomes possible. Lastly, we will elaborate on what we see as the core relational capacities that are intrinsic to the practice of effective grief therapy. Like all of our recommendations regarding treatment, what we have to say reflects our attachment-informed understanding of how people recover from and integrate major losses into their ongoing life experience.

Historical Views of the Therapeutic Relationship

With the development of psychoanalysis, Sigmund Freud revolutionized the practice of psychiatry and laid the foundation for modern psychotherapy. Central to this new method was a focus on the emotional reactions of the patient to the therapist. This unconscious transference of feelings about the client's parent to the relationship with the therapist became the cornerstone of psychoanalytic treatment. The idea of the therapist as a "blank slate" grew out of this approach to psychotherapy, with the clinician remaining, in effect, a non-specific human presence, onto which the patient's feelings could be projected. This way of thinking also proscribed personal disclosure on the part of the therapist, who, it was understood, should reveal as little as possible about themselves or their history.

In contemporary models of psychodynamic treatment, exploration of the client's reactions to their therapist remains a cornerstone of the process. What has changed is the idea that the therapist should strive to be a non-reactive and generic human presence. In the view of modern psychoanalytic theory, the therapeutic encounter takes place in an "intersubjective field"—a place where the unique minds of the therapist and the client come together (Ammaniti & Gallese, 2014). In this view, therapy is a relational process, and the therapist makes explicit use of his or her own experience as a therapeutic tool. Thus, in modern psychodynamic psychotherapy, the therapist is much more likely to share their own personal experience of what is going on for them in the relationship as a way of clarifying the relational dynamics and of modeling the value of self-disclosure in intimate relationships (Orange, 2010; Wallin, 2007, 2014).

The other major psychotherapeutic approach that has influenced our view of grief therapy is the client-centered tradition, founded by Carl Rogers (Rogers, 1951, 1957). As with contemporary psychoanalytic methods, client-centered therapy emphasizes the importance of the therapeutic relationship as a curative factor, but directs the therapist to maintain a specific type of therapeutic stance toward the client: one of unconditional positive regard, emotional empathy and warmth, and congruence. In client-centered approaches, the therapist has always been seen as an authentic, thinking, feeling human being—not a neutral presence. This clinical posture approximates the approach that has been adopted by contemporary psychodynamic clinicians. In the simplest of terms, both of these approaches embody a shift in emphasis from content to process. What the practitioner says is not any more important than how they say it and how they engage with the client (Allen, 2013).

Research on the factors that correlate with therapeutic effectiveness has consistently validated the importance of the therapeutic bond. In his reviews of this literature, Norcross cites research demonstrating the importance of the original Rogerian relational variables, as well as the skill of the clinician at customizing the therapy to the particular personality and defensive style of the client, their ability to arrive at and maintain consensus goals for treatment with the client, their willingness to gather ongoing feedback about the progress of treatment (particularly negative feedback), their ability to repair "ruptures" that develop in the treatment alliance, and their skillfulness at managing their own "counter-transference" reactions to the client (Norcross, 2011; Norcross & Lambert, 2006, 2011; Norcross & Wampold, 2011a).

In the remainder of this chapter, our goal is to operationalize many of these empirically supported variables in the form of what we call the *Core Capacities* of the grief therapist—the skills of the clinician at using his or her self throughout the therapeutic process to enhance the bereaved client's sense of trust, safety, and feeling understood, and hence the effectiveness of grief therapy.

Core Capacities

We make a distinction between the Core Capacities of the attachment-informed grief therapist, which we see as foundational skills, and some of the specific techniques that are described in Chapters 9 and 10. Techniques are explicit procedures used by the therapist at particular times to achieve a particular goal(s). For example, the grief therapist might have a client do some letter writing to the deceased in the service of resolving some "unfinished business" or strengthening the continuing bond with the deceased. When applied with wisdom, skill, and an empathically derived knowledge of the client, such techniques can be invaluable tools in grief therapy.

In contrast to techniques, the Core Capacities presented here are applied throughout the course of therapy, primarily in the service of building, maintaining, and repairing the therapeutic alliance between client and clinician. From the perspective of our model, as outlined in Chapter 7, these capacities serve to make the clinician a trusted attachment figure for the bereaved client, one who uses the relationship itself to underpin the healing process.

Core Capacity One: Fostering Emotional Safety and Trust

Emotional safety is the cornerstone of all secure attachment relationships, including the therapeutic relationship. As described in Chapter 6, mammalian species are hard-wired to pay attention to potential threats in their environment. For human beings, the threat can be psychological as well as physical. As discussed previously, people whose early experience with caregivers has resulted in a less than secure attachment orientation will approach a potentially threatening interpersonal experience (such as therapy) with a learned attachment style meant to protect themselves from interpersonal threats. By definition, threat evokes the attachment system, whether secure or insecure. For clients with a secure orientation to attachment, the likelihood of being able to use the clinician as a transitional attachment figure is usually high. In contrast, for clients with an insecure attachment style, therapy may be a threatening situation (Meij et al., 2007; Mikulincer et al., 2013; Neimeyer, 2012d; Zech & Arnold, 2011). In the case of bereavement, the treatment-seeking individual is often in a psychologically vulnerable state, potentially making the whole notion of talk therapy an unfamiliar and emotionally unsafe interpersonal context (Thomson, 2010). It is no wonder, then, that building trust between therapist and client is the first order of business for grief therapists. *The literature on grief therapy and attachment suggests that the clinician must be able to modify and customize their approach to a given client's attachment orientation, if the therapy is to be successful* (Mikulincer et al., 2013; Zech & Arnold, 2011; Zech et al., 2007; Zech et al., 2010).

How does the clinician build trust with a bereaved client? Our answer is "One step at a time!" Recall that a parent contributes to a secure attachment in their offspring by being reliable in their availability, predictable in their responses, affectively tuned into their child, and skillful in alleviating distress and increasing positive affect in the child. These same principles apply when a grief therapist works to build trust with a bereaved client, particularly one who comes to the encounter with an insecure attachment style—one whose early attachment experiences have left them with expectations that close relationships will lead to emotional disappointment, injury, or abandonment. Just as with the relationship between parent and child, the sense of "felt security" is not created in a single interaction. Rather, it is the result of repeated transactions in which the caregiver proves to be available, trustworthy, benevolent, and skillful in their actions.

Therapeutic Distance

Mallinckrodt and colleagues offer a useful model of the evolution of therapeutic distance over the course of treatment (Mallinckrodt et al., 2009). While originally formulated to describe treatment for attachment based problems in the client's interpersonal life, it also has direct applicability to work with bereaved clients with insecure attachment histories. The authors propose that the practitioner must adjust their own style to reflect the client's attachment-based requirements for feeling safe. They suggest that, over the course of treatment, the clinician gradually moves toward a style of engagement that then challenges the client to explore different ways of being in a close relationship. We propose that in attachment-informed grief therapy, the therapist must monitor and adjust the therapeutic distance with regard to three relevant domains presented by the client: *their relationship with the deceased, with their own grief reactions to the loss, and with the therapist as a helping attachment figure.*

Building Trust with the Avoidant Bereaved Client

In Chapter 4 we discussed some of the factors to consider when working with a client whose attachment style is generally avoidant. As we noted, in the beginning of therapy, the clinician will need to go slowly in asking the client to focus on and tolerate exploration of all three of these domains. They will need to adapt to the client's style and pace, without pathologizing it or communicating impatience (Zech & Arnold, 2011). Over time, as the therapeutic alliance grows, however, the clinician will gradually encourage the client to relate to these three domains in a different way—one that helps them to decrease their psychological distance from their continuing bond with the deceased, from their own grief reactions, and by extension, from the therapist. This evolution over the course of therapy helps to increase the client's repertoire of coping tools as they learn that allowing themselves to approach their loss is a tolerable experience—one that actually leaves them feeling better than simply avoiding it.

Mark

Mark entered grief therapy only after his wife urged him to do so after the death of his older brother in combat in the Middle East. Mark acknowledged that he missed his brother, but also told the therapist that he was "not one to cry in my beer about things like this." Mark felt that he had done as well as could be expected with the loss, and believed that because he had been able to continue working and supporting his family, he was okay. However, his wife revealed a different, more complex story. In a joint session with Mark and the therapist, she indicated that her husband was becoming more and more withdrawn from her and their two children. He was drinking more heavily, sleeping poorly at night, and had recently had three episodes when he uncharacteristically exploded verbally at her or one of their children. She also reported that Mark was reluctant to talk about his brother, despite her attempts to encourage him to do so.

Understanding that Mark was having trouble integrating this painful loss, the therapist decided that he needed to go slowly with him in the beginning. He decided to concentrate on building a relationship with his client. While offering Mark a rationale early on for why he thought grief therapy might be helpful, and stating that he believed that Mark's symptoms were related to his grief, he also told his client that his goal was not to get Mark to "spill his guts" each week. In fact, he explained that his wish would be for Mark to be able to "visit" his grief from time to time at a moment of his choosing, and even symbolically to "visit his brother" through memories of their life together during the sessions, so that he would be free to address the other important things that needed his attention in life now, such as his wife and children.

Following on that pathway, the therapist asked Mark to tell him more about his life now—what he enjoyed and was interested in, and what his goals and ambitions were for his future. They sometimes chatted amiably about sports teams that they mutually admired, or about the work that Mark did and the achievements of his children. As this progressed, the therapist began to inquire about Mark's brother in relation to these particular topics—did he and Mark share an interest in sports (yes); did they talk about how their work and family life were going (yes); were there particularly happy memories or stories about Mark and his brother from childhood (yes). Over the course of the sessions, the therapist would casually point out how important Mark's brother had been in his life, and what a "hole" had been created by his death. As the trust between them grew, and Mark began to open up and invest in the therapy, the therapist started to focus more on the details of his brother's death, and how life had been for him since his brother's demise. Eventually, he was able to ask Mark to share what he thought and felt when he first got the news of his brother's death, what the funeral had been like for him, and more about how he managed his "visits" with his grief now. Mark wept for the first time in that session, but reported in the following session that it had helped—he had been able to sleep better after that, and seemed less possessed by the thoughts about the horror of his brother's death and his yearning to have him back. Further work in the therapy involved the use of some directed techniques, such as having Mark write a letter to his brother, and also visit his brother's grave to read the letter, accompanied by his wife and children. All of these efforts helped Mark to confront his grief, but paradoxically, to also be able to "put it away" when he needed to do so.

Building Trust with the Anxiously Bereaved Client

In keeping with our definition of grief therapy, the goal of the attachment-informed grief therapist is to help the client develop flexible attention to the loss (see Chapter 7). For the client with an avoidant attachment style, and in the language of the Dual Process Model of Bereavement (DPM), this means being able to move toward a Loss Orientation at times and places of their own choosing. For example, with the help of his therapist, Mark was able to move toward his brother, toward his own grief about the loss of his brother, and toward a closer and more self-disclosing relationship with his therapist. In contrast, for the client who has an anxious attachment style, the clinical approach might be quite different with regard to these three domains. Here, the therapeutic work often involves gradually helping the client to flexibly move away from their grief—that is, to be able to move toward a Restoration Orientation. Work with these clients also typically involves transforming the nature of the continuing bond with the deceased in a way that continues the relationship, but in a new form that acknowledges that they are now dead. It may also require helping the client to scale back the emotional dependency that the anxiously attached client often forms with their grief therapist.

Carmella

Carmella felt bewildered and frightened after the death of her husband of 25 years from a difficult struggle with cancer. Carmella described their relationship as "perfect" and reported feeling more overwhelmed than she had ever been in her life. She portrayed her husband as "a rock," someone upon whom she could always rely to help her when she felt unsure or afraid. Carmella had great difficulty handling many of the family tasks without her husband, she yearned intensely to be with him, and although not actively suicidal, she frequently expressed indifference as to whether she lived or died.

Not surprisingly, Carmella frequently looked to the therapist for reassurance and support. Her feelings spilled out more or less continuously in their sessions, as she wept frequently and expressed a great deal of hopelessness about ever feeling better. She talked mostly about her husband's illness and dying experience, and also had trouble ending the sessions, frequently wanting to tell the clinician "just one more thing." Based on Carmella's way of relating to her, the therapist knew that she would initially need to provide some extra support for her client. She told Carmella that she knew she was in tremendous pain, and was also frightened about coping without her husband. She suggested that strengthening Carmella's ability to take care of herself might be one of the major goals for their work together. She also indicated that there might be ways that Carmella could "not let go, but instead find a different way to hold on" to her husband—a goal that Carmella liked. The therapist also allowed Carmella plenty of time to tell her story in her own way and at her own pace, took seriously her suicidal ideation, and offered extra contact time between sessions via e-mail "check-ins."

Over time, the therapist went out of her way to make note of competencies that Carmella had, but did not recognize. She also noted when Carmella had a little easier session ("you didn't cry quite as much this week"), praising her slow but steady progress.

She began to ask Carmella about the things that she was learning that gave her some relief, and encouraged her to do them more deliberately when she found herself upset (e.g., gardening). The therapist encouraged Carmella to join a widows/widowers bereavement group, not only for the support, but also for the chance of making new friends, something that Carmella tried and liked. She also began suggesting that Carmella resume some of the activities that she had enjoyed doing earlier in her life. They discussed engaging in some of these activities with her adult children (going to new restaurants), but also joining a book club where she could begin reading and discussing the literature that she loved.

Lastly, another major component of the therapy consisted of helping Carmella transform the psychological attachment with her husband. The therapist introduced a new idea to Carmella: that although she could not have her husband physically back in her life, she could continue to have a relationship with him, and even count on him as an important source of support. She encouraged Carmella to begin writing to her husband, and also writing back what she felt he might say to her after reading her letters. Over time, Carmella described a growing sense that her husband was now watching over her. She enjoyed talking with him every evening before she went to bed. After about a year, Carmella and the therapist agreed to gradually reduce the frequency of their meetings.

Building Trust with the Disorganized/Unresolved Client

As discussed in Chapter 4, clients with a Disorganized/Unresolved attachment style are often the most emotionally wounded of our clients. Typically, they present for grief therapy not only with issues of a current loss, but also with a great many characterological issues that result from early experiences with caregivers who were abusive, neglectful, or abandoning. People with this classification often have a defensive or guarded edge to their style of relating to people (including the therapist), while also craving contact and support. They also typically suffer from one or more psychiatric and/or substance abuse disorders. Establishing a trusting and productive working alliance with them in treatment can be no small task, one for which the therapist's understanding of attachment dynamics and the role of early relational history is often crucial to helping the client.

Allan

Allan, a 37 year old single man, presented for grief therapy after the death of his girlfriend, Sandi, to cancer. Their relationship had been a stormy one, filled with considerable conflict and numerous separations, followed by reconciliation. Their last reconnection happened when Sandi was diagnosed with ovarian cancer, and Allan returned to be with her. Both Allan and Sandi were heavy drinkers, and suffered from bouts of depression, although Allan's depression was expressed more often as explosive outbursts at Sandi. Allan's drinking had increased since Sandi's death, as had some occasional suicidal ideation. Allan had also recently been fired from a job for excessive absenteeism.

Allan's early history included several losses and disrupted attachment relationships. His father abandoned the family when Allan was 4 years old. Overwhelmed, his mother began to drink heavily. The family moved frequently, as his mother struggled with financial problems and depression. Three and a half years later, his mother remarried a man who was a stable provider, but who was physically and verbally abusive toward Allan and his mother. Conflict between Allan and his stepfather increased in his adolescence, to the point where he moved out of the house at age 17 and joined the Army. Over the years, he maintained periodic contact with his mother, but continued to avoid and despise his stepfather.

Clinical work with Allan occurred over the course of several years, during which Allan would do a piece of work with the therapist, and then drop out of treatment— only to return when new problems (or resurgence of old ones) surfaced in his life. In the first episode of treatment, Allan's narrative about the loss of Sandi, and even more so about his childhood, was very fragmented. He was clearly uncomfortable discussing his thoughts and feelings, and had difficulty putting them into a coherent story. Allan mainly wanted help with his disrupted sleep and the problems that his drinking was creating in his work-life. Allan stayed in therapy for only a short while, but returned about two years later when he remarried, and found himself having intense arguments with his new partner. Likewise, a year and a half after this, when he became a father at the age of 41, Allan found himself flooded with a range of emotions that he thought he had "put behind him," and he returned for the third round of therapy. This third episode resulted in the most productive work that he and his therapist had been able to do. Allan was able to talk for the first time in depth about the impact of his early family life on his development. In their work together, the therapist and Allan were able to identify and mourn the many losses he had experienced in his life, ranging from the initial loss of his biological father, the loss of security as his family life was shattered by the stress of single-parenting and his mother's increased drinking and erratic behavior, and then the further loss of his mother as a safe haven in the face of an abusive stepfather. Allan also began to talk in more depth about the impact of his relationship with and subsequent loss of Sandi.

Over the course of the next two years, Allan came to better understand his use of alcohol and avoidance to cope with his painful feelings of unworthiness, loneliness, and fears of abandonment in close relationships. He developed a newfound clarity about what he wanted for himself in his life, and over time, his ability to be nurturing toward and take pleasure in his new wife and son increased significantly. Likewise, his depression and need to use alcohol to deal with it subsided.

This vignette about Allan illustrates the long term impact of early attachment insecurity that results from unreliable and abusive caregivers, including the resulting disorganized/ unresolved attachment style that combines both avoidant and anxious elements. Allan's problems, while catalyzed by the loss through death of a conflictual but important adult attachment relationship, had deeper roots in the emotional damage he absorbed in his early relationships. The willingness of the therapist to meet Allan allowed progressively deeper layers of his emotional injury and grief to be brought to light, shared, validated, and mourned during each episode of therapy. The stable availability of the therapist over a period of several years, as well as the clinician's skillful tuning of the therapy to Allan's needs and readiness to be more vulnerable, greatly facilitated Allan's growing maturation and capacity to become permanently committed to a partner and child of his own.

Additional Ways to Build Trust with Clients

We believe that the therapist also builds trust by being transparent, that is, making their intentions and perspectives clear to the client, so that the bereaved person understands how their therapist is viewing their problems and the goals and methods of the therapy. In the vignette described previously (Mark), a therapist who believes that successful grief work involves confrontation with the death would likely make this belief clear to the client, along with timely explanations about why they held this belief. Even if the practitioner and client disagree, this transparency allows the client to begin to trust that "my therapist will be direct with me—I can trust his motives and agenda, because he makes them clear to me."

Additional ways of building trust include giving the client a maximum amount of control over the process of treatment, while recognizing the degree of direction or therapeutic leadership the client may need from the clinician. Many bereaved people, particularly those with an avoidant attachment style, fear that therapy will involve an involuntary surrender of control over their emotions and the privacy of their thoughts, as though therapists have the ability to read a person's mind and force them to "open up." To ease this concern the clinician needs to not only explain, but also to demonstrate in their actions, that therapy is a collaborative process, with the client retaining final control over their own internal process, and their disclosure of that process to the therapist. The vignette with Allan illustrates this principle, since the therapist allowed Allan to regulate the psychological distance in their relationship, including the frequency and duration of their contacts.

Finally, therapists build emotional safety and security by demonstrating warmth and genuine respect for the client as an individual. These are the core components of successful therapy identified by Carl Rogers many years ago, and they apply equally well to grief therapy today (Rogers, 1957; Winokuer & Harris, 2012). The empathically attuned grief therapist will have as their goal understanding and then responding appropriately to their client's particular attachment style. They will adjust their own pacing, style, and interventions to the tolerance levels of the client. When the inevitable empathic failures occur in this process, the therapist recognizes the error, and works to repair the relationship so that it is more in synch with the needs of their client.

Core Capacity Two: Empathy

Empathic attunement has come to be recognized as a vital ingredient in a number of contemporary models of psychotherapy, including grief therapy (Allen, 2013; Decety & Ickes, 2009; Elliott et al., 2011; Kauffman, 2012; Neimeyer, 2012d; Rowe Jr & MacIsaac, 1989; Wallin, 2007; Watson & Greenberg, 2009). As we have previously discussed in Chapter 3, the neurobiological underpinnings of human empathy have also become better understood in the last decade, beginning with the discovery in the brains of primates of so-called "mirror-neurons" and the mirror neuron system (MNS) (Keysers, 2011). This finding has been extended to suggest that the capacity for empathy in human beings also involves activation of mirror neurons (Decety & Ickes, 2009; Elliott et al., 2011). As discussed in Chapter 3, Schore has also emphasized the "right brain to right brain," nonverbal communication that occurs between caregiver and infant as a crucial element of attachment based bonding (A. N. Schore, 2002b, 2002c, 2009, 2012; J. R. Schore & Schore, 2014). Thus, the development of empathy between caregiver and infant may well involve activation of these same neurological circuits in both mother and child. This "neuronal resonance," quite possibly involving mirror neurons, is what may allow empathic attunement between a caregiver and their child, and between a therapist and client.

Empathy has both emotional and cognitive components (Decety, 2012; Decety & Ickes, 2009; Hodges & Wegner, 1997; D. J. Siegel, 2012a). Emotional empathy involves the ability to resonate to the emotional state of another: to see or hear the feelings of another person and then to experience the same emotional response in ourselves. The happiness we feel when watching a delighted child play with a pet dog; the sadness we feel when we see a bereaved mother well up in tears: these responses often occur without any higher order cognitive modulation. In the same way that we may find ourselves walking in step with a friend, we can find ourselves feeling in step with another person's emotions.

The resonance that connects people is not without emotional risk, however. Immersion in the feelings of a distressed person can result in emotional flooding on the part of the helper, and can interfere with a responder's ability to take appropriate action. Instead, the ability to feel the emotions of another person becomes most helpful when the empathic observer can also exert what has been called "effortful control," or higher cortical inhibition of the emotions that are evoked in the observer (Hodges & Wegner, 1997; Rothschild, 2006). This ability to maintain a "self–other" distinction ("they are in pain, but their pain is not my pain—instead, I feel badly for their distress") seems to be crucial if the observer is to respond in an engaged, compassionate way, rather than defending themselves from pain by maintaining emotional distance. This capacity to feel the pain of a client without becoming immobilized by it is a crucial empathic skill in grief therapy.

The cognitive component of empathy involves what is generally thought of as perspective taking—that is, understanding not just what a person feels, but why they feel that way. To have perspective on another person's responses, we need to have in mind not just what is happening to the person now, but also what has happened to them in the past—in other words, to consider the impact that previous life experiences may be having on a person's current emotions and behaviors. The ability to make sense of another person's behavior by understanding what is in their mind was identified by Fonagy as mentalizing (Allen et al., 2008; Fonagy et al., 2014). Thus, emotional empathy might arise because "I can see from your face and body posture that you are sad"—a very rapid and largely implicit (unconscious) form of neural processing associated with our remarkable ability to read the meaning of nonverbal cues in others. In contrast, cognitive empathy involves the recognition that "I understand that you are sad *because* your mother has just died. You had a very close relationship with her, and that makes it especially hard to lose her." This is mentalizing—keeping another person's heart and mind in our own heart and mind (Allen et al., 2008).

The capacity to combine both emotional and cognitive types of empathy in the context of a therapeutic relationship, while also holding onto the ability to differentiate between self and other, has direct implications for the complex balancing act that a grief therapist must maintain between being open to the pain of their client, yet not so overwhelmed that it engenders defensive processes in the therapist. This "sweet spot" of empathic attunement appears to offer the most helpful stance for any caregiver of the bereaved individual, whether they are a friend, family member, or grief therapist.

Finally, we want to note that it is crucial in the context of grief therapy that the clinician should not only be able to emotionally resonate with and understand their client, *but that they are also able to successfully communicate this understanding to the client.* Empathic attunement that is not felt by the client is not really empathic attunement. Rather, the client must "feel felt" by their therapist; they must know, in a way that goes beyond words, that they have been understood, and that they are not alone (D. J. Siegel, 2012a, 2012b). The "I felt like you understood" interaction with Carol, mentioned in the opening vignette of this chapter, would seem to include all of these elements of empathy. The therapist felt Carol's emotional distress himself, he reflected on the source of the distress, and then based on his emotional response and cognitive appraisal, he responded in a way that communicated his empathy and desire to comfort her. We believe that this complex integration of empathic skills is essential to an attachment-informed approach to grief therapy.

Core Capacity Three: Non-Defensiveness and Attending to Relational Repair

A strain or rupture in the therapeutic alliance has been shown to dramatically increase the chances of treatment failure, including premature termination of therapy. Conversely, the ability of a therapist to successfully repair these ruptures is one of the best predictors of the ultimate success of treatment (Norcross, 2011; Norcross & Wampold, 2011a, 2011b). Norcross identifies three common types of alliance rupture in psychotherapy (Norcross, 2011). The first is disagreement about the goals of therapy: what does the client want from therapy, and how well does it match what the therapist is trying to achieve? The second is about the tasks of therapy, meaning the methods and processes by which therapy can achieve the agreed upon goals. And the third is the emergence of direct interpersonal strain or tension in the relationship between therapist and client. To provide an example of a rupture of the therapeutic alliance in grief therapy, consider the following hypothetical case:

Jose

Jose, a middle aged male whose wife had recently died, entered therapy wanting help to feel less depressed and to improve his disrupted sleep cycle. The therapist, however, believed that Jose needed to be less avoidant and to confront the reality of his wife's passing, with its attendant emotions and thoughts. The therapist spent the initial sessions trying to get Jose to talk about his feelings about his wife and her death, sometimes pointing out his avoidance of the topic. Instead, Jose tried to discuss the problems created in his life by his wife's death—for example, how to handle discipline issues with his children by himself, and what he could do to get a good night's sleep. He wanted the therapist to give him some "tricks" about how to cope, while the therapist tended to avoid making direct recommendations to Jose, instead trying to help him find his own solutions to his problems. Rather quickly, Jose began to feel frustrated with the process, deciding that it was a waste of time and money. The therapist, meanwhile, was aware of becoming annoyed with Jose, deciding that he was resistant and unwilling to deal with the impact of his wife's death. This culminated in Jose not showing up for his next appointment, and deciding not to return to therapy again.

In this vignette, we can see all three types of relational rupture in the therapeutic alliance. The therapist has different goals for therapy than the client (confronting the death rather than avoiding it), and different expectations about how to go about achieving those goals (getting the client to "open up" and talk about his feelings rather than offering specific suggestions about solving specific problems). As a result, tensions have arisen in their relationship.

What might the clinician have done differently in an empathically attuned therapeutic relationship?

Sensing that Jose was growing frustrated, the clinician made several adjustments, starting with the acknowledgment that they were out of synch: "Sometimes I feel like we're going in different directions here—that I'm trying to get you to do something that doesn't seem right to you. Is that how you see it? If so, that must be frustrating for you, and sometimes it is for me as well. Let's talk about how we can get more on the same page." Listening carefully to the client's explanation that he felt that he was wasting his time, the clinician inquired about what would make Jose feel like they were making more progress. This led to a fruitful discussion in which Jose communicated that he needed to be able to get a good night's sleep, without thinking constantly about his deceased wife. The therapist gently remarked on how difficult that must be for him, and assured him that they could work on some "tricks" (the client's own words) to manage his evenings more easily. The therapist suggested that Jose might be able to use their sessions as the best time to "face the tough facts," but then give himself a "break from the grief" when away from their sessions. Jose could relate to this idea, and agreed to try to talk more about how he feels in the meetings, and to try the suggested sleep technique at home. By the end of the conversation, both Jose and his therapist felt that they understood each other better, and that they were now functioning more as a team.

What capacities are required of the therapist to be able to handle a rupture in the therapy relationship with success? Actually, all of the Core Capacities identified here come into play. Specifically, to respond well to the strain in the alliance, the therapist must maintain a genuine openness and non-defensiveness that allows the issue to be worked through. The ability to mentalize about the experience of the client, about the therapist's own experience in working with the client, and most importantly, about the differences in how they each experience the problems in their relationship, was crucial to resolving the impasse.

Human beings are continually evaluating and passing judgment on their own behavior, feelings, and thoughts, as well as those of other people; this is what our brains are wired to do in order to help us correctly read other people and situations. Although therapists strive to be aware of their own motivation and feelings, we believe that all people can think, feel, and act for reasons about which they are unaware. The defensiveness that can be unconsciously provoked in the therapeutic relationship can be invisible to both the client and the clinician, yet destructive to their alliance. As much as possible, maintaining an open and non-defensive stance and suspending one's own judgments about a given interaction or a given client is vital to doing the work well. What differentiates a well-functioning therapeutic relationship from a less than helpful one is the capacity of the therapist (and to a lesser extent, the client) to recognize when an empathic failure is happening, and to take steps to repair the alliance.

Core Capacity Four: Distress Tolerance

By now, we hope that we have helped the reader to understand that grief, even when it is not debilitating, is dysregulating. This state of disequilibrium, which varies greatly in intensity and persistence, can be eased by the presence of a supportive person or persons. No matter how independent and skilled at taking care of ourselves we may become, there are times when life challenges us with more than we can manage without help from others. As adults, the need for others is generally not as constant, or as desperate, as it is when we are young. But it is a need, nonetheless, and one that tends to be particularly intense in response to loss.

As we have noted, the relationship with an empathic grief therapist serves a reregulating function that is in many respects similar to the reregulation that an attuned caregiver provides to a distressed child. But to serve in this stabilizing and soothing capacity for another person requires that the therapist have a high capacity for distress tolerance—for remaining "present" in the face of the emotional, cognitive, and behavioral storms that bereaved clients may bring to therapy.

This chapter began with a case example (Carol) in which, arguably, the clinician was overwhelmed by his own reactions. In hindsight, it led him to make what was probably the right response, based on Carol's feedback in the following session, but it also might have led to an unhelpful experience for the client. For example, imagine that the clinician broke down in sobs as he listened to Carol's wrenching story. The client then might have become concerned about the well-being of the therapist, and felt compelled to comfort him. Carol might also have found herself wondering "Can this person handle this? This is just like the people at my church—they don't know what to say or do with me. Maybe no one can deal with this." *One of the most difficult aspects of being a grief therapist is learning to tolerate one's own feelings of helplessness in the face of their client's profound suffering, and their presentation of a problem that is existentially "unfixable"—the irrevocable loss of a loved one to death.* Such helplessness has the potential to undermine the clinician's feelings of professional competency and efficacy. It can also bring the clinician face to face with his or her own feelings about their own losses and ultimate mortality.

Sarah

As mentioned in previous chapters, Sarah lost her son to suicide. In addition, she had a number of subsequent losses in her life. These losses included the breakup of her marriage, the loss of her financial security, and a rejection by a new man with whom she had begun to have a romantic relationship. These additional losses, on top of the grief, guilt, and feelings of failure about her son's death, had a significant effect on Sarah's sense of self-worth. They culminated in an acute period of despondency marked by significant suicidal ideation and hopelessness. The therapist monitored this state of mind, and directly encouraged Sarah to contact him if she was having a very difficult time. She did this, and in an emergency session with the clinician, poured out her feelings of despair and shame, and thoughts of ending her life. The therapist listened carefully, with empathy and compassion, as well as some anxiety about the extent to which his client was at risk of making a suicide attempt. For the first part of the session, the therapist's goal was simply to have the client feel that they are not alone with their distress—that he "got it" about how badly she was feeling. As the session unfolded, and the therapist was convinced that Sarah felt the recognition of her emotional pain, he worked to help Sarah reflect on why she was feeling so very badly at this particular point in time. He enumerated the many losses she had experienced (not the least of which was the suicide), and normalized the feelings of unworthiness they had understandably engendered. He also noted the significant progress they had made in their work together, and gently reminded her of the resilience that she had been able to muster in the face of these devastating losses. He also offered a metaphor about what had happened to Sarah, with her "psychological immune system" having been compromised by the losses, so that her ability to ward off assaults on her sense of well-being and self-esteem was not functioning at full capacity. By the end of the session, the combination of being able to freely express her distress, having those expressions be accurately heard by the therapist, and then being helped to view her suffering from a different and more normative perspective, seemed to help Sarah feel better—in other words, to reregulate her emotional arousal back to a range that she could tolerate and manage by herself.

Distress tolerance refers to the capacity of the therapist to remain present for, yet not be overwhelmed by, the emotional storms that grief may elicit in the client. Like a parent who listens to the fears, rage, and unhappiness of their child with calmness and compassion, and thereby helps the child to find their emotional equilibrium again, the grief therapist serves a similar purpose for their clients. In a very real sense, the professional caregiver functions as a kind of emotional shock absorber, softening the impact of the emotional injuries embedded in the loss (and sometimes the subsequent losses that flow from it). In this way, the clinician remains able to protect himself and the client from emotional pain that could otherwise overwhelm them both.

Distressing Thoughts and Behavior

Along with strong feelings, bereaved clients may confront the clinician with a range of thoughts and behaviors that are distressing to the client (and often to the clinician). Hearing that a client is isolating herself from other people, abusing substances to numb her pain, or considering suicide, it is natural to feel concern and to find a course of action that will protect the client but not provoke defensiveness or a withdrawal from treatment. Clients may also behave in a guarded, sullen, or sarcastic manner, rolling their eyes every time the clinician makes a comment or ridiculing the clinician's observations. In most cases these ways of coping have their roots in the client's earliest attachment experiences with caregivers, and these defensive responses are a reflection of their internal working models that have developed at a time when the client was not able to develop healthier forms of self-protection. The challenge for the grief therapist is to simultaneously address the problematic behavior, while also keeping in mind the inner psychic pain and defensive processes that drive the dysfunctional coping patterns.

Finally, we would be remiss if we failed to mention one other form of helplessness that grief therapists must confront: their own existential vulnerability as a mortal human being. Therapists, of course, will have their own history of losses to absorb over the course of their lifetime, many of which will have shaped their own attachment style and frame of mind. And sooner or later, they must also confront their own approaching death. *In a very broad sense, all grief therapy is about the encounter by the client, and the therapist, with the uncertainty and impermanence of life itself.* While primarily focusing on the experience of our clients as they navigate what life has delivered to them, we believe that grief therapists must also work to make their peace with the transience of their own lives and loves. The recognition of their shared human experience—the need to come to terms with the reality of impermanence—can deepen the experience of mutuality between the grief therapist and client that is vital to doing the work well. This leads directly to our last Core Capacity of the attachment-informed grief therapist.

Core Capacity Five: Openness, Mindfulness, and Self-Knowledge

You must be the change you wish to see in the world.

Gandhi

This familiar quotation expresses an essential truth—to bring about change in others, we must manifest those same changes within ourselves. Thus, in order for the grief therapist to be of assistance to a client who is being buffeted by the disruption of loss, they must be aware of, have reflected on, and to a reasonable degree, have come to terms with their own experiences of loss, separation, and psychological trauma. Of particular relevance to the ideas we are offering in this book, we would suggest that grief therapists should be attuned to their own experiences with attachment relationships, beginning with their early developmental experiences in their family of origin, and on up through their current close relationships with partners, parents, children, colleagues, and friends. The goal is for the secure grief therapist to be knowledgeable about and accepting of their own feelings, thoughts, and bodily sensations, such that they are neither dissociated from them, nor controlled by them. This wisdom about one's own inner experience is what allows the attachment-informed grief therapist to foster these capacities in their bereaved clients.

Openness

Openness has been described in Buddhist literature as a "beginner's mind" (Suzuki, 1973)—a receptivity to experience that is, as much as possible, free of assumptions, preconceptions, and prejudices. In the context of grief therapy, openness involves maintaining a non-judgmental stance regarding the experience that the client brings to therapy. It also means retaining an uncluttered curiosity about the client's unique way of construing their loss, as well as their relationship with the deceased and their attempts to live in the world without their loved one. Openness also denotes the therapist's willingness to refrain from prematurely coming to conclusions about who the person in front of them is, what they are capable of, and what they need from therapy. Note that this approach is in marked contrast to a medical model of mental health intervention, in which rapid diagnosis of the patient's problem(s), followed by a straightforward application of the appropriate treatment, is regarded as the therapeutic ideal. Lastly, openness implies what Wallin describes as the "flexibility and freedom" of the secure therapist (Wallin, 2014)—the capacity to change, adjust, and even stretch themselves beyond their usual professional comfort zone to meet the client where they need to be met.

Mindfulness

Mindfulness can be understood as an extension of this stance of openness—essentially the clinician applying this same attitude of openness toward his or her own experience on a moment to moment basis. A number of theorists have noted that while mentalizing denotes the clinician's ability to reflect with *depth* on their own mind and the mind of their client, mindfulness points to the therapist's ability to attend to the great *breadth* of that experience (D. J. Siegel, 2010; R. D. Siegel, 2009; Wallin, 2010). Emerging from 2,500 year old Buddhist meditation traditions, mindfulness practices have entered into Western approaches to therapy as both a valuable generic skill of self-aware clinicians, as well as a specific therapeutic technique in various clinical situations (Cacciatore & Flint, 2011; Germer et al., 2013; Goldin et al., 2012; D. J. Siegel, 2010; R. D. Siegel, 2009; Tang & Posner, 2013; Thompson, 2012). For the clinician, the practice of mindfulness refers to efforts to be aware of the continuous changes in their own subjective experience while conducting therapy: thoughts, emotional reactions, and bodily sensations that arise during their time with a client. In line with modern psychodynamic therapy, this "data" of the therapist's own experience becomes part of the intersubjective field to be examined, understood, and, where helpful, shared with the client (Orange, 2010). As an example of this aspirational goal of remaining open and mindful, consider the following case example:

Wilma

Wilma entered therapy seeking help for her grief after multiple losses: of an important romantic relationship, of a beloved pet, and of her own physical functioning after it was compromised by a medical/surgical error that led to a permanent disability and chronic pain. She had previously been a relatively optimistic and resilient individual, but this series of losses, in close temporal proximity, had left her distressed and bitter. During one session, the therapist needed to end a few minutes early, due to another commitment. Wilma accurately felt the therapist's anxiety about ending the session, and felt cut-off and betrayed by it. At some point Wilma became unable to contain her anger at the therapist's manner, and she let loose with a verbal barrage, telling him that she felt abandoned by everyone in her social network, all of whom were "getting sick of me feeling sorry for myself—now even you." The therapist was aware of the bodily reactions (tightening in the stomach) and strong feelings of anger and shame that Wilma was evoking in him. He had to work hard to sit with these reactions, neither suppressing them, nor acting to defend himself against her attack. Instead, he struggled to reflect on what Wilma must have been feeling in response to what she experienced as the avoidance and dismissiveness of everyone in her social network, which now included her therapist. But he also worked to honor his own experience of feeling unfairly criticized.

He expressed empathy to Wilma about how painful it must be for her to feel "unseen" by those around her, and apologized if he had provoked this feeling in her. And he also clarified what he thought had been going on in him in terms of his own need to end slightly early. He shared that he often felt at a loss as to how to talk with Wilma in a way that did not leave her feeling angry and hurt. His response led to a productive discussion with Wilma about her feelings of abandonment by many people in her life, as well as an empathic apology on her part for becoming so angry. Both Wilma and the therapist agreed that some life situations created dilemmas that were just unsolvable, leaving everyone feeling helpless and upset, in spite of everyone's best efforts.

Self-Knowledge

Self-knowledge is the work done by the therapist to develop insight about their own sources of emotional pain and injury. It includes reflection on their own motivations for doing what they do with clients, and their own characteristic ways of psychologically protecting themselves when they feel threatened. It incorporates both the cultivation of mindfulness about one's interior experience—thoughts, feelings, bodily sensations—and deliberate effort at mentalizing or reflecting on that experience with a minimum of distortion or avoidance. Attachment theory offers one useful perspective from which we can think about the therapist's way of reacting to their clients (Mikulincer & Shaver, 2007). And as Wallin points out, it is useful to understand that in addition to having an overall attachment style, each therapist can fluctuate between different states of mind with regard to attachment at different points in time—sometimes on a moment to moment basis within the ebb and flow of a therapy session (Wallin, 2010, 2014).

When the therapist is in a secure state of mind with regard to attachment, or toward a particular client, they are in a balanced position toward their own experience and toward the communicated experience of their client. They can empathize with their client's feelings and thoughts, yet differentiate between the client's experience and their own. Moreover, they can keep perspective about why their client feels, thinks, and acts the way they do. As Wallin notes, there is room for "two minds"—that of the clinician *and* that of the client (Wallin, 2007). Secure clinicians are also balanced in their need to seek certainty, order, and security for themselves and their client, and to explore the ambiguous and sometimes anxiety provoking possibilities for new meanings and behaviors with the client. In other words, clinicians with a secure attachment style are able to balance their own need for attachment security with their need for originality—that is, their own attachment and exploratory systems. Clinicians in a secure frame of mind can also be flexible in their stance with the client, sometimes taking the lead and acting as the "expert," while at other times being guided by and even corrected by the client. Mistakes in the therapeutic relationship are experienced mostly as opportunities to learn, rather than painful examples of failure. And throughout the therapy, the clinician is free to stay focused on the crucial process oriented question that is central to good therapy: "what does my client need from me now that will be of help?"

However, when clinicians are in an anxious (or preoccupied) state of mind with regard to attachment or a specific client, they are likely to be focused on the client's feelings and thoughts, to the exclusion of their own (Wallin, 2014). They may be worried about how the client will react to them, or whether they will approve of what the clinician is saying or doing. They may feel angry or wounded by what the client is communicating, yet feel immobilized in their freedom to react to it. They are likely to over-identify with the client's experience of grief, and find themselves triggered into remembering their own experiences of loss or trauma. They may devalue clients who intellectualize their grief or who express it with words, rather than with tears and other explicit signals of emotional distress. They may at times be overly serious with a client, and fail to appreciate the humor or absurdity that is part of their mourning, even as these things are a part of life as a whole. In DPM language, they may focus on a Loss Orientation to the exclusion of a Restoration Orientation with clients. They may find that their ability to use their left brain capacities to analyze and reflect on what is happening has been subsumed by a right brain flood of emotion. They may be preoccupied with worry about the client's well-being (e.g., their ability to ever integrate their loss and rebuild their life, or their suicidality), but uncertain about how to be of help. They may experience themselves as incompetent or inconsequential with the individual, and be filled with doubt about whether they can challenge the patient or risk strain or conflict in the relationship. In its more extreme form, the therapist in an anxious state of mind with regard to attachment may fear that the client will fire them—either by leaving them for someone else (e.g., another therapist), or by dying (e.g., suicide). They may be suspicious of clients who seem to recover too quickly, and have trouble letting the client end treatment with them.

In contrast, when the clinician is in an avoidant (or dismissing) frame of mind with regard to attachment or a particular client, they may limit themselves to detached, left brain analysis of the client and their grief, with little or no resonance with the patient's emotional experience. They may find themselves being contemptuous or disapproving of the client and their style of mourning. This may be particularly true of clients who are experienced as overly emotional, dependent, or needy. They may be certain that they understand the client, and what needs to be done to help them, and may be prone to blaming the client for their resistance to accepting their help, or in being slow to recover. They may be overly focused on their own thoughts and feelings, rather than the thoughts and feelings of their client. They may find displays of strong grief emotion from the client to be awkward and uncomfortable, and may steer the therapeutic conversation back to ideas and words, or even to humor. They may find themselves reacting with defensive anger when challenged by a client. They may be reluctant to share anything of a personal nature with the client, even when it might be of help.

Lastly, when a clinician is in a disorganized (or unresolved) state of mind with regard to attachment, or a given client, they are likely to respond to the client with the exaggerated emotionality or significantly distorted thinking associated with counter-transference. Perhaps the hallmark of this state of mind is a feeling of psychological paralysis or immobilization, along with significant bodily cues of hyperarousal. The client may evoke strong feelings of shame, rage, fear, or helplessness in the clinician. The vignette of Wilma offered previously is an example of this kind of intense response on the part of a clinician. Therapists may also find themselves responding with a hostile use of professional skills—for example, a hostile diagnosis ("This person is just a borderline") or attacks on the client via interpretations ("Clearly, you are out to get me, and are attempting to ruin me"). Particularly relevant to grief therapy is the experience of being overwhelmed by the client's bereavement situation (e.g., death of a child when the therapist is also a parent), or their grieving style (e.g., a client whose sadness feels unbearable to the clinician). Extreme feelings of helplessness, often accompanied by global feelings of professional incompetence and inadequacy, are also markers of this state of mind. Clinicians may find themselves wishing to avoid or be rid of the client because of the painful affect they trigger. Most of these states of mind will have been triggered by a specific client, but upon reflection, they are often also rooted in areas of psychological vulnerability and dissociation in the clinician that have their origins in wounding early experiences with attachment figures in the therapist's own development.

A repeated experience of these types of reactions, with many different clients, suggests a possible mismatch between the therapist's personality and skill set, and their choice of profession. Nonetheless, it is also true that at one time or another, all clinicians experience reactions like these with a given client who is very triggering for them. And the appropriate response, not surprisingly, is for the professional to make use of a relationship with someone in their professional setting, such as a trusted supervisor, colleague, or therapist with whom they feel both respect and safety, to reflect on and work through their reactions to the client. In other words, the clinician must make use of a secure attachment figure—someone who can serve as a safe haven and secure base for them—to help them reregulate themselves and mentalize about their experience with the client. This use of such a safe and supportive relationship, in turn, allows the clinician to continue to serve as a helpful attachment figure for their client—restoring their ability to be empathically tuned into their client, without being overwhelmed by them.

Summary

This chapter has focused on what we believe is the heart of attachment-informed grief therapy: the therapeutic relationship between therapist and client. We began with a brief discussion of the substantial body of theory and research on the importance of the therapeutic alliance in all forms of psychotherapy, while noting that this topic has received comparatively little discussion in the grief counseling literature. We then introduced five Core Capacities that we believe the grief therapist must cultivate within themselves in order to foster a strong, collaborative, and effective relationship with their clients. These capacities are: fostering emotional safety and trust; empathy; non-defensiveness and attending to relational repair; distress tolerance; and openness, mindfulness, and self-knowledge. We made the point that these capacities are used throughout the course of therapy, in every session. They differ from specific therapeutic techniques, which are used for targeted purposes from time to time in grief therapy. These types of specific techniques are illustrated in Chapters 9 and 10, where we describe the strengthening in the client of their own capacity for affect regulation and meaning-making after loss.

9   Strengthening Self-Capacities

Thinking about our feelings while we are feeling them is essential to regulating and controlling our emotional states effectively, rather than doing something impulsively to shut off the emotions . . . This is a tall order, and these are skills we develop and refine over a lifetime – not without help.

(Allen, 2003, p.94)

In the preceding chapters we have looked at early attachment experience, and adult attachment orientation, as factors that impact adaptation to significant loss. As we have seen, a substantial body of research from developmental psychology, social psychology, and neuroscience supports the role of attachment security in adaptation to loss, and more broadly, in people's capacity to cope with stressful life events. Coming from different traditions and posing different questions, these streams of research have converged on the importance of emotion regulation in sustaining a healthy relationship with oneself and others (Marganska et al., 2013). In this chapter, we focus on the strengthening of self-regulation as a goal of attachment-informed grief therapy, with examples drawn from our work with a number of clients introduced earlier. These clients include people who, like Vince, have come to see a connection between their difficulties in dealing with grief, and their lifelong habit of suppressing or rejecting their emotions.

Vince

"I'm realizing more and more that I don't know what to do with my feelings. And some of that is because in my family it didn't pay to tell someone what you were feeling. If you said something was wrong you'd just get screamed at. There was no point, and it was easier just to shut down. So now that's what I always do, I just shut down. Or I run away. I don't want to deal with anyone because I feel like I have no way to . . . I don't know how to . . . what my feelings are, or how to talk about them."

For Vince, emotions are uncomfortable reminders of a time in his life when no one saw or heard him, a time when he was left to figure out for himself how to manage all the feelings that occupy the mind and heart of a little boy. When a child's feelings are disregarded or disparaged, he learns to keep them to himself, and eventually, to keep them *from* himself, outside of awareness. Avoidance can be a useful strategy for keeping emotions in check, but in life there are bound to be times when feelings overwhelm this approach. For many people, bereavement is such a time, a time when their way of coping with emotional distress collapses and they have no other strategy on which to fall back.

In Vince's case, the collapse of an avoidant strategy of coping with the loss of a close friend precipitated an escalation of anxiety, and the appearance of trouble-some physical symptoms, the combination of which led him to seek help. With the support of the therapist, Vince was able to make connections between his experience as a child, and his difficulty acknowledging and managing emotion. At the same time, he was encouraged to experiment with alternative ways of relating to his feelings, practices that involved noticing and allowing them to surface. Soon, Vince's physical symptoms began to abate, and while he became more aware of feeling sad and angry, he also found himself less plagued by anxiety and the fear that he was going to "go crazy" and "lose control."

For many people who have lost a loved one, the integration of loss involves a period in which they explore thoughts, feelings, and memories related to the deceased. While most people manage this process without professional help, others decide, after a period of struggle, to talk to someone about their loss. Whatever other support a grief therapist or other professional provides in these circumstances, an important part of their role is to serve as a transitional attachment figure who helps the bereaved individual to achieve a degree of self-regulation sufficient for them to think and talk about their loved one without collapsing into their emotions or steadfastly avoiding them.

In this chapter, we will continue our discussion of attachment orientation as a factor in how people respond to loss, with particular attention to problems in emotion regulation that complicate bereavement in insecurely attached individuals. The literature on emotion and self-regulation reflects the interests and methods of researchers and clinicians from many disciplines. Such diversity inevitably leads to a certain amount of difficulty in communication and integration of knowledge. For example, the terms "emotion" and "affect" and "emotion regulation" and "affect regulation" are used interchangeably by some writers (Mikulincer et al., 2009) but not others (D. J. Siegel, 2012b). For simplicity's sake, we use the term "emotion regulation" throughout this discussion. The treatment recommendations we offer in this chapter reflect what we have described as an important goal of grief therapy, which is to support flexible attention to the loss, particularly in those individuals whose grief has been complicated by their tendency either to become immersed in their feelings or to dismiss them.

Both the Dual Process Model of Bereavement (DPM), and Mikulincer and Shaver's work on the role of insecure attachment in problematic grief, emphasize the need to help bereaved clients who lack core emotional regulatory capacities develop them (Mikulincer & Shaver, 2007, 2008b, 2013; M. S. Stroebe & Schut, 1999). Development of these capacities is also a principle component of therapy for securely attached individuals who have experienced traumatic loss. While all clients may be helped by learning how to soothe themselves and manage painful feelings, there is now substantial evidence that this work is particularly important for individuals who have experienced a traumatic loss or who are survivors of unresolved early relational trauma or loss (Briere et al., 2012; Pearlman & Courtois, 2005; Pearlman et al., 2014).

Given all that we have learned about the diversity of people's response to significant loss, it stands to reason that whatever therapeutic interventions are provided to the bereaved must be correspondingly diverse. When we apply this principle to the use of emotion regulation strategies, the first question that arises is: what is the purpose of introducing these strategies to a particular bereaved individual, and what emotions are we trying to help the bereaved person regulate? The answer to this question will vary from client to client.

Addressing Emotion Regulation Deficits: Fitting the Treatment to the Client

Bereavement is a process that involves reconstruction of meaning and identity, a rebuilding of the self that will continue for the rest of a person's life. Before that process can begin, however, someone who is grieving must find a way to manage the pain of separation. In the immediate aftermath of significant loss, that pain, and the fear, guilt, and other emotions associated with it, can be disabling. The persistence of this level of emotionality is associated with anxious attachment, and is what brings many anxiously attached bereaved people into treatment (Mikulincer & Shaver, 2008a).

As discussed in Chapter 4, anxiously attached individuals are predisposed to sustain or even exaggerate negative emotions in order to attract the attention and care of attachment figures (Mikulincer & Shaver, 2007; Shaver & Mikulincer, 2014). This strategy is apparent in a tendency to ruminate on painful memories and to exaggerate one's inability to cope with current life stressors. Understanding this dynamic as it relates to bereavement is an important consideration in treatment planning. If these tendencies are not addressed, they are likely to interfere with the effectiveness of grief therapy.

In contrast, the grief response of avoidantly attached people is characterized by a tendency to deny the possibility that they might be having difficulty in coping with the loss, thus avoiding activation of their attachment system (Mikulincer & Shaver, 2007; Shaver & Mikulincer, 2014). A list of the emotions that avoidant individuals are most intent on downplaying could also serve as a list of the feelings that most often accompany significant loss: fear, sadness, guilt, distress—in other words, feelings that they associate with vulnerability. In a reversal of the regulatory strategy used by anxiously attached people, avoidant individuals direct attention away from emotion related thoughts and memories and "suppress emotion related action tendencies" (Shaver & Mikulincer, 2014), such as crying or vocalizing their feelings. Also in contrast to anxiously attached individuals, avoidant individuals operate on the principle that negative emotions are something to be managed without the help of others, who are viewed as unable, or not inclined, to provide support. Like anxiously attached people, individuals who are avoidantly attached can benefit from emotion focused interventions, but given the differences in their way of managing their feelings, the interventions that help each group will be different.

Attachment orientation influences the choice of defensive strategies, and is likewise reflected in the problems that arise from overuse of these strategies. Thus, it is reasonable to conclude that interventions to support emotion regulation (and grief interventions on the whole) must address the specific difficulties of a bereaved client (Zech et al., 2010). We will return to this proposition after a brief orientation to techniques that can be used to assist in the regulation of affect.

Emotion Regulation Strategies

In the second edition of the *Handbook of Emotion Regulation*, Gross explains that regulatory processes do one of two things: they either down-regulate negative emotions, or up-regulate positive emotions (Gross, 2014, p.8). He describes five "families" of regulatory processes, which are listed with examples here.

Situation selection: The "most forward thinking approach to emotion regulation" (Gross, 2014, p. 9), situation selection, involves taking actions that are likely to end up in a situation that will relieve negative feelings or give rise to positive ones.

For example, a widow might arrange to have dinner with a friend on the anniversary of her husband's death. Another approach to helping clients plan for what are expected to be difficult anniversaries or situations is visualization, where the client is directed to think about the situation, bring up the thoughts and feelings he imagines will arise at that time, and with the clinician's help, imagine what he will do to help himself manage his feelings (Taylor et al., 1998).

Situation modification: "Directly modifying a situation so as to alter its emotional impact" (Gross, 2014, p. 9).

For example, a widow might avoid driving past the cemetery where her deceased husband was buried. At a family gathering, she might choose to avoid interacting with a family member who routinely makes insensitive remarks about her deceased husband.

Attentional deployment: "Directing attention within a given situation in order to influence one's emotions" (Gross, 2014, p.10).

This is often used when situation modification is not possible; for example, a widow might recall pleasant memories of her husband, or look at pictures of him taken when he was healthy and active. Techniques for redirecting attention can also be used to promote oscillation between a Loss Orientation and a Restoration Orientation (Mikulincer & Shaver, 2013). A simple way to do this is to encourage a person to let themselves think about something sad, and then redirect their attention so that they are thinking about something happy. More concretely, a widow could be coached to plan her day around activities like cleaning out her husband's desk, or having lunch with a friend. In each case, the idea is to encourage an awareness of the possibility of *choosing* where one's attention is directed, rather than having one's state of mind externally, and randomly, determined.

Cognitive change: Modifying "how one appraises a situation so as to alter its emotional significance" (Gross, 2014, p.10).

Techniques to help clients restructure dysfunctional thoughts can be an important component of therapy with anxiously or avoidantly attached clients, as the previous discussion suggests, and can take a number of forms, from reinterpreting the importance of a past mistake, to reevaluating one's ability to manage in the face of external stressors (Neimeyer, 2006b, 2012f). The widow, for example, might develop a different perspective on her ability to take care of herself and her children, or she might be taught the use of the ABC model of Rational Emotive Behavioral Therapy (REBT) to minimize self-defeating thoughts (Malkinson, 2012). This activity of reframing how one looks at the self or a situation is closely linked with the meaning-making process that will be discussed in more depth in Chapter 10.

Response modulation: Response modulation refers to "directly influencing experiential, behavioral, or physiological components of the emotional response" (Gross, 2014, p.10).

For example, a therapist could provide instruction in deep breathing or muscle relaxation techniques, or suggest that a bereaved person engage in some form of regular physical exercise.

This final category of regulatory strategies summarized by Gross includes many of the techniques that clinicians use to help people who are in distress, whether their distress is related to an ongoing problem or a traumatic event. These techniques are described more fully in a number of excellent clinical manuals by Pearlman (Pearlman et al., 2014) and Leahy (Leahy et al., 2012).

Attachment Orientation and Emotion Regulation

Taking into account all of these processes, we can propose some answers to the questions raised at the beginning of this chapter about the role of emotion regulation in integration of a loss. While these observations will be true in most cases, they hold particularly for the insecurely attached, where interventions that *strengthen people's capacity to experience, understand, express, and manage their emotions can help restore the dynamic oscillation described in the DPM.* As we have noted throughout, people with different kinds of insecure attachment orientation exhibit different types of difficulties that require different treatment approaches. Table 9.1 provides a summary of some of these projected difficulties.

Table 9.1 Attachment Related Complications in Grief (Kosminsky and Jordan, 2016)

Attachment Style	Complications
Anxious	Dependency in relationship; intensity of loss related emotions interferes with oscillation and integration of the loss
Avoidant	Dismissive of attachment; ambivalence about the person and avoidance of feelings about them interfere with oscillation and integration of the loss
Disorganized	Difficulty in tolerating and managing emotion and lack of mentalizing capacity interfere with processing intense and conflicting feelings relating to the deceased and interfere with integration

Taking this a step further, Table 9.2 summarizes the kinds of interventions that we tend to use with clients who have these different types of insecure attachment orientations.

Table 9.2 Emotion Regulation Techniques by Attachment Style (Based on Expected Problems in Integration of Loss) (Kosminsky and Jordan, 2016)

Attachment Style	Treatment Recommendations
Anxious	Emotion regulation; address cognitions that sustain negative emotions
Avoidant	Affect awareness; address negative cognitions regarding emotion
Disorganized	Establish safety; restore mentalizing

In the next section, we present examples of techniques for emotion regulation that address the problems associated with different types of insecure attachment. Note, however, that like all therapeutic interventions, *approaches to strengthening emotion regulation should be chosen based on the needs of the individual client*; what is offered here is not prescriptive. The references cited are all excellent sources for learning more about the wide range of approaches to strengthening these capacities.

Anxious Attachment: Emotion Regulation; Addressing Cognitions that Sustain Negative Emotions

"I wake up, I remember that he's gone, and I'm not just sad, I'm terrified."

Trudy

The neediness of anxiously attached clients can produce a variety of reactions in therapists, from sincere sympathy to active resentment. Which of these responses is elicited depends on a number of factors, including the therapist's own attachment orientation, what kind of day they are having, and the cumulative level of stress in their personal and professional life. That being said, as a general rule the desperate unhappiness of anxiously attached bereaved clients cannot help but provoke, in the helping professional, a desire to provide comfort and to offer someone deep in grief the hope that their pain will ease. In short, grief therapists do not need to be told to provide the comfort that anxiously attached bereaved people want. They may, however, be reluctant to intervene in more confrontational ways. Yet there will be times when this approach is what is needed.

Trudy

"My parents always said I needed someone to take care of me and they were right. Now they're gone, and my husband is gone, and I can't get over this terrible feeling that I'm not going to make it."

Trudy, who was described in Chapter 4 as having an anxious attachment style, remained tearful and hopeless five years after her husband's death. Notwithstanding her insistence that she was incapable of caring for herself and her two almost adult children, she had done exactly that, and arguably, had done it more consistently than her husband. Like many bereaved individuals, Trudy wanted to feel better—more energetic, less worn out, more able to manage several life challenges that were on the horizon such as selling her house, finding a new job, and finding a suitable placement for her son, whose presence at home was increasingly stressful for Trudy and her teenage daughter. Trudy's speech was rapid, as was her breathing. Gently pointing this out, the clinician asked Trudy to slow down and take a few deep breaths, after which she was able to proceed at a more regulated pace. The clinician commented on how sometimes "our feelings take so much energy that we don't have much left over to do the things we want to do." She went on to suggest that one of the things they could work on together was helping Trudy manage her emotions a bit, so that she didn't always feel so tired and stressed (see the next section, *Modulating Feelings*). Before she left, the clinician taught Trudy some breathing exercises she could practice at home during the week. The clinician ended the session by assuring her client that she would be there to help—Trudy was not alone—and that together, they would help her find a way to feel better and move on with her life.

Although a clinician may be tempted to reassure a client like Trudy that she is an adult and can surely take care of herself, making this observation before a strong bond has been established is likely to result in a rupture in the relationship, and even the withdrawal of the client. Following the well-established principle that we begin where the client is, we start by offering sympathy and reassurance. As discussed previously, anxiously attached clients will at times sustain an agitated emotional state in order to ensure the attention and care of the therapist. Of course, we want people to know that they are not helpless. But someone like Trudy, who genuinely feels unable to care for herself, has to be helped to come to her own conclusion about her competence and strength. Faith, as we know, has to come from within, and that includes faith in oneself.

After a few weekly sessions with the clinician, Trudy was able to talk about her husband's death without dissolving into tears, and the narrative she had constructed of her own helplessness and her husband's strength began to change. With her attention directed to evidence of her accomplishments and what these accomplishments said about her ability to survive independently, Trudy became increasingly self-confident. She was able to understand the roots of her tendency toward excessive dependence, and this too helped her let go of it. Strength built upon strength, and over the next year Trudy put her house on the market and found a new job. She found a placement for her son, and after a difficult period of adjustment, concluded that it was the best thing she could have done for him. Along the way, Trudy decided to take dance classes and try online dating. In short, Trudy made the kind of progress we hope to see in people who come to us for help, especially those who have been through years of unrelieved suffering. After five years of being on her own, Trudy was ready to shed the identity of "china doll," an identity that no longer fitted, and that no longer served her.

Modulating Feelings

To modulate feelings is to exercise control over their intensity, rather than letting the feelings overtake you. One of the many approaches to modulating feelings involves focusing on the physical sensations that accompany emotions—discomfort, tightness, rapid breathing—and "reporting" to oneself on these sensations without attaching meaning to them. Often simply shifting attention from thoughts that sustain and intensify emotions to physical sensations is enough to bring down the level of emotional arousal (Leahy et al., 2012; Linehan, 1993).

An alternative approach involves examining the emotion with the intention of identifying what information it contains ("What is this emotion trying to tell me?"). Like the approach previously described, focusing on the meaning of an emotion—shifting from the physiological to the cognitive, and regarding the emotion as a source of information rather than an overwhelming force—can help a person feel more in control. Also important is the realization that emotions vary in intensity, and that there are things we can do to moderate the intensity of emotion.

Calming Breath

The way a person is breathing is one of the most readily available measures of their emotional state, and also one of the most direct paths to changing it. People are quick to pick up on the connection between how they are breathing (rapidly, shallowly, or hardly at all), and their level of emotional and physiological discomfort. With practice, in session and at home, taking a breath becomes a habituated response to feeling stressed, and taking "breathing breaks" to regulate their internal state becomes part of clients' daily self-care. To get them started, it helps to offer some simple and easy to remember instructions like the ones here.

> *Sit in a comfortable position, your body softening into your chair. Soften your gaze at your surroundings, or close your eyes. Now take a slow breath in, for a count of four; hold it for a count of four; and slowly breathe out for a count of four. Do this a total of four times.*

In Chapter 4 we also met Gloria, another client whose grief was complicated by the anxious nature of her attachment. Gloria was described as someone who was "tormented by her persistent feelings of failure as a daughter; she weeps continually in sessions . . . only stopping briefly when the therapist draws her into discussion and encourages her to breathe." The following paragraph picks up on the narrative of Gloria's therapy.

Gloria

"She was my everything. I just don't know how I can go on without her."

Two months into treatment, Gloria continued to weep. The clinician often found herself drawing her chair closer to Gloria's in an effort to convey more fully her attention and care. When the clinician did this, Gloria would calm down. The resulting interaction resembled a kind of dance: Gloria would weep, the clinician would bring her chair in closer, and Gloria would stop weeping. Although she recognized this pattern, the clinician was not sure what to say or do about it. One day, when she had drawn closer and Gloria had stopped weeping, the clinician moved her chair back to its original position. Within moments, Gloria was gasping for breath, and her tears resumed. The clinician's response was likewise immediate and intense. Looking Gloria in the eyes, she said in a firm voice: "Stop! You were fine just a moment ago! Nothing has changed! You can be fine now!" And with that, Gloria stopped crying.

Many years later, this experience is a reminder of how a clinician can be drawn into the drama of a client's efforts to get her attachment needs met. Once it became an explicit focus of treatment, Gloria was able to trace the history of her intense and anxious attachment to her mother and to see how it had been reenacted in therapy. In response to the therapist's gentle inquiries, Gloria confirmed that her mother did not pay much attention to her, except when she was hurt or sick. She had learned that the surest way to ensure her mother's attentive care was through the expression of extreme distress.

After this discussion, Gloria was less prone to prolonged crying jags, and more able to talk about changing her day to day routines in ways that would help her feel better and more in control. She was encouraged to find ways to soothe herself and to occupy the many hours she had previously devoted to her mother's care. She eventually returned to school and began a new career that restored some sense of meaning and purpose to her life. Her feelings about her mother and her longing for her return did not dissipate, however, at least during the time when she was in treatment, and in the several years following when she was in periodic contact with the therapist.

Addressing Cognitions that Impede Healing

The past exerts a powerful influence on how we experience what is happening in the present. While it is helpful to know this, knowing it is often not enough to keep us from reacting in a manner that is beyond our understanding and that of those around us. Someone who, like Gloria, grew up with a mother who was inattentive except when she was sick or crying may find herself weeping in response to a therapist's moving her chair back a foot. Someone whose father died when he was young may feel panic at the thought of his teenage son going on a school trip. Jon Allen describes these as "90/10" moments, where 90% of a response is connected to past events, and 10% is related to what is happening in the moment. The idea that their response to a given situation is not unreasonable in light of their history is reassuring to many people. As Allen writes, they are not "making a mountain out of a molehill"; in truth, there is "a real mountain in their past, and their sensitized nervous system inclines them to react to molehills as mountains" (Allen, 2013, p.60).

In Gloria's case, what turned out to be an effective intervention (firmly instructing the client to stop crying and resume the conversation) was born of the therapist's frustration with the client's collapse into an old behavior pattern. The literature on mindfulness based psychotherapy practices (Germer et al., 2013; Hanson, 2013; D. J. Siegel, 2010; R. D. Siegel, 2009) offers a good many more considered techniques for helping clients stay in the moment (see the discussion of Mindfulness).

Finally, we return to Trish, another client who benefited from recognizing the impact of her past on her present reactions and functioning.

Trish

> "I never feel like I can trust that my feelings are really mine. My feelings are always so tied up with my mother, my sisters, my husband. I'm always trying to figure out what someone else wants, what would be good for someone else."

In contrast to Gloria, Trish was able to talk about her emotions without crying; she was analytical and dispassionate in describing a childhood in which she often felt alone, helpless, and afraid. When she first came to therapy Trish described her mother's death as a relief. But within a short time, she began to feel frighteningly unsure of herself, and was unable to bring herself to make the decisions that were necessary to settle her mother's estate.

Trish's mother was always unwell, and as a child Trish worried about her constantly, often getting up in the middle of the night to make sure that she was breathing. Only as an adult and with input from others had she come to understand that the illness of alcoholism made her mother unsteady on her feet, drove her to bed in the middle of the day, and was the reason for her periodic, sudden hospitalizations. Trish remembered her mother as being "fine one minute and falling down the next," and she recalled her mother insisting that it was Trish and her sisters who were making her sick, and who would be the death of her.

Early in therapy, Trish explained that there was "no point in getting angry or upset" when she was growing up because "mom would get more angry or more upset, and then she would leave the room and you would feel guilty and be afraid that she was going to die." With a slight nod of understanding, the clinician gently asked Trish what she was feeling now as she talked about her childhood then. After a few moments' hesitation she said, "Like a mess." The clinician smiled and said, "That's good to know, but that's not a feeling." Trish was shown a list of feelings and asked to choose one or two that were closest to the feelings she had when she talked about her childhood. "Fear" was Trish's response. "Because thinking about that time is hard, and I don't know if I can do it and not fall apart." The clinician noted that fear was a reasonable way to feel when you're starting to think about revisiting painful memories. "But feeling afraid is a lot different than feeling like a mess, don't you think? A mess is something you are; fear is something you feel." Trish nodded, and the clinician added: "And it's good to know that fear is what you're feeling, because now that you know that, and now that you've told me, I can say something that may help you feel less afraid. I can tell you that you don't have to do this alone, and you don't have to do it all at once."

Returning the following week, Trish said more about the stress of being the executrix of her mother's estate. "How can I talk to lawyers and accountants? How can I talk to anyone, when I'm afraid I'm going to say the wrong thing, make the wrong move?" Her mother had always told her what to do, and as much as she had resented her for it, Trish now realized that she had no idea of how to think for herself. She was terrified that without her mother she would have no one to go to for help when problems came up; her sisters were as useless as she was. The clinician suggested that Trish try asking herself what she should do when a decision had to be made; she might know more than she suspected. Trish replied: "I know what you're saying, but when you say it, I get very afraid and every part of my body says no." Acknowledging the fear Trish felt and why it made sense, the clinician immediately withdrew her suggestion, saying, "Well, I certainly don't want to recommend your doing anything that your whole body tells you not to do. But I wonder, could I have a word with your pinkie?" This seemingly nonsensical inquiry was in fact an invitation for Trish to close her eyes and relax into a trance state, something she had previously found allowed her to explore ideas that were otherwise too frightening or uncomfortable to consider. In a gentle voice, the clinician began to speak of Trish's pinkie as a place where a lot of undiscovered self-knowledge could be found. Her pinkie indicated agreement (with a little nod) and the clinician continued, emphasizing that Trish had it in herself to find her way. She could always ask for help, but before asking others she could ask herself. When she opened her eyes Trish smiled and said, "I like that. Because my pinkie is always with me." When she returned the following week, Trish reported that she had taken to asking herself "WWPD?" (what would Pinkie do) rather than always turning to others for answers.

The utilization of trance, as illustrated here, owes much to the teachings of Milton Erickson (Erickson & Rossi, 1979; Rosen, 1991) and to the interpretation and expansion of Erickson's work by his student Stephen Gilligan (Gilligan, 2012, 2013; Gilligan & Price, 1993).

Avoidant Attachment: Becoming Aware of Feelings; Suspending Judgment

"Don't expect me to sit here and cry. I don't do that. What's the point?"

Hannah

If the neediness of the anxious client challenges the clinician's capacity for compassion, the dismissiveness of the avoidant client can cause her to question her competence. It is important to remember, in the face of such a person's lack of confidence in the value of therapy and frequent assertions that she doesn't need anyone's help, that her presence in the clinician's office provides countervailing evidence to these claims. When allowed to take their time and draw their own conclusions, avoidant clients will often get to a point where they can let down the defenses they have erected against their own emotions, and the help offered by others.

Hannah

"I don't expect anyone to help me, including you."

From the outset, Hannah made it clear that her expectations for therapy were limited at best. She continued to articulate her low opinion of the value of therapy on a weekly basis for several months, arriving with the announcement that she had almost canceled, and concluding each session with a comment about how she was "no better off than when I came." She stopped treatment after three months and returned three months after that at the urging of a friend, and because she was not feeling well physically or mentally.

Soon after she returned, the clinician repeated a question that Hannah had previously dismissed, asking where she had learned that the best way to deal with her emotions was to suppress them. This time, instead of waving away the clinician's question, Hannah asked: "Why is any of this important? It's not what I'm here to talk about." The clinician responded by briefly explaining that the way parents respond to us as children when we're afraid or upset has a lot to do with the way we think about our feelings—whether or not we think they're worth paying attention to, or sharing with other people. Hannah's parents traveled a great deal, and they were not very involved with her in the intervening times when they were at home. The very independent little girl she remembered herself as being had grown into a woman who was determined not to need anyone's help. She achieved this goal by controlling her feelings. Seeing that Hannah was still listening, the clinician said, "I think it's really important for you to think of yourself as independent, someone who doesn't need anyone else. So, it's a risk for you to feel your feelings. If you let yourself feel really sad, you might need someone to comfort you. And that's not something you want to have to do, because deep down you figure no one is going to comfort you." Hannah's strategy had worked quite well for much of her life; it had gotten her through an isolated

childhood and then through her husband's illness and death. But under the load of every-
thing she had been through, this strategy was starting to break down and her feelings were
coming to the surface. The clinician suggested that Hannah needed a different way of being
strong, one that allowed her feelings to be part of her life.

It would be nice to be able to say that Hannah heard what the clinician said and was convinced that it would be a good thing for her to feel her feelings. But what happened instead was that Hannah rolled her eyes and changed the subject. More often than not, this is what happens the first or fifth time a clinician talks to someone like Hannah about what it might be like to relax the defenses they have erected against their emotions. So it is a good idea for the clinician to be prepared to have that happen. If clients continue to come, as Hannah did, they will often find themselves less avoidant and critical of their feelings and more inclined to allow space for them to exist. They can be encouraged to notice their feelings during the week, and also to notice what they say to themselves about their emotions when they are aware of them. They can practice letting go of judgments about what they feel.

This kind of growth is one of the goals of what Christopher Germer describes as "compassion based psychotherapy" (Germer et al., 2013, p.99), so called because it emphasizes the cultivation of an attitude of acceptance toward oneself and one's feelings. Rather than treating their emotions as enemy intruders, clients are encouraged to let them in; rather than thinking of themselves as weak when they feel sad, or unforgiving when they feel angry, they are encouraged to recognize that every human emotion is just that—a part of being human.

Soften, soothe, and allow

Sit comfortably and either close your eyes or soften your gaze. Slowly let your attention come to your breath, and as you do, become aware of any tightness in your body. Take another breath, and as you do, pay attention to what you are thinking and feeling. Notice the connection between what you are thinking and feeling, and the tightness in your body. Now, think about softening that part of your body. If your stomach is feeling tight or your heart is hurting, you can rest your hand there, and just let yourself be comforted by your own gentle touch. You can speak to yourself in a soothing way, or you can simply repeat the word soft, saying it quietly to yourself as you continue to breathe, slowly and deeply. Whatever discomfort is there, notice it, and let it be what it is. You can repeat the word "allow" on each breath. Continue to repeat the words "soften, soothe, allow."
Adapted from Germer (Germer et al., 2013)

Margaret

"Why am I even talking about my anger? It's stupid for me to be angry, because there's nothing I can do about it."

"I don't know how you listen to this stuff all day. It must be so boring for you."

Margaret's declaration in this instance was both a hedge against her fear that the therapist would openly declare her desire for Margaret to simply stop talking and leave so that the therapist could go home, and a hint as to her attitude toward the importance of emotions, her own in particular. Margaret, who was introduced in Chapter 4, was aware of her emotions, but she did not trust them. If she was angry or disappointed, it was only because she had unrealistic expectations of others and of life in general. If she was anxious or worried, it was only because she was irrational and unable to think clearly about whatever was causing her distress.

Contrary to Margaret's assumption, we believe that most mental health professionals and grief therapists do not usually find it boring to listen to people talk about their feelings. What can cause a certain amount of frustration is listening to someone relentlessly judge and criticize their feelings. When the time is right, in can be worth suggesting to the client that the antagonistic relationship they have with their emotions may have originated as an adaptation to an early environment that was unresponsive to their feelings and needs. This dislike of one's emotions can be amplified by the messages that people may be getting from their current relationships, and by the social pressure to "get over" their loss or suppress grief related feelings.

As discussed in Chapter 4, avoidance is by no means an ineffective strategy for managing emotion, but there is some evidence that it can collapse under conditions of extreme stress (Wijngaards-de Meij et al., 2005; Wijngaards-de Meij et al., 2007a). At worst, the collapse of an avoidant strategy can manifest itself in impaired physical or emotional functioning. But impaired functioning is not the only potential downside of trying to overcome or ignore emotions rather than learning to live with them, particularly when the emotion is grief. Given our assumption about the importance of flexible attention in bereavement and the role of emotion in healing, we spend a fair amount of time talking with avoidant clients about how they can develop a kinder and more accepting attitude toward their feelings.

Avoidant clients, as we have suggested, can be expected to resist the idea that they might benefit from adopting this more accepting attitude. Such a suggestion conflicts with what they believe is a constructive approach to limiting the impact of emotions that they should not have.

- It's crazy for me to be angry with him for being dead.
- It's stupid for me to think that I should have been able to save her.
- It's been six months since she died. There must be something wrong with me if I'm still so upset.

These thoughts/statements, which we have all heard (and may sometimes even think), sustain a negative trajectory of self-evaluation, and drain an individual of energy and hope. Rather than helping a bereaved person to put their chin up and carry on, this kind of thinking usually only serves to reinforce the bereaved person's sense of futility and despair.

For people who have become accustomed to managing their emotions in this way, the shift to an emotion friendly attitude does not happen overnight. It helps to explain that like any habit, the habit of attacking one's emotions is mentally sticky, but given time and practice, the mind can learn to let it go. Mindfulness and the cultivation of self-compassion, topics we will return to later, are approaches that can help in developing a more favorable and accepting attitude toward emotions.

Disorganized Attachment: Establish Safety; Restore Mentalizing

Children classified as disorganized by Main and her colleagues in the Strange Situation were those who, upon reunion with their caregivers, exhibited behavior that alternated in a confused and sometimes bizarre manner between approach and avoidance, and included episodic displays of "freezing" or collapse. In contrast to anxious or avoidantly attached infants, these children seemed to have no coherent internal working model directing their behavior and little ability to soothe themselves when stressed. The mothers of these children were described as "frightened and frightening," a reference to the difficulty they appeared to experience in managing their response to a needy infant, and to the behavior exhibited toward the infant.

Allen describes early trauma as a failure of mentalizing: the parent is not attuned to the child's internal state, cannot understand what the child may be feeling, and responds to expressions of need with anger, or not at all (Allen, 2013). The child feels unseen, invisible, and alone. Among the developmental deficits that result from the parent's lack of mentalizing is a lack of mentalizing capacity in the child, a breakdown in their ability to understand what other people are feeling and to recognize internal emotional cues. Therapy, above all, is an opportunity to explore the world of emotion in the company of a reassuring guide. The therapist's attunement to the client provides a model of mentalizing, and the safety of the therapeutic environment provides a space in which the client's own mentalizing capacity can develop.

Mentalizing

The idea that understanding another person's point of view can sometimes, though not always, reduce our antipathy toward that person is not new. We have found, however, that describing something in a new way can help people *think* about it in a new way. In our experience, clients (particularly those who are more easily engaged by talking about ideas than about feelings) are interested in hearing about mentalizing, how it develops, and why it is important. The idea that mentalizing is *a skill that they can learn* as opposed to an innate capacity they are lacking is encouraging to many people. They can appreciate how learning this skill will help reduce conflict in their current relationships, and how it can also help lighten the emotional burden of anger that they have been carrying toward other people, living and dead.

The clinician in the following exchange had previously explained mentalizing as a skill that Audrey (who was introduced in Chapter 4) might find helpful. This suggestion was part of a broader discussion of the toxic effect of Audrey's lingering anger toward her father on her current relationships with family, friends, and co-workers. Audrey regularly got into arguments with people over what she took to be hostile or critical remarks. In this dialogue, the clinician models the skill of mentalizing, while also affirming Audrey's empathic response to her mother.

Audrey

"So I've been living with my mother, and then my friend asked me to stay at her place for a week and take care of her cat, and my mother is asking me all these questions, like how much is she paying me, and do I really think I should be taking this on. She's still treating me like a child! She thinks I can't make my own decisions! And when I was ready to leave to go over there, she comes at me with these files and wants me to look at them, and why is she doing that right then?"

("What do you think?")

"I don't know. . . . But it makes me so angry! Like here it is again, no one in my family knows me, no one knows who I am or what I'm capable of!"

("I know, and that's a bad feeling, an old, bad feeling.")

"It's my whole life, that feeling."

("Yes . . . You felt that way so much growing up, mostly because of your father, all the criticism, the accusations, the yelling. . . . This reminds you of him, when what you're trying to do is to not think about him all the time.")

"When my mother talks to me that way it's like I never left, like he never died."

("I know you and your mother don't always get along, and you figure that anything that comes out of her mouth is a judgment, a criticism. I'm wondering, though, what do you think she was expecting it would be like when you moved in? I get the sense from things you've said that she was looking forward to it, she was kind of happy about it. And now, even though you don't always get along, I think maybe she likes having you around.")

"That could be."

("Uh huh. So, is it possible that she said those things about you going to cat sit because she didn't want you to be away for a week? Maybe she's going to miss you.")

"Well, I don't know about that. But maybe. It has been kind of nice, just not being alone. We usually sit together and eat dinner. And now that you mention it, right after she handed me the files, she went into the kitchen and got her supper and brought it out to where I was standing and looking at the files, and I said, you know, these files are interesting. I want to look at them for a minute. Why don't we sit down and I'll look at them while you eat your dinner."

("That was kind of you.")

As this conversation proceeded, Audrey's body began to relax, and she began to breathe more deeply. This apparent "softening" was noted by the clinician, and it was suggested that Audrey might want to think about how "softening" might become a goal for her, in her relationship with her mother, and also in her relationship with herself.

"I guess I'm carrying a lot of anger around all the time. Maybe if I could be softer with other people, and with myself, I could let some of that go. I did one of those visualizations this week, I listened to one, and it helped me go to sleep. I could do more of that."

("I'm glad that worked for you, and that sounds like a good idea. Just remember that you don't have to push yourself. Think about softening.")

"I want to do that. I want to be softer, especially with myself."

Feeling "softer," as Audrey imagined, is a more comfortable way to feel. When she feels softer, Audrey feels like a more mature and nicer person. She is less self-critical, and less inclined to think that others are judging her. Physiologically, she is more relaxed; her breathing is deeper, and her body is less tense. All of these responses have the effect of giving her back some of the energy that her father's death, and her preoccupation with it, have taken from her.

The cultivation of what is described here as "softness" is one small example of practices that have been used for thousands of years to reduce human suffering and enhance human happiness. In the next section we discuss some of these ideas.

Mindfulness, Forgiveness, Self-Compassion: Developing Attitudes that Promote the Integration of Loss and Other Painful Experiences

Mindfulness

> Inescapable physical or mental discomfort is the "first dart" of existence. As long as you live and love, some of those darts will come your way. First darts are unpleasant ... But then we add our *reactions* to them. These reactions are "second darts" – the ones we throw ourselves. Most of our suffering comes from the second darts.
>
> (Hanson, 2009, p.50)

Everything we have written in this chapter relates in one way or another to the question of how to help people manage the disruption of mental peace that is the wellspring of suffering. The emotional suffering we call grief is caused by the deprivation of someone or something we cherish. Our suffering is amplified by the vivid reminder that the world can be chaotic and unpredictable, and that much of what happens to us is outside of our control. This secondary wave of suffering, the part that comes from struggling against reality because it is not what we want, is part of what Buddhists call the "second dart" (Bodhi, 2005). Mindfulness practices (see Chapter 8, as well), and the cultivation of an attitude that *what is, is*, can help ease people away from their struggle against reality. This is, of course, a struggle they are bound to lose if they are seeing the world other than as it is, and persist in trying to change what they cannot change. In work with bereaved clients, mindfulness can be introduced as a way for them to have an interlude of peace even as they are continuing to grieve, by focusing attention on the present moment. A simple exercise that we have used with clients is to have them focus on something beautiful in the therapist's office and to simply gaze at it for a few minutes, while breathing slowly in and out (R. Shapiro, 2005). This exercise can be particularly helpful for clients who tend to ruminate about their loss (Zech et al., 2010).

As an alternative to the use of structured exercises, Pat Ogden describes a process in which mindfulness is an integral part of the interaction between therapist and client (Ogden, 2009; Ogden & Fisher, 2015). She suggests asking questions that bring the client's attention to what is happening in the moment. "Directed mindfulness," Ogden writes, is an "application of mindfulness that directs the patient's awareness toward particular elements of experience considered important to therapeutic goals" (Ogden, 2009, p.222).

In the following exchange, the clinician used this approach with Audrey, who was beginning to grimace and clench her jaw at the conclusion of her session:

> "I know I have to be *more understanding with my mother.* I know she's *old and sick and I have to try to be nicer to her.*"
> ("Okay, so as you say that, I notice your body is tightening again, and your jaw is clenched, and you have a scary kind of smile on your face. How does it feel?")
> (Laughing) "Not very good. Like I can hardly breathe, I'm so tight."
> ("Okay, great, so how about you take a breath. And now relax your jaw. Maybe let yourself smile, just a little. And try saying it again.")

This time Audrey's voice was quieter, her tone softer, her body more relaxed. It felt better, and since feeling better is what Audrey wants, she is motivated to be mindful of the messages she sends to her body through her expressions, her tone of voice, and her breath.

> ("Remember how we talked about the messages you send to your body, about whether you're safe or not—and how if you breathe, and smile a little, your body gets the message that you're not in danger, and that helps you feel calmer and more in control.")

As a final example, an invitation to soften and allow can also be extended by bringing attention to the connection between the therapist and client. When clients become upset about the past or afraid of the future, the following can be used to ground them in the present moment.

Right now in this moment, I can see that you are suffering, because you miss her so much . . . And *right now in this moment* you're here with me, we're here together. Outside, there are trees, and the breeze is blowing the branches, and right now we're just here, looking at each other, and it feels good, just sitting here together and not having to do anything but be here, now. No place to go, nothing to do. We're just here, together. Right now in this moment we can feel good about just being together.

Forgiveness

People have different views concerning the importance of forgiveness. We have had many conversations with bereaved people about forgiveness, and what we have come to believe is that while it may be a relief to forgive someone, it is not always possible. Making forgiveness a goal can sometimes interfere with whatever degree of emotional healing *is* possible, rather than facilitating healing. If someone was hurt as a child, that person may need to hold onto anger *on behalf of the child* she was, because not to do so is tantamount to leaving the child unprotected. To forgive can feel too much like a denial that the injury occurred, and just as important, that the child survived. People may also be reluctant to forgive because of the connection between "forgiving" and "forgetting." They may feel that if they forgive, the memory of what happened will recede, and with it, a piece of their past that is a key to understanding who they are. People may have similar feelings about injuries suffered in their adult lives. That is, they may feel that they have a right to be angry, and that to let go of that anger would be a betrayal of some part of who they are. The question then becomes one of how they can retain the memory of what was done to them, and yet not remain attached in an unhealthy and self-destructive way to the person who hurt them.

One way to help clients get past feelings about old hurts in situations in which forgiveness is not possible, or not yet possible, is to guide them toward identifying some of the negative thoughts about themselves—feelings of self-blame, failure, vulnerability— that may keep those old wounds from healing (F. Shapiro, 2012). For example, if someone lied to them, they may blame themselves for their gullibility. If someone hurt them physically, they may hate themselves for not having fought back. These kinds of thoughts are another example of the "second dart" of suffering.

Angry thoughts associated with old hurts are "sticky" thoughts, and letting go of them takes practice. Clients can be advised that what they are letting go of is not the memory of what happened, but some of the discomfort generated by the memory. It may be helpful for a person to remember that they do not have to see, or interact with, the person who hurt them. Some people like to imagine having a force field that protects them from the influence of another person. Some people like to imagine that the person who hurt them is very small, or very far away (Hayes et al., 2011). This approach can be suggested with a statement such as: "When someone is taking up too much space in your mind it can be helpful to imagine that they are too little or too distant to be concerned about." Any of these practices for working with painful feelings can be suggested for clients who want to be able to moderate their feelings of anger. What should be emphasized in recommending these practices is that the goal is not to "forgive and forget," but to loosen the hold of negative thoughts and feelings that interfere with peace of mind and detract from the individual's ability to focus on what is important and meaningful to them.

Self-Compassion

Self-compassion is another kind of forgiveness, and another kind of letting go. What we need to let go of is the idea that we can be as perfect in reality as the ideal self of our imagination. To be compassionate is to embrace human imperfection, our own, and that of others. For many people, nothing is more difficult than befriending the self.

Vince

"This week I've been very frustrated with myself, I feel like I'm not able to say what I want to say clearly, I can't articulate . . . and I felt that in a meeting with my supervisor and I got very angry at myself last night, like, what is wrong with me? Why can't I express myself? And it's weird because my supervisor actually commented that I was well prepared for the supervision, that I presented my cases well. But I couldn't take it in, what he said. And actually it made me a little uncomfortable."

("Any idea what that might be about?")

"Well, you know, we've talked about how I'm not comfortable sometimes being *seen*. I'd rather not be seen."

("If someone sees you . . .")

"They're going to see that I'm not a good person. I feel like part of me is not a good person. And that's also why it's hard for me to take it in when someone says something good about me, because I don't feel like I deserve it.

("It's hard to have a relationship with another person if you think they're going to judge you or get angry at you. And that's true for your relationship with yourself, too. That's why it's important to be able to be OK with yourself, to accept your feelings, to accept how you are, even if it's not exactly how you think you should be or want to be. To start from the position that you're OK, that there's nothing wrong with you.")

"Like that book you gave me, that's a good book and I'm going to read it again (Huber, 2001). There's one passage in that book that I like a lot, where she talks about self-improvement. The problem with thinking about how you're going to improve yourself is that it brings you back to the feeling that you're not good enough the way you are. And thinking so much about how you're going to improve just ends up making you feel worse about yourself, so what's the point of even trying to be better if you're such a screwup?"

("So, another way to talk to yourself could be: 'I don't have to perfect. I just have to be trying. I don't have to know everything. I just have to be learning.'")

"That's being compassionate with myself. And if I can be more that way, I can feel better about letting other people be close to me. And also, if I feel better about myself I don't have to be so angry at my mother for what she did. I don't have to forgive her. But at some point, you have to accept your parents for who they are, or were. And just live your life."

Summary

Our goal in this chapter has been to illustrate a number of approaches to helping clients develop Core Capacities for emotional self-regulation. In many ways, these overlap with, or are the same as, the Core Capacities described in Chapter 8 for grief therapists. Implicit in this emphasis on these capacities is the belief that what a grieving person needs from a therapist is not to be healed, fixed, or even "treated," but to be helped in a gentle and attuned manner to be present with the experience of loss, and to access the internal resources needed to integrate that experience. Helping clients learn how to manage emotion is by no means the *only* task of a grief therapist, but it is a *necessary foundation* for treatment with many bereaved individuals. The cases in which such work is particularly important have been identified in previous chapters, and include people with early attachment trauma, and people who have suffered particular kinds of traumatic and kinship loss.

The clinical examples included here, it should be emphasized, illustrate only part of the treatment with the clients presented. As in any grief oriented intervention, treatment in these cases included many other elements, including exploration of the full range of emotions related to the person and the loss, discussion of the bereaved's self-blame in relation to how the person died, and reconstruction of the bereaved's identity. What we have tried to do here is to pick out one aspect of treatment that we find is not always given the attention it warrants in accounts of work with the bereaved—that is, the effect of problems with emotion regulation as a factor in problematic grief. We are suggesting that when a grief therapist helps a client develop resources for affect management, the result is that they are better able to tolerate the other work that is involved in addressing their loss. When people are taught skills such as mentalizing, they often find that they are less reactive to the people in their lives (like Audrey) and more able to understand, if not forgive, the behavior of the deceased (like Vince). The net result is that they are able to recapture emotional energy that has been diverted to an unhealthy continuing bond.

A person who is able to understand their own motivations and behaviors and those of others is less prone to confusion and hopelessness in life, and in grief. Sadness and yearning may be inescapable parts of loss, but terror is not—nor is unrelenting anger or self-blame. A capacity for flexible attention, which is associated with secure attachment, but which we believe can be cultivated in the context of secure relationships at any time in life, enables a person to have a respite from painful emotions, and in those periods of respite, to enjoy what is good in the present moment, to identify what possibilities in life still exist, and to plan for a future guided by an understanding of what they most value. In the following chapter we look at another important part of this process of self-discovery, the reconstruction of meaning, with an eye toward illustrating how this process is managed within the context of attachment-informed grief therapy.

10 Meaning-Making in Adaptation to Loss

> Give sorrow words; the grief that does not speak knits up the o-er wrought heart and bids it break.
>
> William Shakespeare, *Macbeth*

> As a proponent of talk therapy, I employ one all-purpose technique: conversation.
>
> (Allen, 2013, p.211)

Chapter 9 focused on affect regulation as a central task of grief therapy. In this chapter, we focus on meaning-making as the complement of affect regulation, and an equally important element in the alchemy of adjustment to loss. In bereavement, the changes that must be accommodated include not only the loss of the person who has died, but also the loss of parts of ourselves, and the world as we knew it—what has been described as our "assumptive world" (Neimeyer, 2001; Pearlman et al., 2014). Although the term "meaning-making" brings to mind a process that is more cognitive than emotional, as described in Chapter 9, the construction of meaning is a process that is intimately and emotionally affecting for the client (and therapist), one that at times relies on metaphor, poetry, and other non-linear forms of thinking and communication (Neimeyer, 2001, 2006a; Neimeyer & Sands, 2011; Neimeyer et al., 2011). It is a process that is facilitated within the context of a trusting, secure bond, the creation of which, we suggest, is aided by the therapist's awareness of the client's attachment history and attachment related needs.

We begin this chapter by describing the process of meaning-making in bereavement. We then link these concepts to related constructs from attachment theory, specifically reflective functioning and mentalizing. The remainder of the chapter offers case illustrations and discussion of how meaning-making can be facilitated in grief therapy. The emphasis in this part of the chapter will be on the particular difficulty, and importance, of meaning-making in the aftermath of violent, sudden, and otherwise traumatic losses.

The Role of Meaning-Making in Bereavement

A number of theorists have conceptualized grieving as a process of meaning recon-struction (Attig, 2011; Kauffman, 2002; Neimeyer, 2001; Neimeyer & Sands, 2011;

Neimeyer et al., 2002). In particular, Robert Neimeyer and his colleagues have made this the center of their thinking about the mourning process, providing extensive evidence of the crucial role that meaning reconstruction plays in this process (Coleman & Neimeyer, 2010; Currier et al., 2009; Gillies et al., 2013; Lichtenthal et al., 2011; Lichtenthal et al., 2013; Neimeyer, 2015). They have also contributed innovative clinical techniques to help facilitate the practice of meaning reconstruction in grief therapy (Neimeyer, 2012f; Thompson & Neimeyer, 2014). Constructivist approaches to mourning begin with the premise that the self is not a fixed entity, but rather the malleable outcome of an individual's life experiences, along with the individual's attempts to integrate those experiences into their ongoing self-narrative (Neimeyer, 2009).

A group of empirical studies over the last decade have buttressed this perspective by examining the meaning related variables that have significant predictive power in identifying individuals who will have greater difficulty in their bereavement recovery: these are *sense-making, benefit finding*, and *identity reformation* (Gamino & Sewell, 2004; Gillies & Neimeyer, 2006; Holland et al., 2007; Keesee et al., 2008; Lichtenthal et al., 2013). Sense-making is the ability of the mourner to organize the events of the loss into an understandable sequence (emplotment) and to find a purpose or reason for a loss, rather than to experience it as incomprehensible (thematic deconstruction) (Currier & Neimeyer, 2006). Benefit finding is the capacity to find positive outcomes in the loss experience, despite its painful and unwelcome nature. And identity reformation is the ability to restore an old, and/or to rebuild a revised self-narrative in the face of the challenges presented by a death. It is worth noting that both clinical and empirical research suggests that all of these components are likely to be more difficult to achieve in the wake of deaths that are sudden, unexpected, violent, or untimely (i.e., out of the perceived developmental order of life, such as the death of a child) (Currier, Holland et al., 2008; Currier et al., 2009; Keesee et al., 2008; Lichtenthal et al., 2013; Pearlman et al., 2014).

Tom

Tom was a 64 year old man who was raised in a conservative religious tradition, and continued to follow that tradition in his adult life. Tom's lifelong conviction was that God rewards those who are obedient to his will and punishes those who ignore his commandments. The arrival of his first grandchild was experienced by Tom as a gift from God that filled him with love and gratitude. He was thus shocked, outraged, and deeply bereaved when, at 4 months of age, his grandchild developed a severe respiratory infection that eventually led to his death. This loss was shattering for Tom. It resulted in many symptoms of being dysregulated—his sleep was disrupted, he had trouble concentrating at work, and his mood alternated between being depressed and extremely irritable. The death of his grandson also forced Tom into an excruciating reevaluation of his religious faith. How could God take this child from him, when his grandson could not yet have sinned? How could he continue to believe that God was always just and righteous, when something this unjust could happen? Could this somehow be God's punishment of Tom for his own transgressions? These agonizing questions were the result of the shattering of Tom's assumptive world about how the universe operated, and the nature of the God who he believed ran the world. They were both a cause of and a result of the profound feelings of anger, sorrow, and grief that Tom felt about the death of his grandson.

This brief story about Tom conveys the pervasive emotional and spiritual damage that the loss of an important relationship can inflict. In working with someone like Tom, who has suffered both a painful loss, and a profound disruption of their assumptive world, meaning-making becomes a requisite part of restoring self-regulatory capacity. In the absence of a revised understanding of such a sudden and untimely death, it will be difficult for many clients to let go of painful rumination and speculation about the disconnect between what they expected and believed, and what has actually occurred.

Mentalizing, Reflective Functioning, Coherence, and Perspective-Taking

One of our goals in this book is to make linkages between the theoretical domains of attachment theory and thanatology. As discussed in Chapters 2, 4, and 9, mentalizing theory is based on the recognition that as children develop they gradually recognize that other people have minds that are separate from their own, with distinct thoughts and feelings. The development of this capacity to mentalize—to reflect on one's own mind, and the unique minds of other people—is crucial to the development of a separate, differentiated identity in the child (Allen, 2013). As with affect regulation, the capacity for mentalizing develops through interaction with our early attachment figures. The parents of the growing child, through repeated, empathically attuned transactions with their offspring, mirror back the child's internal affective and cognitive states, and thereby help the child to recognize their own experience as separate from their parents' and unique to themselves. High levels of this capacity are related to the development of good mental health and emotional resilience in the face of stressor events in children and adults, and conversely, the failure to adequately develop these resources is related to a vulnerability to the impact of traumatic events and a propensity toward psychiatric disorder (Ensink et al., 2014; Fonagy et al., 2014). It has also been postulated that activation of the attachment system is neurologically the reciprocal of and inhibits the brain functions that allow mentalizing to occur (Jurist & Meehan, 2009). Thus, helping with the restoration of mentalizing in therapy may be a key element of reducing activation of the attachment system and reduction of the trauma response (Allen, 2013).

As used in attachment theory, reflective functioning (RF) is the operationalization of the construct of mentalization on the Adult Attachment Interview (AAI) (Fonagy et al., 1991; Fonagy et al., 1998). The RF Scale of the AAI assesses the ability of the subject to reflect on their own mental states, as well as that of others, and has been found to be associated with a number of other mental health variables. Moreover, a mother's RF score around a trauma history with attachment figures has been found to be predictive of the attachment security of her child and the mother's ability to invest in her child and her marriage (Ensink et al., 2014). Likewise, psychotherapy has been found to improve the RF scores of clients (Levy & Kelly, 2009).

Another concept that resonates in both attachment theory and meaning-making approaches to bereavement is the idea of the *coherence of a narrative* (Hesse, 2008; Main et al., 2008). Recall from Chapter 2 that the AAI is scored with regard to loss and trauma in terms of the linguistic coherence of the narrative given by the respondent to the probes about relationships with early attachment figures. A lack of coherence in a narrative is viewed as a reflection of unresolved trauma and loss in the respondent's attachment history (Steele & Steele, 2008). In a similar fashion, meaning reconstruction theorists have emphasized the disruption of the coherence of the self-narrative and assumptive world as a central impact of traumatic losses, as well as a prime focus of meaning reconstruction oriented interventions (Armour, 2006; Hibberd, 2013; Landsman, 2002; Nadeau, 1998; Neimeyer & Sands, 2011; Owens et al., 2008). This convergence of thinking from these two very different intellectual traditions is impressive, and informs the conceptual foundation of this chapter as well.

Meaning-making can also be understood as critical for the reregulation of an individual's emotional equilibrium that has been disrupted by a loss. Jurist and Meehan have referred to the strengthening of "mentalized affectivity" as a goal in psychotherapy (Jurist & Meehan, 2009). This construct refers to the capacity to reflect, in particular, on the emotions that drive our behavior, as well as on the emotions and behavior of others (see Chapter 9). And as Allen has emphasized, the ability to mentalize about one's experience is a component of all forms of psychotherapy, and is crucial to the healing of trauma, whether early attachment trauma, or current traumatic losses (Allen, 2013). From our attachment-informed point of view, the restoration and strengthening of this capacity for self-reflection meaning-making is thus a central task in the process of affect regulation as described in Chapter 9. This becomes particularly salient in the circumstances of traumatic losses, which are much more likely to challenge a bereaved person's assumptive world and arouse very strong affective reactions (Currier, Holland et al., 2008; Pearlman et al., 2014).

Facilitating Meaning-Making after Loss

How does the process of grief therapy help a client whose assumptive world has been shattered by a death? What elements of the format and structure of therapy allow this vital repair work to proceed? Are there specific techniques that may be used during therapy that can enhance this activity? These questions will be the focus of the remainder of this chapter.

The Arc of Grief Therapy

Holmes (Holmes, 2010, 2013) proposes a simple but useful tripartite model of the "phases" of all psychotherapeutic activity: Attachment, Meaning-Making, and Change. Respectively, these involve the building of a secure and trusting attachment relationship with the client, the exploration of the meaning and origins of the presenting problem(s), and the fostering of new ways of thinking, feeling, and behaving in response to those presenting problems. Much of what we have said in previous chapters about the role of attachment orientation in the response to loss is relevant here. Clients begin grief therapy with expectations about what kind of help they may receive in the context of an intimate relationship with a professional caregiver at a time of great distress in their life. These expectations directly reflect the attachment orientation (and secondary attachment strategies) that the client has developed as a result of their life experiences. (See Chapter 4 for a discussion of some of these factors and related considerations regarding the customization of treatment in grief therapy.)

Almost all people who seek grief therapy have, by definition, had their attachment system (or in the case of bereaved parents, their caregiving system) activated by the loss, i.e., they are experiencing acute separation distress. In addition, as noted previously, the activation of the attachment system creates a state of emotional arousal that can interfere with higher order processing, including the capacity to mentalize. In traumatic bereavement, the mourner may have developed alexithymia—the inability to put feelings into words. The experience of trauma can sometimes be so fragmented and dissociated that it cannot be processed with language (Van der Kolk, 2014). The progression from dysregulation to reregulation is represented here:

Reactive/Dysregulated → Reflective → Reintegrated/Reregulated

Most individuals seeking professional assistance have been thrust into a *Reactive* stance with regard to their loss, in which they are dysregulated on physical, emotional, cognitive, and behavioral levels. This dysregulation may take the form of hyperarousal, usually associated with an anxious attachment style, hypoarousal, generally found in people with an avoidant attachment style, or a complex mixture of the two that is associated with a disorganized attachment style. This last category is usually accompanied by an exacerbation of typically pre-existing psychiatric and personality disorders that have been intensified by the death.

One goal of grief therapy is to support and promote the bereaved person's progress from a dysregulated state to one in which the individual is able to reflect on and make sense of their loss. This process is accomplished in the context of a secure and trusted attachment relationship with the grief therapist, and requires that the therapist help the client with both affect regulation and meaning-making about the death. This process of integration also involves helping the client to change. In the context of bereavement, change means adapting to the inevitable alterations in life functioning, identity, and ways of being in the world that significant losses demand of a mourner. It also means the acquisition of new skills and ways of thinking that can promote psychological coherence, and even growth, in clients (Cozolino, 2010; Holmes, 2010, 2013).

Note that in addition to being dysregulating and inhibiting the capacity for meaning-making, the death of a loved one also usually constrains the reciprocal of the attachment behavioral system, i.e., the exploratory system of the individual. As Sbarra and Hazan outline, a reciprocal relationship of co-regulation exists between people who are bonded to one another (Sbarra & Hazan, 2008), and the loss of this other (whether parent, child, partner, or friend) results in dysregulation. Thus, it is common to begin grief therapy with a newly bereaved client who has been "hibernating" or "hunkering down" in their life. This withdrawal can take many forms. Many severely or traumatically bereaved individuals, for example, will show emotional constriction, numbing, and sometimes full blown dissociative responses (particularly when they are also traumatized by the mode of death), with little capacity to feel their normal range of emotions, or to put their experience into words. Likewise, bereaved persons may present with a cognitive constriction that entails ruminative thinking about a yearned-for reunion with the loved one and a diminished ability to imagine or problem solve about a world without the deceased. In extreme cases, this diminished problem-solving capacity results in suicidality in the mourner, where ending one's life can appear to be the only option for the mourner to obtain relief from their suffering and end the separation from the deceased (Johnson et al., 2008; Latham & Prigerson, 2004; Szanto et al., 2006). Lastly, many mourners will also have withdrawn from their usual social relationships, avoiding engagement in their previous social roles involving work, family, and friendships. *All of these common signs of bereavement can be understood as manifestations of the deactivation of the mourner's exploratory system, and protracted hyperactivation of their attachment system as manifested in the psychological need to "search" for the lost individual.* A central goal of grief therapy, then, can be understood as the restoration of a healthier and more balanced equilibrium between the attachment and exploratory systems in the bereaved individual. This is also another way of stating what we have previously noted in the Dual Process Model of Bereavement (DPM): that the oscillation between grieving (seeking proximity to the deceased) and restoration (exploration of the changed world) needs to be reactivated when it has become frozen.

What Does Meaning-Making Mean for This Client?

The core stance of the therapist in psychotherapy, particularly in exploratory therapies such as client-centered and psychodynamic approaches, has frequently been described as one of curiosity. That is, therapy is an effort by a clinician to engage in a shared exploration of and conversation with the client about the origins of and their efforts to ameliorate the presenting problem(s) (Holmes, 2009, 2010). We believe that this is also the case in grief therapy. In one sense, the presenting problem in grief therapy seems obvious, i.e., the client has lost a loved one to death. Yet in another sense, the problem is not always so clear to either the therapist or the client until this type of mutual investigation has been conducted. Thus, the presentation by clients of seemingly similar presenting problems may reflect quite different core issues. Consider the following three case vignettes:

> *Susan entered therapy after the suicide of her husband. She had endured a verbally and occasionally physically abusive marriage to this man for almost 30 years. Finally, she announced to him that she was done with the marriage, and moved out. After a week or two of pleading with her to return, and her persistence in saying "no," he shot himself. Susan simultaneously felt a sense of liberation, along with a deep feeling of guilt—one that was compounded by the anger of one of her adult children who blamed her mother for her father's death.*
>
> *Carol sought grief therapy for herself after the suicide of her husband, who had been depressed after getting himself and the family into significant financial difficulty. Carol felt confused and worried about how to help their 3 year old son deal with the death of his father. She also was furious with her husband for deserting the family and leaving her with what seemed to be overwhelming challenges as a single parent, including the financial difficulties. She resented her mother-in-law, whom she believed blamed her for her son's death, and who laid strong claim to the raising of her grandson. Carol was unsure about how to deal with her mother-in-law's frequent intrusive visits, which were usually framed as efforts to "help out" after the death.*

Jim was deeply bereaved by the suicide of his wife. She had been depressed on and off throughout much of their five year marriage, and had made a previous suicide attempt. But their relationship had been one of childhood sweethearts who befriended and supported each other in separating from their conflictual and hurtful families of origin. Without the one person whom he had come to trust in life, Jim found himself feeling lost, afraid, and unsure about how he could have a life without his wife. He wondered if suicide was now the only option for him as well, and fantasized that death would reunite him with his missing partner.

All three of these vignettes involve the suicide of a life partner, a similarity in the presenting problem that might lead one to expect a similarity in the main issues faced by the bereaved spouse. Nonetheless, the core issues that will need to be addressed in grief therapy are quite different for each of these individuals. They range from guilt over feeling relief, to anger at being abandoned, to intense fearfulness about being alone. *Put differently, the meaning of these three losses was unique to each of these bereaved individuals.*

Thematic Questions for Meaning-Making

The process of exploring the meaning of a loss for a particular client, and the ways in which the self-narrative of the client has been damaged or frozen by the death, has been termed "mapping the terrain of loss" by the first author (Kosminsky, 2012). It can be described in a series of broad, thematic questions that are revisited over and over again during the course of the therapeutic journey. Some version of these questions will be raised as part of almost every session, including the first session, of grief therapy. In parallel fashion, over the course of treatment, as the individual moves from a reactive, to a reflective, to a reintegrated stance, these questions will occupy a varying portion of each session. Conversation about all of these thematic questions facilitates the psychological integration of the individual's experience into a coherent narrative, and quite likely helps with integration on a neurological level as well, as the client uses higher order cortical functioning to process experiences that may previously have been processed mainly by the affective systems of the brain, (i.e., the limbic system), (Cozolino, 2010; A. N. Schore, 2012).

- *How are you doing now?* Therapy must begin with an assessment of the client's objective functioning, as well as their subjective experience, in the here and now. This includes the client's physical functioning (disruption of bio-rhythms; health issues; concerns about the bodily impact of the loss; loss of energy and stamina; use of prescription and non-prescription drugs, etc.), social functioning (availability and quality of social connection and support; changes emerging in relationships both inside and outside the family; desire to connect with others vs. withdrawal into the self, etc.), and psychological functioning (symptoms of anxiety, post-traumatic stress disorder (PTSD), and anhedonia; rumination about the death and particular aspects of the death; suicidal thoughts and/or behaviors, etc.). As we have previously discussed, getting a sense of the bereaved person's general attachment orientation, and their characteristic ways of dealing with psychological pain, is also crucial.

This process can also include history taking about the client's prior experience with other losses and traumatizing events (which will frequently have been retriggered by the current loss), as well as the nature of their history of other close relationships with attachment figures. Some approaches to grief therapy advocate the initiation of treatment with a careful and systematic assessment of the client before beginning treatment (Pearlman et al., 2014). We understand and appreciate the merits of such a method. However, we also believe that treatment begins with the first moment of therapy, and we do not view assessment as a discrete and separate process that precedes therapy. In our opinion, an excessive focus on assessment with a newly bereaved and traumatized client, to the exclusion of building safety and the feeling of being understood in the therapeutic relationship, runs the risk of empathic failure with clients. With the exception of certain information about the client's safety (e.g., suicidal ideation, use of addictive drugs, etc.), we generally prefer to allow the history gathering process to evolve in parallel with the growth of the therapeutic alliance during the early phases of treatment.

• *Can you tell me about the death/dying?* The "death narrative" or "event story" (Neimeyer, 2012e) almost always plays some role in the mourning process, though it may not be the most prominent or problematic aspect of the loss. In cases of traumatic bereavement, the nature of the death, including the client's actual or imagined mental pictures of the suffering and death of the deceased, should always be a part of the conversation, and quite likely a major focus of treatment. However, the timing of an intensive confrontation with the horrifying or terrifying aspects of the death is a matter of clinical judgment and experience. It should be viewed in the context of the client's preferred way of dealing with very disturbing thoughts and feelings, which is a function of their attachment orientation. Such exposure work usually should not be pursued in depth unless and until a solid therapeutic relationship with the client has been established, and both client and clinician agree that the time for such work is appropriate (Allen, 2013). The clinician needs to be particularly cautious with a client who could be categorized as having a disorganized frame of mind with regard to attachment. A client with this type of defensive style is particularly likely to become emotionally dysregulated when asked to relive traumatic memories, experiencing therapy as a threatening, rather than helpful experience.

• *Can you tell me about the life of the person?* The narrative or "back story" of the life of the deceased and the client's relationship with their loved one is a key part of the mourning process (Neimeyer, 2012e), and is often central to understanding complicated grief. The development of a coherent story of the life of the deceased is considered by Walter to be a principal task of mourning (Walter, 1996). Note that this parallels the emphasis placed on narrative coherence in the assessment of attachment styles in the AAI. From the storytelling done at funerals, to the reminiscing and reflection about the person done years later, reviewing the life of the deceased is a necessary part of the work of internalizing the relationship with the deceased (Pearlman et al., 2014; Rando, 1993). This is particularly true if the deceased served as an attachment figure for the mourner, or, in the case of parents, was the recipient of caregiving from the mourner (see section on fostering and repairing continuing bonds). The narrative of the life of the deceased is also typically intertwined with the larger life narrative of the mourner, including their family of origin experiences with caregivers, and the trajectory of their physical, psychological, and social development.

- *What have you lost?* This question is central to the work of *sense-making* in grief therapy. This core thematic inquiry embodies a host of subordinate questions for exploration over the course of grief therapy. What are the tangible and symbolic aspects of the loss (e.g., the death of a spouse might involve the loss of a companion to have breakfast with each morning, and the dream of a happy retirement in Florida)? How will the mourner's world change without this individual in it? What must be relearned to live in the world going forward (Attig, 2011)? What has been, to use Neimeyer's phrase, the life imprint of this individual on the client's life (Neimeyer, 2012c)? What must the individual let go of, and how will she be able to do that? What does she need to hold onto, and how will she bring that about? How does this loss evoke or connect with other losses in the mourner's life (Kosminsky, 2012)?

- *Who are you now?* This thematic question pertains to the *changes in identity* that can often accompany loss. To an extent that is often under-appreciated, our identity is deeply involved with our relational world. Bereaved parents often question "Am I still a parent?" when a child dies, and bereaved spouses will report that "I still feel married" for long periods of time after the death of their partner. Thus, loss often involves the reworking of identity for the mourner. Consideration of identity related questions such as "How do you think of yourself now?", "How have you changed?", "Has your purpose in life changed?" and "What have you learned from this experience?" allow the client to reflect on their view of themselves, and how the loss has altered their identity and purpose in life.

- *What do you need to hold onto?* This question addresses the meaning of the continuing bond with the deceased. Embedded in this inquiry is the idea that people can and do maintain a connection with their dead (see Chapter 5). There are, of course, as many ways to stay connected to a dead loved one as there are mourners who wish to do so. Some mourners will cultivate memories of the deceased, others will pursue the bond through spiritual means such as prayer or meditation, and still others will maintain connection by honoring the values and the unfinished business of the deceased. In emphasizing the value of continuing bonds, it is important to keep in mind that some people may also benefit from allowing themselves to distance themselves from aspects of the relationship that may have been hurtful, and detract from, rather than enhance, their well-being and healing.

- *Has anything good come out of this experience for you?* This question relates to the *benefit finding* component of meaning-making. This is obviously a theme that should not be the focus of attention early in the grief therapy process, when the individual typically still views the death of a loved one as a uniformly negative experience. It is usually only when people have been able to move toward a more reflective and reintegrated stance that they begin to discern benefits in the bereavement experience. Benefit finding may also take different forms for different people. Some people will find a new resilience in themselves or that their appreciation of life and relationships has been enhanced. Still others may find a new or renewed sense of purpose in their life.

- *What is the future that you want?* Nearly all models of the mourning process suggest that healthy mourning must end in a reinvestment by the griever in their own life trajectory (Attig, 2011; Pearlman et al., 2014; Worden, 2009). These are some of the questions that reflect a shift toward what the DPM calls a Restoration Orientation (see Chapter 4): What will the client's future be without this person? What do they want it to be like, and how can they move on with their life? What holds them back from moving on with their life? What lies unfinished and unaccepted about the loss for the mourner? What new skills must they learn to go forward? And who do they know themselves to be without this person in their life? Who will they be in the future? Who do they want to be?

Grief Therapy Techniques

Therapeutic techniques are usually thought of as deliberate activities, engaged in by the therapist to help the client achieve a certain goal or goals. In the context of grief therapy, these goals can include saying goodbye to a loved one, making peace with someone from whom they were estranged, or reestablishing or repairing the connection with the deceased. Techniques can also be used to help a person come to terms with the reality of a death, find meaning in the loss, or reduce the symptoms associated with the loss.

While we understand the value of techniques in grief therapy, we also believe that, like all tools, the efficacy of therapeutic techniques depends on the skill and clinical wisdom of the person using them. From the moment the client walks in the door, we are employing our best skills at engaging with and helping the bereaved person. At times, these skills will involve the explicit use of specific techniques. *But over the course of therapy, most of what we do is in direct response to what is happening in the moment with the client.* Our interventions emerge from the kind of attunement we have described in the therapeutic relationship in Chapter 8. In this sense, the therapeutic encounter is directed by the client and by what they seem to need from us, here and now. In our opinion, the application of technique, without this kind of therapeutic resonance and wisdom, is at best a hollow exercise, and, at worst, has the potential to be actively harmful to the client.

The Therapeutic Conversation as Technique

While meaning-making after a loss may seem to be primarily an intrapsychic process, in fact, it is also a transpersonal activity that is greatly facilitated (or hindered) by our dialogue with other people (Neimeyer & Jordan, 2001; Neimeyer et al., 2000). The careful exploration of variation after variation of the thematic questions noted previously, with a supportive clinician, is central to our view of grief therapy. Thus, the very process of asking good questions of the client and listening with skilled and empathic attunement to the answers—what Allen calls "plain old therapy" (Allen, 2013)—facilitates the entire progression of meaning-making.

There have been many debates within the psychotherapy literature about the merits or drawbacks of manualized and technique oriented therapies versus a more relational and improvisational style of conducting treatment (Allen, 2013; Neimeyer, 2012d). It is beyond our scope or intention here to take a firm stand on one side of this debate or another. Even carefully designed approaches to grief therapy acknowledge the importance of a foundational therapeutic alliance and flexibility on the part of the therapist as necessary components of a successful treatment protocol (Pearlman et al., 2014). Likewise, even less structured approaches to therapy have implicit agendas and goals on the part of the clinician and the client, and skill sets on the part of the therapist that help clients to achieve these goals (Allen, 2013; Neimeyer, 2012d).

It is probably obvious from our earlier discussions that in our own work, we emphasize customization of the therapy to the needs of the client, both on a moment to moment basis in a given session, and over the whole course of the therapy. We believe that attachment theory offers one highly useful framework for doing that. And we have also argued that the foundation of attachment-informed grief therapy is the therapeutic relationship itself, again based on our understanding of attachment dynamics. *In a sense, the cultivation of a safe haven and secure base through the medium of the therapist–client bond is the core "technique" of attachment-informed grief therapy.* It is the medium of empathically attuned conversation that allows the development of this bond. And above all, it is to this factor that we encourage grief therapists of all therapeutic orientations to pay attention.

As an example of a technique that is embedded in the context of the therapeutic conversation, recall that we earlier discussed the concept of "mentalized affectivity" (Jurist & Meehan, 2009)—the idea that gaining insight into emotions can be tremendously helpful to clients. This is particularly true in therapy with bereaved clients, many of whom must cope with feelings that are unfamiliar and more intense than any they have experienced in the past.

Stewart

Stewart was stunned by the motor vehicle skidding accident that took his wife from him on a snowy winter evening. Her death initially left Stewart disoriented and in shock. The intensity of his conflicting and powerful emotions was frighteningly unfamiliar to him. Moreover, as the initial shock wore off, he found himself starting to feel worse, as waves of grief began to alternate with surges of anxiety, so Stewart sought grief counseling. After some initial assessment, the clinician decided that his client needed help just understanding what was happening to him. Stewart's only other experience of loss had been the death of his best friend in high school in a reckless boating accident. By asking Stewart to reflect on what he was noticing in his emotions and in his bodily reactions, and by offering psychoeducation about normal grief and trauma responses, the therapist was able to help Stewart identify, label, and begin to gain a sense of control over his responses. He also taught Stewart some specific breathing exercises that helped him to stay calmer when the anxiety overtook him.

Later on in the treatment, Stewart and his therapist had an important, breakthrough session. Noticing that Stewart often looked tense and flushed when he spoke about the circumstances of his wife's death, the therapist asked Stewart whether some of what he might be feeling could be anger. Stewart initially rejected this idea, saying that he knew that his wife's death was "not anyone's fault." The therapist persisted, however, noting that grief can sometimes bring up thoughts and emotions that seem irrational, until they are understood from a different perspective. He asked Stewart if he had ever had anything stolen from him, and Stewart recalled having a prized baseball glove stolen as a teenager. When asked how he felt, Stewart immediately said "angry—really furious." The therapist then noted that the Latin root of the word bereavement actually meant to be robbed of something—and a look of recognition immediately came over Stewart's face. He realized that while it may not have been anyone's fault that his wife died, it was still understandable that he might feel quite angry about having his wife "stolen" away from him. Further, when asked if he could recall ever feeling that way before, Stewart quickly remembered that he was also very angry when his best friend had died. He realized that he had felt furious with the friend for the reckless behavior that had needlessly cost him his life. With this discovery of what the loss of his wife, and his friend, had meant to him emotionally, Stewart began to notice a lighter, calmer feeling in his emotions. This also showed itself in his posture and facial expressions—like a heavy burden was beginning to lift from his shoulders.

By carefully using the security of the therapeutic bond, along with some well-timed questions and observations over the course of their conversation, the clinician was able to help his client reflect on (i.e., mentalize about) his own emotional reactions and gain a different perspective on his mourning experience. This process helped Stewart to make sense of his bereavement and to move toward a more reflective and eventually reregulated and integrated stance toward his loss.

Writing Techniques

There are a number of specific writing or journaling techniques that directly ask the client to reflect on the meaning of a loss, or a particular aspect of a loss (Graybeal et al., 2002; Lichtenthal & Neimeyer, 2012; Neimeyer, 2012b; Neimeyer et al., 2008; Pennebaker et al., 2007). Writing seems to offer a number of possible benefits for the bereaved, ranging from emotional catharsis to an enhancement of perspective about the loss. Writing may also enhance the work of transforming the relationship with the deceased into an internalized continuing bond. These writing activities can range from simply asking the client to keep a journal about their thoughts and feelings to more directed writing exercises such as writing letters to the deceased, writing letters from the deceased to oneself, and writing letters from one part of the self to another part (Lichtenthal & Neimeyer, 2012).

Nancy

Nancy felt great guilt over the suicide death of her daughter. She believed that had she been more vigilant about her daughter's eating disorder and depression, she could have prevented the suicide. But another part of Nancy's mind knew that this was an unfair verdict about her functioning as a parent and her vigorous efforts to find help for her daughter. Nancy was asked to write out a dialogue between these two parts of herself, and then to read this out loud. In doing this exercise, Nancy began to see that there was some merit in what both of the voices had to say, and that they both came out of the same deep well of sorrow at the loss of her daughter. Engaging in this activity seemed to help Nancy gain more perspective about her inner conflict, as well as to feel more kindheartedness toward herself.

In a sense, this technique helped Nancy to become more of a wise and compassionate attachment figure for herself. In addition to being emotionally cathartic, such writing facilitated the process of meaning-making about her loss and to gain insight into some of the distress that had been engendered by the loss—the strong feelings of failure and guilt that she felt, which were in conflict with her more reasonable sense that she had done all that she could to help her daughter.

Visualization and Enactment Techniques

This third category of technique involves asking the client to be more mentally and sometimes physically active with their grief by engaging in a specific kind of activity. Visualization, sometimes also called guided imagery (Brown, 1990; Creagh, 2005; Jordan, 2012), asks the client to summon mental images so that they can be confronted and mastered, or so that they can provide a different vision of the dying process or of the deceased loved one now.

One common use for these techniques is in the case of traumatic bereavement. When a death is sudden, unexpected, and/or violent, it is common for mourners to experience not only grief, but also trauma (Litz, 2004; Pearlman et al., 2014). As we discussed in Chapter 6, this can lead to real complications in the mourning process, and require attention by the clinician to both the separation distress *and* the traumatic distress of the client. Intrusive memories, re-experiencing of certain sensory aspects of the death, avoidance of stimuli associated with the death that trigger memories and physiological arousal, and amnesias regarding the event itself are all signs that the individual has likely been traumatized by the death. Since trauma intensifies emotional arousal while at the same time reducing the person's ability to engage in higher order processing, i.e., meaning-making, this aspect of grief may need to be dealt with early in the treatment process. Nonetheless, we caution clinicians about prematurely encouraging clients to confront and relive the horrifying or terrifying aspects of the death scene until a trusting therapeutic alliance has been established. The clinician and client must agree that going further into the death related memories will be helpful (Allen, 2013). Note that this does *not* mean that the client has to be free from any trepidation about confronting the traumatic components of their grief—usually, traumatized clients will be fearful of anything that asks them to "go back there." But the client must feel secure with the therapist, and believe that doing the trauma work will be helpful to their recovery, before it can safely begin. Lastly, it is important to recognize that although eyewitnesses are probably more likely to develop PTSD type symptomatology, a person does *not* need to have been a direct eyewitness to the death of their loved one to be traumatized by it—they simply must have developed a mental picture of the event.

One example of a technique that affords the client the opportunity to confront and become desensitized or habituated to a disturbing traumatic scene is called Eye Movement Desensitization and Reprocessing (EMDR) (Kosminsky & McDevitt, 2012; F. Shapiro, 2012; F. Shapiro & Forrest, 2004). EMDR begins by teaching people self-soothing activities to help down-regulate the mind and body. These also provide a tool that the client can use when away from the therapist to self-regulate their autonomic arousal when triggering events happen. After learning and practicing these self-soothing techniques, the client then deliberately attempts to recall the traumatic material, while simultaneously receiving bilateral stimulation from the therapist. This means rhythmic and alternating sensory stimulation of the left and right hemispheres of the brain. In the original EMDR protocol, this was accomplished by having the client follow the therapist's fingers moving back and forth across their visual field. The range of techniques for producing bilateral stimulation has since been expanded to include devices that provide auditory or tactile bilateral stimulation instead. This process seems to amplify and "reprocess" the traumatic memories, allowing the client full access to the memories while also increasing their experience of catharsis and mastery over the disturbing (and often dissociated) recollections. Finally, time is spent integrating the experience by discussing and cognitively restructuring the self-perceptions that have been distorted by the trauma (e.g., it was my entire fault; I am a failure or bad person because my loved one died, etc.). This last segment of EMDR affords the client an opportunity for reflection and integrative meaning-making about the traumatic death.

Other forms of visualization and enactment techniques that promote meaning-making, particularly after traumatic loss, are worth consideration (see Pearlman et al., 2014, for a rich compendium of such techniques). Almost all of the writing activities discussed previously can equally well be imagined in the mind's eye of the mourner and/or enacted, rather than written out. Thus, empty chair techniques, where the mourner speaks to an empty chair that represents the deceased, or some other person or aspect of their own self, are familiar techniques for many grief therapists (Neimeyer, 2012a). The case vignette of Nancy just presented could have also been done as a guided imagery application, or an empty chair enactment in which Nancy had a conversation with her daughter, rather than parts of herself. This would have been a slightly different focus for the guilt that Nancy felt (dialogue with her daughter, rather than a part of herself), but utilizing similar methods. The common element of all of these modalities is symbolic conversation with someone: the dead, a part of the self, or another living person. When done in the context of addressing the deceased, they can help greatly with repairing and consolidating an internal sense of connection to the deceased, i.e., a continuing bond.

Also along the lines of visualization techniques that may help with both trauma reduction and development of continuing bonds with the deceased, the second author of this book has been developing a technique tentatively called "In Heaven." In this technique, the client is led through a guided imagery in which they imagine their loved one as being in heaven, or a paradise-like place. The client is told that they do not need to believe in an afterlife to do the activity, since its goal is not to affirm a belief in heaven, but rather to help the mourner feel better and to cultivate an alternative image of the deceased that differs from the actual death scene. The mourner is invited to view their loved one as being in heaven or paradise as they imagine it to be, completely healed, both physically and psychologically. The technique can also be extended to include an imagined dialogue with the deceased about unfinished business and a transformation of the continuing bond with the loved one (Jordan, 2012).

Sarah

Sarah was devastated by the suicide of her son. She found his lifeless body hanging in the basement of their house. She was haunted by the remembered shock and horror of first discovering his body, and the attempt to cut him down, summon help, and futilely try to revive him. Three years later, the imagery still intruded on her consciousness, unbidden and alien. In an effort to provide some relief from the PTSD symptoms, two procedures were used by the therapist. The first was to do a single session of EMDR, which was quite powerful in producing a strong abreaction of tears and physical shaking as Sarah deliberately summoned the mental pictures that she had of that morning. However, she also reported a feeling of relief at the end of the procedure. Three sessions later, the "In Heaven" technique was also employed to strengthen the trauma reduction work. Sarah wrestled a great deal with the question of whether she should allow herself to believe in a "heaven" or an afterlife for her son. She agreed to try the technique, however, when it was explained that the goal of the activity was to help calm her agitated physical and emotional state with regard to the details of her son's death, and to give her an alternative picture that she could "switch to" when the bad memories returned.

After doing a relaxation exercise, Sarah was guided to imagine her son as now being in heaven, whatever that meant to her. She proceeded to picture her son sitting in a dining room with her deceased parents, having a meal together and enjoying the classical music that was a favorite of them all. Sarah reported that this experience helped her to "maybe allow myself to believe that he is still alive, and that he is not lonely. I have worried that he somehow was lonely." The therapist affirmed that mothers are "wired" to continue to worry about the well-being of their children, even after they have died. Sarah has subsequently used this experience to slowly cultivate an internal connection with her son, finding herself comfortably talking with him, both in times of stress, and just as a way of feeling closer to him when she is missing him more intensely.

The combination of the EMDR and In Heaven exercises allowed Sarah to develop more soothing images of her son, while leaving her mostly free of intrusions of the distressing memories. She also reported feeling that her son is "with me now, everywhere," even though she remains unsure whether she actually believes in an afterlife. This shift from the traumatic details of the death has freed Sarah to reflect more on the experience of facing a life without her son and her beliefs about an afterlife, and even to reevaluate other aspects of her life unrelated to the death. She has adapted to significant changes in her marriage and work relationships, and has begun exploring new interests and ways of relating to people in her life. The evolution of the focus in her grief reflects Sarah's movement from a reactive to a more reflective and ultimately reintegrated stance, as well as an ongoing shift from a Loss Orientation to a Restoration Orientation and a reawakening of her exploratory behavioral system.

Retelling Techniques

A fourth category of related techniques involves retelling and reworking the death narrative in a way that can also help with trauma reduction and the building of a continuing bond with the deceased. The principle of asking the mourner to retell the story of the death is appearing in more guidelines for working with complicated bereavement (Neimeyer, 2012e; Shear et al., 2005; Shear et al., 2011). Rynearson, in particular, has also done pioneering work in which bereaved clients not only retell the story of the death, but also then rework the narrative in a fashion that makes it more bearable and less traumatizing (Rynearson, 2001, 2006; Rynearson & Salloum, 2011). The

In Heaven technique just described is an example of a visualization procedure that allows the mourner to develop a more tolerable image of the loved one, rather than a deeply disturbing memory of the deceased at the moment of their death. In all of these retelling and trauma reduction techniques, after first learning self-soothing procedures, the mourner re-exposes themselves to the death scene and narrative, and/or changes that narrative in a fashion that "pacifies" the imagery, calms the physiological hyperarousal associated with their trauma response, and allows the emergence of a transformed continuing bond with the deceased and a revised perspective about the loss.

Harriet

Harriet's situation was described previously in Chapter 6, on trauma and bereavement. Recall that Harriet was deeply bereaved after the death of her young adult son in a hiking accident. Her son had been hiking with friends in the desert canyons of the American southwest, and became separated from his companions at one point in the trip. It appeared that he fell and broke a leg, and was, for a time at least, knocked unconscious by the fall. The body was not discovered until almost 72 hours later, where it was found at the bottom of a small ravine. Since the death, Harriet had been haunted by the fear that her son had died a protracted and painful death—alone, in great physical and psychological pain, and calling out for his mother. After exploring this image of the death, the therapist introduced the idea of being able to rework the imagery in a way that might make it more bearable. Harriet agreed to try this. After a brief relaxation procedure, Harriet was asked to imagine her son dying in the worst possible way—a painful, slow, frightening, and terribly isolated passage. This was, understandably, upsetting for her to do. Then, however, she was invited to reimagine the death under circumstances that would have been more tolerable for her. Harriet chose to imagine her son having access to pain medication, warm blankets, and water to drink. She also imagined her and her son's spirits meeting before he died. This allowed them to do a tender leave-taking before he fell unconscious again and died peacefully and quickly. Harriet reported significant comfort from this "version" of her son's passing, and has subsequently been able to "switch the channel" to this scene when troubling thoughts of his passing return, which they have tended to do with much less frequency since completing this exercise.

In imagining the details of an alternative ending to her son's life, Harriet was able to gain some sense of control over and some relief from the intrusive images of his death. What she envisioned was a scenario in which she was able to continue to be her son's caregiver and to express her love for him one last time. It also allowed her to move beyond the specific details of his dying, and on to greater reflection about his life and the love that they felt in their relationship with one another.

Meaning-Making as a Lifelong Process

Grieving is a developmental process in the sense that the significance of a loss unfolds over time. In the beginning, it is impossible to know everything that a loss will mean. Rather, the implications of living one's life without an important person reveal themselves to us only as we go through our life, continuing on without that individual. The process of making sense of a loss, and reflecting on the emerging meanings of living a life without the loved one, is actually a lifelong process that is at the very heart of meaning reconstruction in mourning.

Jack

The father of the second author (JRJ) died in 1974, while the author was a graduate student in psychology. His father had been a public school teacher and then an administrator for all of his professional life. At the time of his father's death, the author was not married, nor was he a parent. But in 1998, as the author was about to attend the graduation of his firstborn child from high school and then send her off to college, he found himself experiencing a wave of missing his father—at this point in his life, a relatively rare occurrence. Reflecting on the significance of this unanticipated upsurge of grief, it occurred to him that "My dad should be here for this—he would have loved this." He realized that this was an aspect of living his life without his father that he could not possibly have understood at the time of his father's death. He recognized that the meaning of his loss was still unfolding, even 25 years after his father's death.

Summary

The reconstruction of meaning-making is an inescapable part of rebuilding a life in the aftermath of significant loss. It is an emotional, as well as an intellectual, process, and one that contributes to the bereaved individual's ability to gain a sense of mastery with respect to what can be unbearably painful thoughts and feelings. It is particularly relevant in the case of traumatic death, where the circumstances of the death increase the loss of coherence in the individual's assumptive world.

This process of discovering, and/or creating, layers of meaning in the loss is one that is tremendously facilitated by the support of an attachment figure—an attuned and skilled "expert companion" who serves as a confidant, a guide, and an audience to bear witness to the journey of healing (Tedeschi & Calhoun, 2003). It is the complement of emotional reregulation in bereavement recovery, and is a central focus of the process of attachment-informed grief therapy. As we help individuals to reflect on and integrate their loss, we help them to put the loss in the wider perspective of their larger life narrative. The death of their loved one becomes an important part of their life story, but only a part—not the entire story that it may seemed to have been when the loved one first died. This enhanced capacity to make sense of the loss is central to the transition from the reactive stance toward the loss that comes at the beginning of the mourning process, to the reflective, and then eventually to the reregulated and reintegrated place where we hope our clients will be able to arrive with the help of grief therapy.

11 Conclusions

Our goal in writing this book has been to bring together attachment theory, relevant neuroscience research, and contemporary models of bereavement in order to better understand how people respond to loss, how they recover, and how we can promote healing when the process has been disrupted. In this chapter, we offer some final commentary on the value of a cross-disciplinary approach to understanding grief and providing grief therapy, and we consider avenues for future work in the realms of theory, research, and practice relating to grief therapy.

From birth, human beings seek to establish and maintain connection with other human beings. In infancy, certain primary attachment figures become the main objects of the instinct and desire to connect, the first in most cases being the infant's mother. As people grow, they begin to transfer their attention from this first love object to friends, then to romantic partners, and, if they have them, to children of their own. The same instinct that drives human beings to attach also activates an emotional and behavioral response to separation and loss. When a loved one dies, the sadness, yearning, and need to search are likely to be intense, and for a time at least, inescapable. Grief is the inevitable result of the loss of someone we love and to whom we are attached. The ways in which people grieve are as varied as the ways in which they love.

An Attachment Perspective on Adaptation to Loss

Attachment theorists, starting with Bowlby, Ainsworth, and Main, proposed that attachment behaviors are rooted in infancy and early childhood, and reflect the child's best efforts to ensure that the attachment figure will remain available to them. As children grow into adulthood, they continue to engage with people largely on the basis of assumptions and models developed in relation to early attachment figures. These ways of relating carry over into the way people react when someone to whom they are deeply attached or bonded is taken from them by death. In other words, an individual's attachment style will be a major determinant of how they grieve, and that style helps to account for variations in grief response. Those who experienced secure attachment in their early relationships, while no less saddened by loss, are likely to have an easier time adjusting to it. Time, in fact, usually will help to heal their psychological wounds. Those with an insecure attachment orientation may well have a more problematic adjustment to loss, and those problems may intensify over time. The types of issues they are likely to face will differ depending on the type of insecure attachment at the root of their suffering—avoidant, anxious, or disorganized.

In the mid-1990s, Peter Fonagy and his colleagues set in motion a second wave of investigation into the role of early attachment experience on mental health and relationships. These researchers suggested that while many people with early attachment trauma had difficulty regulating their emotions, managing their relationships, and coping with stress, a significant number of them seemed to be functioning well as individuals, partners, and parents. In accounting for this apparent triumph over early experience, Fonagy proposed that these healthier individuals had been able to reflect on their experiences, integrating them rather than dissociating from them. In other words, they had found a way to make sense of the behavior of their caregivers (without necessarily having to forgive it), while remembering and feeling compassion for their younger selves. From this place of understanding, they were more able to decide for themselves how to behave, how to think, and how to feel, and to convey this acceptance and love to their children. What set these individuals apart, Fonagy and his team proposed, was a capacity for mentalization—the ability to recognize the mental states of themselves and others, and to differentiate between the two. This core capacity also plays a critical role in people's ability to make meaning of the stressful life events they have experienced, including the death of important people in their life.

Attachment Style and Models of Grief

Another major advance in the evolution of an attachment-informed approach to grief and grief therapy was the introduction of the Dual Process Model of Bereavement (DPM) by Stroebe and her colleagues. The DPM postulates that healing from loss involves oscillation between thoughts and feelings related to the loss (a Loss Orientation) and the psychological and practical issues surrounding a future life without the deceased (a Restoration Orientation). Research has identified at least some of the factors influencing oscillation between loss and restoration, and has demonstrated the significant role of attachment orientation in this process. Those whose attachment insecurity is considered anxious may become entrapped in a Loss Orientation. Avoidant individuals, in contrast, have a tendency to focus on restoration, without revisiting or seeking to reflect on the meaning of their loss. Individuals whose orientation to attachment includes elements of disorganization, particularly those who experienced early abuse or neglect, may present with a range of symptoms related to deficits in both emotion regulation and mentalization, deficits that become most evident when a person must shoulder the emotional load of bereavement. Regardless of type, attachment insecurity often results in grief related complications that suggest the need for therapeutic intervention, though the techniques and approaches indicated will vary depending on the tolerances and attachment orientation of the mourner.

Neuroscience and Attachment

In recent years, a series of developments in the field of neuroscience, in particular interpersonal neuroscience, has established models of brain development that support much of what has been observed about attachment by researchers in the fields of developmental and social psychology. Findings from these disciplines help us to understand the developmental origins of our capacities to make sense of our own thoughts and behavior, manage emotions, form relationships, and cope with traumatic life events, including the death of a loved one.

Research findings on brain development in the first two years of life are yet another lens through which to view the connection between attachment security and adaptation to loss. Secure attachment supports the development of emotion regulatory capacities in the brain. The stress of insecure attachment, and the more profound impact of ongoing neglect or abuse, adversely affect the development of these capacities. Indeed, attachment figures throughout our lifespan serve a homeostatic and regulatory function for our psychological and physiological stability. Conversely, the loss of people to whom we are attached, and the absence of such figures in times of great stress in our life, can be understood as a profoundly dysregulating experience. In this sense, grief therapy, as we have described it, is a process that helps people to integrate the loss and reregulate themselves on a physiological, emotional, and cognitive level.

The Therapist as a Transitional Attachment Figure

Bowlby was the first to draw attention to the parallels between the activation of the attachment system in childhood and the grief response of adults in the wake of the death of a loved one. This book is part of what has become a decades-long project to explore the implications of Bowlby's profound insight. We have looked at the concept of grief as the loss of an attachment figure (or its reciprocal, the loss of a care-seeking figure, in the case of the death of a dependent child). In many cases, the death of a loved one takes away the very person to whom the mourner would have turned for help in surviving and making sense of a traumatic experience. It is a logical extension of Bowlby's premise that in order for a loss to be integrated and for reregulation of the attachment system to occur, bereavement requires the support of other individuals who serve as attachment figures, be they family member, friend, or a good therapist. This is why we have emphasized the crucial role of the therapist as a transitional attachment figure who is empathically attuned to the psychological needs, and limitations, of the mourner. The therapist must carefully titrate the bereaved person's exposure to painful reality, and gradually help to increase the mourner's capacity to tolerate painful emotions, thoughts, and memories—a process guided by the therapist in light of the client's attachment orientation and evolving capacities for emotion regulation. In this way, it becomes possible for a person to learn and grow through the experience of therapy. In the course of this kind of therapeutic work, the client's comfort zone gradually expands, and with it the potential for further psychological growth. The therapeutic bond thus becomes another way of activating the "broaden and build" cycle of growth that occurs when a person is embedded in a protective and nurturing attachment relationship.

As we have seen, an attachment-informed approach to any type of psychotherapy should be viewed as a complement to, rather than a replacement for, existing therapeutic models and approaches. Slade has made what seems to us a highly practical suggestion:

> What I think would be most helpful is to find a way to expose clinicians to the measures and methods of attachment research so that they can more fully appreciate

its core elements. The aim of such an effort would not be to teach clinicians to administer research measures per se, but to use methods to inform clinical listening and formulation.

(Slade, 2008, p.778)

In our case, we have suggested that understanding attachment, affect regulation, and related concepts can help grief therapists in formulating treatment goals and strategies, and building a strong, trusting bond with clients. Also, familiarity with research instruments like the Adult Attachment Interview (AAI) can provide new avenues of exploration with clients, and an incentive for clinicians to mine the rich stores of data that are contained not just in the story a client tells, but also in how they tell it.

Promoting Integration in Grief Therapy

Losing a loved one is painful, and confronting that pain is something that people do not readily or easily accept. But to avoid the pain, we have to avoid the truth. The result can be a kind of emotional purgatory, in which the mourner is suspended between the poles of pain and healing, between grief and reengagement in life. As clinicians, we do not like causing people pain—quite the opposite; we want to help alleviate their suffering. But to help them move toward integration, it is often necessary to bring people face to face with what is painful and frightening, and to say things that direct their attention to what they want to avoid. *We can say these things, and people can hear them, but only if they feel safe with us.* This is what Porges (2011) tells us is the beauty of the evolved nervous system, i.e., we can decide that someone is safe, and we can decide to listen to them and be comforted by them. The feeling of safety is what makes relationships possible, and that includes the therapeutic relationship. And because fear is so often a part of grief, clinicians who work with the bereaved need to be particularly attuned to verbal and nonverbal expressions of anxiety and trepidation, as well as anger, helplessness, and despair. Attention to the body may help both the therapist and the client to better understand their emotional state, and therefore to facilitate movement toward integration and wholeness of experience.

The need for therapists to pay attention to these cues is an underdeveloped idea in the literature on grief therapy. It is part of what we have described as a new paradigm of psychotherapy that calls upon clinicians to use their whole brains to engage the whole brains of clients, paying attention to and stimulating the emotional brain as well as the thinking brain. Siegel has said that it is emotional experience that changes us. Emotions engage mind and body, and trigger a higher level of awareness that enables us to see something new, or to see something old in a new way. While we might understand what Siegel is describing as moments of insight, we believe that this is more than insight, because it is more than an intellectual awareness. It is a change in the whole of our person, and it is what we experience when the physical synapses in our brain have changed to adapt to a new reality. Something inside has shifted and we are different than we were before.

Audrey
"I know that I've changed. My father abused me, and I've abused myself. This is an eternal game I've been playing with myself. I could cry. But I'm not going to."

I've reached a new plateau, and I don't want to go back. I'm not going to fight with anybody anymore about who I am as a human being. Last week, you said something to me that was hard for me to hear, and I said: I'm tired of this. And I know you thought I was tired of therapy, tired of hearing things I don't want to hear. But I trust you, and I know why you said what you did. And during the week what I've realized I was saying was: *I'm tired of myself.* I've been fighting for people to see who I really am. *Don't you see who I really am?* I'm not doing that anymore. I can live with myself now. What I want now is to fill my soul. I want to fill my soul with love and light and happiness, with graciousness and kindness."

The Future of Attachment-Informed Grief Therapy—What Comes Next?

Attachment theory, and its neurobiological foundation, has opened new vistas for us in our work with bereaved clients. Still, there are many areas of attachment-informed theory, research, and practice that remain in their infancy, with new discoveries that await us in the next decade and beyond. In this next section, we would like to sketch out the terrain of this new frontier, and suggest some initial lines of exploration. This includes topics that we believe require more study and research, as well as linkages between intellectual domains that, like a healthy brain, require better integration of content and structure to enhance the depth of our understanding in thanatology.

We defined grief therapy (Chapter 7) as: "*a concentrated form of empathically attuned and skillfully applied social support, in which the therapist helps the bereaved person reregulate themselves after a significant loss by serving as a transitional attachment figure.*" In this book, we have mostly equated grief therapy with one-on-one, individual psychotherapy. While in one sense this is appropriate, since the great majority of grief counseling is probably delivered in the modality of one therapist working individually with one client, we nonetheless recognize that there are not only other forms of therapy, but also other forms of social support that may serve the same functions as a grief therapist. For example, family therapy may be an effective way of helping bereaved family members support one another. Group interventions, whether professionally led or peer facilitated, may also provide an environment in which members (with the help of the facilitator) serve individually and collectively as transitional attachment figures for one another. And of course, friendships have always played a vital role in helping bereaved people reregulate themselves after the death of a loved one.

Our point is that the healing role of empathically resonant human relationships in the process of mourning is not limited to the domain of professional grief therapists. This is why we fundamentally view grief therapy as a form of social support, albeit a focused and specialized one that people often cannot find in their immediate social network. The work of understanding how all social relationships (not just professional ones) can help or hinder the process of recovery after loss, and how an attachment perspective can help inform this understanding, remains largely unfinished and in need of further study.

It also is clear that considerable work remains to be done to apply findings in the rapidly advancing field of neuroscience to the field of thanatology. Unlike traumatology, where there has been a concerted effort to tie advancements in the understanding of the neurobiological mechanisms of the trauma/fear response to clinical practice, surprisingly little research has focused on the neurobiology of the separation/grief response (see O'Connor, 2005). Moreover, to the best of our knowledge, no studies have been done to explore the specific neurological impact of social connection on facilitating recovery from bereavement. These are, indeed, exciting times in terms of new discoveries in the brain sciences, and we strongly encourage researchers in the field to include in their theoretical models and empirical studies the universal experience of loss and separation, as well as the neurophysiological role of attachment relationships (or lack thereof) in recovery from loss.

Related to this, we believe that more needs to be understood about the relationship between the trauma response, the bereavement response, and attachment. While there are likely differences in the neurobiology of trauma (which is fundamentally a fear/anxiety response) and bereavement (which is basically a response to separation), it is clear that they also have much in common. Both trauma and bereavement represent a psychological, and sometimes a physical, threat to human beings. They produce considerable distress with many common symptoms, particularly emotional distress, and both can lead to a crisis in meaning-making for the affected individual. Moreover, both trauma and bereavement have similar risk and protective factors, not least of which is a history (or an absence) of secure attachments, and the importance for recovery of supportive attachment figures. And, as we have noted in Chapter 6, when the death of a loved one evokes both the trauma and the bereavement response, the trajectory of mourning is likely to be made more complicated. We hope to see in the future much more cross-fertilization between the fields of traumatology and thanatology, since so many of the phenomena that are the focus of both disciplines are found together in traumatic bereavement situations.

Further, there remains much to be learned about the role of attachment style in the response to loss, and about our understanding of how a client's attachment style can be used to customize therapy. We have described ways in which we try to customize therapy in our own work, and in support of this approach, we have drawn on the extensive body of literature in attachment theory about attachment styles. Still, a great deal of refinement and testing lies ahead, and we urge others to join in this task.

Much of the field of psychotherapy has been dominated by the medical model of treatment that characterizes modern psychiatry. This approach emphasizes the crucial role of differential diagnosis, followed by the application of evidence based treatments for a particular diagnosis. For example, the entire movement to define a new diagnostic entity related to complicated grief has emerged mostly out of this medicalized tradition of psychosocial intervention. As we stated earlier, we do not seek to replace this model, and certainly not to reject the benefits of controlled research into interventions that may help with complicated grief.

But we also believe that this paradigm has built-in biases and limitations, particularly when applied to manualized treatments for grief. Such treatments usually emphasize fidelity to a given protocol of applied techniques. This type of consistency is important in a research setting in order to provide the reliable, measurable results that make an evidence based therapy possible. Unfortunately, manualized treatments typically pay little attention to the nature of the relationship between therapist and client. The result is a treatment that, in principle, could be delivered by anyone as long as they are trained in the proper protocol. Thus, one approach to advancing the field of grief therapy is to continue to develop better manualized treatments, and there is a role for that. However, our approach is more focused on continuing to develop better therapists, by enabling them to respond empathically and effectively to the attachment oriented needs of each particular client—regardless of the therapist's therapeutic orientation or allegiance.

Lastly, we would like to make some observations about psychological development after loss, sometimes referred to as Post-Traumatic Growth. Like most theories or models in psychology, attachment theory can perhaps legitimately be challenged for focusing too much on pathology—on what can go wrong in early developmental processes that lead to insecure attachment styles, and on the damage that can be done by the loss of important attachment or caregiving relationships in childhood or adult life. Our book also likely has a bias toward that "dark side" of attachment insecurity, as well. At the same time, we encourage the field of thanatology to spend more of its energy in understanding how losses are the source of psychological and spiritual growth in life.

Mikulincer and Shaver, at the conclusion of their encyclopedic book on adult attachment, write eloquently about the tremendous benefits of attachment security (Mikulincer & Shaver, 2007). These benefits include the clear and empirically established outcomes of attachment security such as better mental health, greater self-esteem, more security enhancing marital and parenting skills, and a general resilience to adverse life events such as the death of a loved one. But the authors also speculate about the possible benefits of attachment security in facing the existential issues that are inherent in being human—the encounter with impermanence, suffering, and our own mortality. The inner sense that one's life has purpose and meaning, and that one is valued and loved by others, helps us face these difficult, but intrinsic aspects of human life. We welcome clinical and research investigation into how growth enhancing attachment relationships (and we include here the client/therapist relationship) can help grieving people not only find their way back to physical and psychological balance after a loss, but also to grow into a new and deeper experience of well-being.

Closing Thoughts

> All day I think about it, then at night I say it.
> Where did I come from, and what am I supposed to be doing? I have no idea.
> My soul is from elsewhere, I'm sure of that. And I intend to end up there.
>
> (Rumi, 1995)

Anyone who, day after day, year after year, has conversations with people about death, is bound to be acutely aware of his or her own mortality. As grief therapists, we know better than most how fleeting and unpredictable life is, and how little control we ultimately have over what happens to us and to the people we love. Is there anyone among us who has not wondered, at the end of a long day filled with dark stories, where we ourselves have come from, and where we are going? Like each of our clients, we are all on an uncertain journey toward an unknown destination.

In the face of this existential truth about life, we have come to share with many of our colleagues a deep sense that human connection can bring relief from suffering. This is the belief that brought us to this work, and that continues to influence the way we relate to our clients and do our work as grief therapists. We believe in the healing power of relationships, including the therapeutic relationship. We understand the fundamental sameness of human response to loss, and that insight supports our ability to hopefully respond to the suffering of a bereaved person with openness, compassion, and empathy. Only someone who is grieving knows the weight of their grief. But we do not need to know how heavy another person's burden is to help them bear it.

To work with people who are grieving is to know both the fragility of human life and the strength of the human spirit. We hope that what we have shared here of our own ideas and work will be of use to all those who read this book, in their role as grief therapists and healers.

Phyllis S. Kosminsky and John R. Jordan

References

Ainsworth, M. D. S. (1967). *Infancy in Uganda: Infant care and the growth of love*. Baltimore, MD: Johns Hopkins University Press.

Ainsworth, M. D. S., Blehar, M. C., Waters, E., & Wall, S. (1978). *Patterns of attachment: A psychological study of the strange situation*. Hillsdale, NJ: Lawrence Erlbaum Associates.

Albom, M. (2002). *Tuesdays with Morrie: An old man, a young man, and life's greatest lesson*. New York, NY: Broadway Books.

Allen, J. G. (2001). *Traumatic relationships and serious mental disorders*. New York, NY: John Wiley & Sons Ltd.

Allen, J. G. (2003). Mentalizing. *Bulletin of the Menninger Clinic, 67*(2), 91–112.

Allen, J. G. (2013). *Restoring mentalizing in attachment relationships: Treating trauma with plain old therapy*. Arlington, VA: American Psychiatric Publishing.

Allen, J. G., Fonagy, P., & Bateman, A. (2008). *Mentalizing in clinical practice*. Arlington, VA: American Psychiatric Publishing.

Allumbaugh, D. L., & Hoyt, W. T. (1999). Effectiveness of grief therapy: A meta-analysis. *Journal of Counseling Psychology, 46*(3), 370.

Ammaniti, M., & Gallese, V. (2014). *The birth of intersubjectivity: Psychodynamics, neurobiology, and the self*. New York, NY: W. W. Norton & Company.

Archer, J. (1999). *The nature of grief: The evolution and psychology of reactions to loss*. Florence, KY: Routledge/Taylor & Francis Group.

Armour, M. (2006). Meaning-making for survivors of violent death. In E. K. Rynearson (Ed.), *Violent death: Resilience and intervention beyond the crisis* (pp. 101–121). New York, NY: Routledge.

Attig, T. (2011). *How we grieve: Relearning the world* (revised ed.). New York, NY: Oxford University Press.

Azevedo, F., Carvalho, L., Grinberg, L., Farfel, J., Ferretti, R., Leite, R. et al. (2009). Equal numbers of neuronal and nonneuronal cells make the human brain an isometrically scaled-up primate brain. *Journal of Comparative Neurology, 513*(5), 532–541.

Bakermans-Kranenburg, M. J., & van IJzendoorn, M. H. (2009). The first 10,000 Adult Attachment Interviews: Distributions of adult attachment representations in clinical and non-clinical groups. *Attachment & Human Development, 11*(3), 223–263.

Balk, D. E. (2013). Life span issues and loss, grief, and mourning: Adulthood. In D. K. Meagher & D. E. Balk (Eds.), *Handbook of thanatology: The essential body of knowledge for the study of death, dying, and bereavement* (pp. 157–169). New York, NY: Routledge.

Bartholomew, K., & Horowitz, L. M. (1991). Attachment styles among young adults: A test of a four-category model. *Journal of Personality and Social Psychology, 61*(2), 226–244.

Baumann, M., Frank, D. L., Liebenstein, M., Kiffer, J., Pozuelo, L., Cho, L. et al. (2011). Biofeedback in coronary artery disease, type 2 diabetes, and multiple sclerosis. *Cleveland Clinic Journal of Medicine, 78*(Suppl. 1), 220–220.

Berant, E., Mikulincer, M., & Shaver, P. R. (2008). Mothers' attachment style, their mental health, and their children's emotional vulnerabilities: A 7-year study of children with congenital heart disease. *Journal of Personality, 76*(1), 31–66.

Berking, M., Poppe, C., Wupperman, P., Luhmann, M., Ebert, D., & Seifritz, E. (2012). Emotion-regulation skills and psychopathology: Is the ability to modify one's negative emotions the ultimate pathway by which all other skills affect symptoms of mental disorders? *Behavior Research and Therapy, 43*(2012), 931–937.

Bodhi, B. (Ed.). (2005). In the Buddha's words. *An anthology of discourses from the Pāli Canon.* Somerville, MA: Wisdom Publications.

Boelen, P. A., & Klugkist, I. (2011). Cognitive behavioral variables mediate the associations of neuroticism and attachment insecurity with Prolonged Grief Disorder severity. *Anxiety Stress Coping, 24*(3), 291–307.

Boelen, P. A., Stroebe, M. S., Schut, H. A. W., & Zijerveld, A. M. (2006). Continuing bonds and grief: A prospective analysis. *Death Studies, 30*(8), 767–776.

Bonanno, G. A. (2009). *The other side of sadness: What the new science of bereavement tells us about life after loss.* New York, NY: Basic Books.

Bonanno, G. A., & Boerner, K. (2008). Trajectories of grieving. In C. B. Wortman, M. S. Stroebe, R. O. Hansson, H. Schut, & W. Stroebe (Eds.), *Handbook of bereavement research and practice: Advances in theory and intervention* (pp. 287–307). Washington, DC: American Psychological Association.

Bonanno, G. A., Wortman, C. B., & Nesse, R. M. (2004). Prospective patterns of resilience and maladjustment during widowhood. *Psychology and Aging, 19*(2), 260–271.

Bornstein, M. H. (2014). Human infancy . . . and the rest of the lifespan. *Annual Review of Psychology, 65*, 121–158.

Bowlby, J. (1944). Forty-four juvenile thieves: Their characters and home-life. *International Journal of Psychoanalysis, 25*(19–52), 107–127.

Bowlby, J. (1951). *Maternal care and mental health* (Vol. 2). Geneva, Switzerland: World Health Organization.

Bowlby, J. (1960). Grief and mourning in infancy and early childhood. *Psychoanalytic Study of the Child, 15*(1), 9–52.

Bowlby, J. (1977). The making and breaking of affectional bonds. I. Aetiology and psychopathology in the light of attachment theory. An expanded version of the Fiftieth Maudsley Lecture, delivered before the Royal College of Psychiatrists, 19 November 1976. *British Journal of Psychiatry, 130*(5), 420–431.

Bowlby, J. (1980). *Attachment and loss: Loss, sadness and depression.* New York, NY: Basic Books.

Bowlby, J. (1982). *Attachment and loss: Attachment* (Vol. 1). New York, NY: Basic Books.

Bowlby, J. (2005). *A secure base: Clinical applications of attachment theory.* New York, NY: Taylor & Francis.

Bowlby, J. (2008). *A secure base: Parent–child attachment and healthy human development.* New York, NY: Basic Books.

Bowlby, J., & Parkes, C. M. (1970). Separation and loss within the family. In E. J. Anthony (Ed.), *The child and his family,* (pp. 197–216). New York, NY: John Wiley & Sons Ltd.

Braun, K. (2011). The prefrontal–limbic system: Development, neuroanatomy, function, and implications for socioemotional development. *Clinics in Perinatology, 38*(4), 685–702.

Briere, J., Godbout, N., & Runtz, M. (2012). The Psychological Maltreatment Review (PMR): Initial reliability and association with insecure attachment in adults. *Journal of Aggression, Maltreatment & Trauma, 21*(3), 300–320.

Brown, J. C. (1990). Loss and grief: An overview and guided imagery intervention model. *Journal of Mental Health Counseling, 12*(4), 434–445.

Buckle, J. L., & Fleming, S. J. (2011). Parenting challenges after the death of a child. In R. A. Neimeyer, D. L. Harris, H. R. Winokuer, & G. F. Thornton (Eds.), *Grief and bereavement in contemporary society: Bridging research and practice* (pp. 93–105). New York, NY: Routledge/ Taylor & Francis Group.

Bureau, J. F., Martin, J., & Lyons-Ruth, K. (2010). Attachment dysregulation as hidden trauma in infancy: Early stress, maternal buffering and psychiatric morbidity in young adulthood. In R. A. Lanius, E. Vermetten, & C. Pain (Eds.), *The impact of early life trauma on health and disease: The hidden epidemic* (pp. 48–56). New York, NY: Cambridge University Press.

Burke, L. A., & Neimeyer, R. A. (2013). Prospective risk factors for complicated grief: A review of the empirical literature. In M. S. Stroebe, H. Schut, & J. van den Bout (Eds.), *Complicated grief: Scientific foundations for health care professionals* (pp. 145–161). New York, NY: Routledge/ Taylor & Francis Group.

Burke, L. A., Neimeyer, R. A., & McDevitt-Murphy, M. E. (2010). African American homicide bereavement: Aspects of social support that predict complicated grief, PTSD, and depression. *Omega: Journal of Death and Dying, 61*(1), 1–24.

Byrne, G. J. A., & Raphael, B. (1997). The psychological symptoms of conjugal bereavement in elderly men over the first 13 months. *International Journal of Geriatric Psychiatry, 12*(2), 241–251.

Cacciatore, J., & Flint, M. (2011). ATTEND: Toward a mindfulness-based bereavement care model. *Death Studies, 36*(1), 61–82.

Carr, D., & Jeffreys, J. S. (2011). Spousal bereavement in later life. In R. A. Neimeyer, D. L. Harris, H. R. Winokuer, & G. F. Thornton (Eds.), *Grief and bereavement in contemporary society: Bridging research and practice* (pp. 81–92). New York, NY: Routledge/Taylor & Francis Group.

Carr, D., Nesse, R. M., & Wortman, C. B. (Eds.). (2006). *Spousal bereavement in late life.* New York, NY: Springer Publishing Company.

Cassidy, J., & Kobak, R. R. (1987). Avoidance and its relation to other defensive processes. In J. Belsky & T. M. Nezworski (Eds.), *Clinical implications of attachment theory.* New York, NY: Routledge.

Cassidy, J., & Shaver, P. R. (Eds.). (2008). *Handbook of attachment: Theory, research, and clinical applications* (2nd ed.). New York, NY: Guilford Press.

Cheng, H.-L., McDermott, R. C., & Lopez, F. G. (2015). Mental health, self stigma, and help-seeking intentions among emerging adults: An attachment perspective. *The Counseling Psychologist, 43*(3), 463–487.

Chisholm, J. S., Quinlivan, J. A., Petersen, R. W., & Coall, D. A. (2005). Early stress predicts age at menarche and first birth, adult attachment, and expected lifespan. *Human Nature, 16*(3), 233–265.

Coan, J. A. (2008). Toward a neuroscience of attachment. In J. Cassidy & P. R. Shaver (Eds.), *Handbook of attachment: Theory, research, and clinical applications*, (pp. 241–265). New York, NY: Guilford Press.

Coleman, R. A., & Neimeyer, R. A. (2010). Measuring meaning: Searching for and making sense of spousal loss in late-life. *Death Studies, 34*(9), 804–834.

Collins, N. L., & Feeney, B. C. (2004). Working models of attachment shape perceptions of social support: Evidence from experimental and observational studies. *Journal of Personality and Social Psychology, 87*(3), 363.

Costello, P. C. (2013). *Attachment-based psychotherapy: Helping patients develop adaptive capacities.* Washington, DC: American Psychological Association.

Cozolino, L. J. (2010). *The neuroscience of psychotherapy: Healing the social brain* (2nd ed.). New York, NY: W. W. Norton & Company.

Cozolino, L. J. (2014). *The neuroscience of human relationships: Attachment and the developing social brain* (2nd ed.). New York, NY: W. W. Norton & Company.

Cozolino, L. J., & Santos, E. N. (2014). Why we need therapy—and why it works: A neuroscientific perspective. *Smith College Studies in Social Work, 84*(2–3), 155–157.

Creagh, B. A. (2005). Transformative mourning: The Bonny Method of Guided Imagery and Music for widowed persons. Unpublished doctoral dissertation. Cincinnati, OH: Union Institute and University.

Currier, J. M., Holland, J. M., Coleman, R. A., & Neimeyer, R. A. (2008). Bereavement following violent death: An assault on life and meaning. In R. G. Stevenson & G. R. Cox (Eds.), *Perspectives on violence and violent death* (pp. 177–202). Amityville, NY: Baywood Publishing Company.

Currier, J. M., Holland, J. M., & Neimeyer, R. A. (2006). Sense-making, grief, and the experience of violent loss: Toward a mediational model. *Death Studies, 30*(5), 403–428.

Currier, J. M., Holland, J. M., & Neimeyer, R. A. (2009). Assumptive worldviews and problematic reactions to bereavement. *Journal of Loss and Trauma, 14*(3), 181–195.

Currier, J. M., & Neimeyer, R. A. (2006). Fragmented stories: The narrative integration of violent loss. In E. K. Rynearson (Ed.), *Violent death: Resilience and intervention beyond the crisis* (pp. 85–100). New York, NY: Routledge/Taylor & Francis Group.

Currier, J. M., Neimeyer, R. A., & Berman, J. S. (2008). The effectiveness of psychotherapeutic interventions for bereaved persons: A comprehensive quantitative review. *Psychological Bulletin, 134*(5), 648–661.

Danquah, A. N., & Berry, K. (Eds.). (2013). *Attachment theory in adult mental health: A guide to clinical practice.* New York, NY: Routledge/Taylor & Francis Group.

Davis, D., Shaver, P. R., & Vernon, M. L. (2003). Physical, emotional, and behavioral reactions to breaking up: The roles of gender, age, emotional involvement, and attachment style. *Personality and Social Psychology Bulletin, 29*(7), 871–884.

Decety, J. (2012). *Empathy: From bench to bedside.* Cambridge, MA: MIT Press.

Decety, J., & Ickes, W. (Eds.). (2009). *The social neuroscience of empathy.* Cambridge, MA: MIT Press.

De Leo, D., Cimitan, A., Dyregrov, K., Grad, O., & Andriessen, K. (2014). *Bereavement after traumatic death: Helping the survivors.* Boston, MA: Hogrefe Publishing.

Delespaux, E., Ryckebosch-Dayez, A.-S., Heeren, A., & Zech, E. (2013). Attachment and severity of grief: The mediating role of negative appraisal and inflexible coping. *Omega: Journal of Death and Dying, 67*(3), 269–289.

Denckla, C. A., Mancini, A. D., Bornstein, R. F., & Bonanno, G. A. (2011). Adaptive and mal-adaptive dependency in bereavement: Distinguishing prolonged and resolved grief trajectories. *Personality and Individual Differences, 51*(8), 1012–1017.

Deno, M., Miyashita, M., Fujisawa, D., Nakajima, S., & Ito, M. (2013). The influence of alexithymia on psychological distress with regard to the seriousness of complicated grief and the time since bereavement in the Japanese general population. *Journal of Affective Disorders, 149*(1), 202–208.

DeOliveira, C. A., Moran, G., & Pederson, D. R. (2005). Understanding the link between maternal adult attachment classifications and thoughts and feelings about emotions. *Attachment & Human Development, 7*(2), 153–170.

Didion, J. (2007). *The year of magical thinking.* New York, NY: Random House LLC.

Dozier, M., Stovall-McClough, C. K., & Albus, K. E. (2008). Attachment and psychopathology in adulthood. In J. Cassidy & P. R. Shaver (Eds.), *Handbook of attachment: Theory, research, and applications* (2nd ed.), (pp. 718–744). New York, NY: Guilford Press.

Duncan, B. L., Miller, S. D., Wampold, B. E., & Hubble, M. A. (2010). *The heart & soul of change: Delivering what works in therapy* (2nd ed.). Washington, DC: American Psychological Association.

Dykas, M. J., & Cassidy, J. (2011). Attachment and the processing of social information across the life span: Theory and evidence. *Psychological Bulletin, 137*(1), 19.

Dyregrov, K. (2005). Experiences of social networks supporting traumatically bereaved. *Omega: Journal of Death and Dying, 52*(4), 339–358.

Dyregrov, K., & Dyregrov, A. (2008). *Effective grief and bereavement support: The role of family, friends, colleagues, schools, and support professionals.* Philadelphia, PA: Jessica Kingsley Publishers.

Elliott, R., Bohart, A. C., Watson, J. C., & Greenberg, L. S. (2011). Empathy. In J. C. Norcross (Ed.), *Psychotherapy relationships that work: Evidence-based responsiveness* (2nd ed.), (pp. 132–152). New York, NY: Oxford University Press.

Ensink, K., Berthelot, N., Bernazzani, O., Normandin, L., & Fonagy, P. (2014). Another step closer to measuring the Ghosts in the Nursery: Preliminary validation of the Trauma Reflective Functioning Scale. *Frontiers in Psychology, 5*(5).

Epstein, R., Kalus, C., & Berger, M. (2006). The continuing bond of the bereaved towards the deceased and adjustment to loss. *Mortality, 11*(3), 253–269.

Erickson, M. H., & Rossi, E. L. (1979). *Hypnotherapy, an exploratory casebook.* New York, NY: Irvington Publishers.

Feigelman, W., Jordan, J. R., McIntosh, J. L., & Feigelman, B. (2012). *Devastating losses: How parents cope with the death of a child to suicide or drugs.* New York, NY: Springer Publishing Company.

Field, N. P. (2006). Unresolved grief and continuing bonds: An attachment perspective. *Death Studies, 30*(8), 739–756.

Field, N. P. (2008). Whether to relinquish or maintain a bond with the deceased. In M. S. Stroebe, R. O. Hansson, H. Schut, & W. Stroebe (Eds.), *Handbook of bereavement research and practice: Advances in theory and intervention* (pp. 113–132). Washington, DC: American Psychological Association.

Field, N. P., & Filanosky, C. (2010). Continuing bonds, risk factors for complicated grief, and adjustment to bereavement. *Death Studies, 34*(1), 1–29.

Field, N. P., & Friedrichs, M. (2004). Continuing bonds in coping with the death of a husband. *Death Studies, 28*(7), 597–620.

Field, N. P., Gal-Oz, E., & Bonanno, G. A. (2003). Continuing bonds and adjustment at 5 years after the death of a spouse. *Journal of Consulting and Clinical Psychology, 71*(1), 110–117.

Field, N. P., Gao, B., & Paderna, L. (2005). Continuing bonds in bereavement: An attachment theory based perspective. *Death Studies, 29*(4), 277–299.

Field, N. P., Nichols, C., Holen, A., & Horowitz, M. J. (1999). The relation of continuing attachment to adjustment in conjugal bereavement. *Journal of Consulting and Clinical Psychology, 67*(2), 212–218.

Field, N. P., Packman, W., Ronen, R., Pries, A., Davies, B., & Kramer, R. (2013). Type of continuing bonds expression and its comforting versus distressing nature: Implications for adjustment among bereaved mothers. *Death Studies, 37*(10), 889–912.

Field, N. P., & Wogrin, C. (2011). The changing bond in therapy for unresolved loss: An attachment theory perspective. In R. A. Neimeyer, D. L. Harris, H. R. Winokuer, & G. F. Thornton (Eds.), *Grief and bereavement in contemporary society: Bridging research and practice* (pp. 37–46). New York, NY: Routledge/Taylor & Francis Group.

Foa, E. B., Keane, T. M., Friedman, M. J., & Cohen, J. A. (2009). *Effective treatments for PTSD: Practice guidelines from the International Society for Traumatic Stress Studies* (2nd ed.). New York, NY: Guilford Press.

Fonagy, P., Bateman, A. W., Lorenzini, N., & Campbell, C. (2014). Development, attachment, and childhood experiences. In J. M. Oldham, A. E. Skodol, & D. S. Bender (Eds.), *The American Psychiatric Publishing textbook of personality disorders* (pp. 55–77). Arlington, VA: American Psychiatric Publishing.

Fonagy, P., Steele, M., Steele, H., Leigh, T., Kennedy, R., Mattoon, G., & Target, M. (2000). Attachment, the reflective self, and borderline states: The predictive specificity of the Adult Attachment Interview and pathological emotional development. In S. Goldberg, R. Muir, & J. Kerr (Eds.), *Attachment theory: Social, developmental, and clinical perspectives*, (pp. 233–278). Hillsdale, NJ: The Analytic Press.

Fonagy, P., Steele, M., Steele, H., Moran, G. S., & Higgitt, A. C. (1991). The capacity for understanding mental states: The reflective self in parent and child and its significance for security of attachment. *Infant Mental Health Journal, 12*(3), 201–218.

Fonagy, P., Target, M., Steele, H., & Steele, M. (1998). *Reflective-functioning manual, version 5.0, for application to adult attachment interviews.* London, UK: University College London.

Fraley, C. R., & Bonanno, G. A. (2004). Attachment and loss: A test of three competing models on the association between attachment-related avoidance and adaptation to bereavement. *Personality and Social Psychology Bulletin, 30*(7), 878–890.

Fraley, C. R., Fazzari, D. A., Bonanno, G. A., & Dekel, S. (2006). Attachment and psychological adaptation in high exposure survivors of the September 11th attack on the World Trade Center. *Personality and Social Psychology Bulletin, 32*(4), 538–551.

Fraley, C. R., Roisman, G. I., & Haltigan, J. D. (2013). The legacy of early experiences in development: Formalizing alternative models of how early experiences are carried forward over time. *Developmental Psychology, 49*(1), 109–126.

Gallo, L. C., Smith, T. W., & Ruiz, J. M. (2003). An interpersonal analysis of adult attachment style: Circumplex descriptions, recalled developmental experiences, self-representations, and interpersonal functioning in adulthood. *Journal of Personality, 71*(2), 141–182.

Gamino, L. A., & Sewell, K. W. (2004). Meaning constructs as predictors of bereavement adjustment: A report from the Scott & White Grief Study. *Death Studies, 28*(5), 397–421.

Gaudet, C. (2010). Pregnancy after perinatal loss: Association of grief, anxiety and attachment. *Journal of Reproductive and Infant Psychology, 28*(3), 240–251.

George, C., Kaplan, N., & Main, M. (1985). Attachment interview for adults. Unpublished manuscript. Berkeley: University of California.

George, C., & Solomon, J. (2008). The caregiving system: A behavioral systems approach to parenting. In J. Cassidy & P. R. Shaver (Eds.), *Handbook of attachment: Theory, research, and clinical applications*, (pp. 833–856). New York, NY: Guilford Press.

Germer, C. K., Siegel, R. D., & Fulton, P. R. (2013). *Mindfulness and psychotherapy.* New York, NY: Guilford Press.

Gillath, O., Bunge, S. A., Shaver, P. R., Wendelken, C., & Mikulincer, M. (2005). Attachment-style differences in the ability to suppress negative thoughts: Exploring the neural correlates. *Neuroimage, 28*(4), 835–847.

Gillies, J., & Neimeyer, R. A. (2006). Loss, grief, and the search for significance: Toward a model of meaning reconstruction in bereavement. *Journal of Constructivist Psychology, 19*(1), 31–65.

Gillies, J., Neimeyer, R. A., & Milman, E. (2013). The Meaning of Loss Codebook: Construction of a system for analyzing meanings made in bereavement. *Death Studies, 38*(4), 207–216.

Gilligan, S. G. (2012). *Generative trance: The experience of creative flow.* New York, NY: Crown House Publishing.

Gilligan, S. G. (2013). *Therapeutic trances: The co-operation principle in Ericksonian hypnotherapy.* Bethel, CT: Crown House Publishing.

Gilligan, S. G., & Price, R. (1993). *Therapeutic conversations*. New York, NY: W. W. Norton & Company.

Goldin, P., Ziv, M., Jazaieri, H., & Gross, J. J. (2012). Randomized controlled trial of mindfulness-based stress reduction versus aerobic exercise: Effects on the self-referential brain network in social anxiety disorder. *Frontiers in Human Neuroscience, 6*(295).

Graybeal, A., Sexton, J. D., & Pennebaker, J. W. (2002). The role of story-making in disclosure writing: The psychometrics of narrative. *Psychology & Health, 17*(5), 571–581.

Gross, J. J. (2014). *Handbook of emotion regulation* (2nd ed.). New York, NY: Guilford Press.

Gross, J. J., & John, O. P. (2003). Individual differences in two emotion regulation processes: Implications for affect, relationships, and well-being. *Journal of Personality and Social Psychology, 85*(2), 348.

Gross, J. J., & Muñoz, R. F. (1995). Emotion regulation and mental health. *Clinical Psychology: Science and Practice, 2*(2), 151–164.

Grossmann, K., Grossmann, K. E., & Kindler, H. (2005). Early care and the roots of attachment and partnership representations: The Bielefeld and Regensburd Longitudinal Studies. In K. Grossman, K. Grossman, & E. Waters (Eds.), *Attachment from infancy to adulthood: The major longitudinal studies* (pp. 98–136). New York, NY: Guilford Press.

Hall, C. (2014). Bereavement theory: Recent developments in our understanding of grief and bereavement. *Bereavement Care, 33*(1), 7–12.

Hankin, B. L., Kassel, J. D., & Abela, J. R. Z. (2005). Adult attachment dimensions and specificity of emotional distress symptoms: Prospective investigations of cognitive risk and interpersonal stress generation as mediating mechanisms. *Personality and Social Psychology Bulletin, 31*(1), 136–151.

Hanson, R. (2009). *Buddha's brain: The practical neuroscience of happiness, love, and wisdom*. Oakland, CA: New Harbinger Publications.

Hanson, R. (2013). *Hardwiring happiness*. New York, NY: Random House, Incorporated.

Harlow, H. F., & Zimmermann, R. R. (1959). Affectional responses in the infant monkey. *Science, 130*, 421–432.

Hart, H., & Rubia, K. (2012). Neuroimaging of child abuse: A critical review. *Frontiers in Human Neuroscience, 6*(52).

Hayes, S. C., Strosahl, K. D., & Wilson, K. G. (2011). *Acceptance and commitment therapy: The process and practice of mindful change*. New York, NY: Guilford Press.

Hazan, C., & Shaver, P. R. (1987). Romantic love conceptualized as an attachment process. *Journal of Personality and Social Psychology, 52*(3), 511–524.

Herman, J. L. (1992). *Trauma and recovery*. New York, NY: Basic Books.

Herman, J. L. (1995). Complex PTSD: A syndrome in survivors of prolonged and repeated trauma. In G. S. Everly, Jr. & J. M. Lating (Eds.), *Psychotraumatology: Key papers and core concepts in post-traumatic stress* (pp. 87–100). New York, NY: Plenum Press.

Hesse, E. (2008). The Adult Attachment Interview: Protocol, method of analysis, and empirical studies. In J. Cassidy & P. R. Shaver (Eds.), *Handbook of attachment: Theory, research, and clinical applications* (2nd ed.) (pp. 552–598). New York, NY: Guilford Press.

Hesse, E., & Main, M. (2000). Disorganized infant, child, and adult attachment: Collapse in behavioral and attentional strategies. *Journal of the American Psychoanalytic Association, 48*(4), 1097–1127.

Hibberd, R. (2013). Meaning reconstruction in bereavement: Sense and significance. *Death Studies, 37*(7), 670–692.

Ho, S. M. Y., Chan, I. S. F., Ma, E. P. W., & Field, N. P. (2012). Continuing bonds, attachment style, and adjustment in the conjugal bereavement among Hong Kong Chinese. *Death Studies, 37*(3), 248–268.

Hodges, S. D., & Wegner, D. M. (1997). Automatic and controlled empathy. In W. Ickes (Ed.), *Empathic accuracy* (pp. 311–339). New York, NY: Guilford Press.

Hofer, M. A. (1996). On the nature and consequences of early loss. *Psychosomatic Medicine, 58*(6), 570–581.

Holland, J. M., Neimeyer, R. A., Currier, J. M., & Berman, J. S. (2007). The efficacy of personal construct therapy: A comprehensive review. *Journal of Clinical Psychology, 63*(1), 93–107.

Holmes, J. (2001). *The search for the secure base: Attachment theory and psychotherapy.* New York, NY: Routledge/Taylor & Francis Group.

Holmes, J. (2009). From attachment research to clinical practice: Getting it together. In J. H. Obegi & E. Berant (Eds.), *Attachment theory and research in clinical work with adults* (pp. 490–514). New York, NY: Guilford Press.

Holmes, J. (2010). *Exploring in security: Towards an attachment-informed psychoanalytic psychotherapy.* New York, NY: Routledge/Taylor & Francis Group.

Holmes, J. (2013). Attachment theory in therapeutic practice. In A. N. Danquah & K. Berry (Eds.), *Attachment theory in adult mental health* (pp. 16–32). New York, NY: Routledge/ Taylor & Francis Group.

Huber, C. (2001). *There is nothing wrong with you: Going beyond self-hate. A compassionate process for learning to accept yourself exactly as you are.* Murphys, CA: Keep It Simple Books.

Innamorati, M., Pompili, M., Amore, M., Vittorio, C. D., Serafini, G., Tatarelli, R., & Lester, D. (2011). Suicide prevention in late life: Is there sound evidence for practice? *Evidence-based practice in suicidology: A source book* (pp. 211–232). Cambridge, MA: Hogrefe Publishing.

Jerga, A. M., Shaver, P. R., & Wilkinson, R. B. (2011). Attachment insecurities and identification of at-risk individuals following the death of a loved one. *Journal of Social and Personal Relationships, 28*(7), 891–914.

Johnson, J. G., Zhang, B., & Prigerson, H. G. (2008). Investigation of a developmental model of risk for depression and suicidality following spousal bereavement. *Suicide and Life-Threatening Behavior, 38*(1), 1–12.

Jones, J. D., Cassidy, J., & Shaver, P. R. (2015). Parents' self-reported attachment styles: A review of links with parenting behaviors, emotions, and cognitions. *Personality and Social Psychology Review, 19*(1), 44–76.

Jordan, J. R. (2000). Introduction: Research that matters: Bridging the gap between research and practice in thanatology. *Death Studies, 24*(6), 457–467.

Jordan, J. R. (2012). Guided imaginal conversations with the deceased. In R. A. Neimeyer (Ed.), *Techniques of grief therapy: Creative practices for counseling the bereaved* (pp. 262–265). New York, NY: Routledge/Taylor & Francis Group.

Jordan, J. R., Kraus, D. R., & Ware, E. S. (1993). Observations on loss and family development. *Family Process, 32*(4), 425–440.

Jordan, J. R., & McIntosh, J. L. (2011). *Grief after suicide: Understanding the consequences and caring for the survivors.* New York, NY: Routledge/Taylor & Francis Group.

Jordan, J. R., & Neimeyer, R. A. (2003). Does grief counseling work? *Death Studies, 27*(9), 765–786.

Jordan, J. R., & Ware, E. S. (1997). Feeling like a motherless child: A support group model for adults grieving the death of a parent. *Omega: Journal of Death and Dying, 35*(4), 361–376.

Juffer, F., Bakermans-Kranenburg, M. J., & van IJzendoorn, M. H. (2012). *Promoting positive parenting: An attachment-based intervention.* New York, NY: Routledge/Taylor & Francis Group.

Jurist, E. L., & Meehan, K. B. (2009). Attachment, mentalization, and reflective functioning. In J. H. Obegi & E. Berant (Eds.), *Attachment theory and research in clinical work with adults* (pp. 71–93). New York, NY: Guilford Press.

Kagan, R. (2004). *Rebuilding attachments with traumatized children: Healing from losses, violence, abuse, and neglect.* Binghamton, NY: Haworth Maltreatment and Trauma Press/The Haworth Press.

Kandel, E. R. (1998). A new intellectual framework for psychiatry. *American Journal of Psychiatry, 155*(4), 457–469.

Kandel, E. R., Markram, H., Matthews, P. M., Yuste, R., & Koch, C. (2013). Neuroscience thinks big (and collaboratively). *National Reviews Neuroscience, 14*(9), 659–664.

Kaniasty, K. (2012). Predicting social psychological well-being following trauma: The role of postdisaster social support. *Psychological Trauma: Theory, Research, Practice, and Policy, 4*(1), 22.

Kato, P. M., & Mann, T. (1999). A synthesis of psychological interventions for the bereaved. *Clinical Psychology Review, 19*(3), 275–296.

Katz, M., Liu, C., Schaer, M., Parker, K. J., Ottet, M.-C., Epps, A. et al. (2009). Prefrontal plasticity and stress inoculation-induced resilience. *Developmental Neuroscience, 31*(4), 293.

Kauffman, J. (2002). *Loss of the assumptive world: A theory of traumatic loss.* New York, NY: Brunner-Routledge.

Kauffman, J. (2012). The empathic spirit in grief therapy. In R. A. Neimeyer (Ed.), *Techniques of grief therapy: Creative practices for counseling the bereaved* (pp. 12–15). New York, NY: Routledge/Taylor & Francis Group.

Keesee, N. J., Currier, J. M., & Neimeyer, R. A. (2008). Predictors of grief following the death of one's child: The contribution of finding meaning. *Journal of Clinical Psychology, 64*(10), 1145–1163.

Keysers, C. (2011). *The empathic brain: How the discovery of mirror neurons changes our understanding of human nature* (Kindle edition).

Keysers, C., & Perrett, D. I. (2004). Demystifying social cognition: A Hebbian perspective. *Trends in Cognitive Sciences, 8*(11), 501–507.

Kiecolt-Glaser, J. K., McGuire, L., Robles, T. F., & Glaser, R. (2002). Emotions, morbidity, and mortality: New perspectives from psychoneuroimmunology. *Annual Review of Psychology, 53*(1), 83–107.

Kim, B.-R., Stifter, C. A., Philbrook, L. E., & Teti, D. M. (2014). Infant emotion regulation: Relations to bedtime emotional availability, attachment security, and temperament. *Infant Behavior and Development, 37*(4), 480–490.

Klass, D. (1997). The deceased child in the psychic and social worlds of bereaved parents during the resolution of grief. *Death Studies, 21*(2), 147–175.

Klass, D. (1999). *The spiritual lives of bereaved parents.* Philadelphia, PA: Brunner/Mazel.

Klass, D. (2006). Continuing conversation about continuing bonds. *Death Studies, 30*(9), 843–858.

Klass, D., Silverman, P. R., & Nickman, S. L. (1996). *Continuing bonds: New understandings of grief.* Philadelphia, PA: Taylor & Francis.

Kooiman, C. G., van Rees Vellinga, S., Spinhoven, P., Draijer, N., Trijsburg, R. W., & Rooijmans, H. G. M. (2004). Childhood adversities as risk factors for alexithymia and other aspects of affect dysregulation in adulthood. *Psychotherapy and Psychosomatics, 73*(2), 107–116.

Kosminsky, P. S. (2007). *Getting back to life when grief won't heal.* New York, NY: McGraw Hill.

Kosminsky, P. S. (2012). Mapping the terrain of loss. In R. A. Neimeyer (Ed.), *Techniques in grief therapy: Creative practices for counseling the bereaved* (pp. 30–32). New York, NY: Routledge/Taylor & Francis Group.

Kosminsky, P. S., & McDevitt, R. (2012). Eye Movement Desensitization and Reprocessing (EMDR). In R. A. Neimeyer (Ed.), *Techniques of grief therapy: Creative practices for counseling the bereaved* (pp. 95–98). New York, NY: Routledge/Taylor & Francis Group.

Kübler-Ross, E. (1997). *On death and dying.* New York, NY: Simon and Schuster.

Landsman, I. (2002). Crises of meaning in trauma and loss. In J. Kauffman (Ed.), *Loss of the assumptive world: A theory of traumatic loss* (pp. 13–30). New York, NY: Brunner-Routledge.

Lanius, R. A., Vermetten, E., & Pain, C. (2010). *The impact of early life trauma on health and disease: The hidden epidemic*. New York, NY: Cambridge University Press.

Latham, A. E., & Prigerson, H. G. (2004). Suicidality and bereavement: Complicated grief as psychiatric disorder presenting greatest risk for suicidality. *Suicide and Life-Threatening Behavior, 34*(4), 350–362.

Leahy, R. L., Tirch, D. D., & Napolitano, L. A. (2012). *Emotion regulation in psychotherapy: A practitioner's guide*. New York, NY: Guilford Press.

Levy, K. N., Ellison, W. D., Scott, L. N., & Bernecker, S. L. (2011). Attachment style. In J. C. Norcross (Ed.), *Psychotherapy relationships that work* (2nd ed.) (pp. 279–300). New York, NY: Oxford University Press.

Levy, K. N., & Kelly, K. M. (2009). Using interviews to assess adult attachment. In J. H. Obegi & E. Berant (Eds.), *Attachment theory and research in clinical work with adults* (pp. 121–152). New York, NY: Guilford Press.

Lichtenthal, W. G., Burke, L. A., & Neimeyer, R. A. (2011). Religious coping and meaning-making following the loss of a loved one. *Counselling and Spirituality/Counseling et spiritualité, 30*(2), 113–135.

Lichtenthal, W. G., & Neimeyer, R. A. (2012). Directed writing to facilitate meaning-making. In R. A. Neimeyer (Ed.), *Techniques of grief therapy: Creative practices for counseling the bereaved* (pp. 165–168). New York, NY: Routledge/Taylor & Francis Group.

Lichtenthal, W. G., Neimeyer, R. A., Currier, J. M., Roberts, K., & Jordan, N. (2013). Cause of death and the quest for meaning after the loss of a child. *Death Studies, 37*(4), 311–342.

Linehan, M. M. (1993). *Skills training manual for treating borderline personality disorder*. New York, NY: Guilford Press.

Liotti, G. (2014). Disorganised attachment in the pathogenesis and the psychotherapy of borderline personality disorder. In A. N. Danquah & K. Berry (Eds.), *Attachment theory in adult mental health: A guide to clinical practice* (pp. 113–128). New York, NY: Routledge/Taylor & Francis Group.

Litz, B. T. (2004). *Early intervention for trauma and traumatic loss*. New York, NY: Guilford Press.

Lobb, E. A., Kristjanson, L. J., Aoun, S. M., Monterosso, L., Halkett, G. K. B., & Davies, A. (2010). Predictors of complicated grief: A systematic review of empirical studies. *Death Studies, 34*(8), 673–698.

Loman, M. M., & Gunnar, M. R. (2010). Early experience and the development of stress reactivity and regulation in children. *Neuroscience & Biobehavioral Reviews, 34*(6), 867–876.

Lopez, F. (2009). Clinical correlates of adult attachment organization. In J. H. Obegi & E. Berant (Eds.), *Attachment theory and research in clinical work with adults* (pp. 94–120). New York, NY: Guilford Press.

Lorenz, K. (1957). Companionship in bird life. In C. H. Schiller (Ed.), *Instinctive behavior: The development of a modern concept* (pp. 83–128). New York, NY: International Universities Press.

Luecken, L. J. (2008). Long-term consequences of parental death in childhood: Psychological and physiological manifestations. In M. S. Stroebe, R. O. Hansson, H. Schut, & W. Stroebe (Eds.), *Handbook of bereavement research and practice: Advances in theory and intervention* (pp. 397–416). Washington, DC: American Psychological Association.

McIntosh, J. L. (1992). Epidemiology of suicide in the elderly. *Suicide and Life-Threatening Behavior, 22*(1), 15–35.

MacLean, P. D. (1990). *The triune brain in evolution: Role in paleocerebral functions*. New York, NY: Springer Publishing Company.

Main, M. (1996). Introduction to the special section on attachment and psychopathology: 2. Overview of the field of attachment. *Journal of Consulting and Clinical Psychology, 64*(2), 237–243.

Main, M. (2000). The organized categories of infant, child, and adult attachment: Flexible vs. inflexible attention under attachment-related stress. *Journal of the American Psychoanalytic Association, 48*(4), 1055–1096.

Main, M., Goldwyn, R., & Hesse, E. (1998). Adult attachment scoring and classification system. Unpublished manuscript. Berkeley, CA: University of California.

Main, M., & Hesse, E. (1990). Parents' unresolved traumatic experiences are related to infant disorganized attachment status: Is frightened and/or frightening parental behavior the linking mechanism? In M. T. Greenberg, D. Cicchetti, & E. M. Cummings (Eds.), *Attachment in the preschool years: Theory, research, and intervention. The John D. and Catherine T. MacArthur Foundation series on mental health and development* (pp. 161–182). Chicago, IL: University of Chicago Press.

Main, M., Hesse, E., & Goldwyn, R. (2008). Studying differences in language usage in recounting attachment history: An introduction to the AAI. In Steele, H. & Steele, M. (Eds.), *Clinical applications of the Adult Attachment Interview* (pp. 31–68). New York, NY: Guilford Press.

Main, M., Kaplan, N., & Cassidy, J. (1985). Security in infancy, childhood, and adulthood: A move to the level of representation. In I. Bretherton & E. Waters (Eds.), *Growing points in attachment theory and research. Monographs of the Society for Research in Child Development, 50*(1–2, Serial No. 209), 66–104.

Main, M., & Solomon, J. (1986). Discovery of a new, insecure disorganized/disoriented attachment pattern. In T. B. Brazelton & M. Yogman (Eds.), *Affective development in infancy* (pp. 95–124). Norwood, NJ: Ablex.

Malkinson, R. (2012). The ABC of rational response to loss. In R. A. Neimeyer (Ed.), *Techniques of grief therapy: Creative practices for counseling the bereaved* (p. 129). New York, NY: Routledge/ Taylor & Francis Group.

Malkinson, R., Rubin, S. S., & Witztum, E. (2006). Therapeutic issues and the relationship to the deceased: Working clinically with the Two-Track Model of Bereavement. *Death Studies, 30*(9), 797–815.

Mallinckrodt, B., Daly, K., & Wang, C.-C. D. C. (2009). An attachment approach to adult psychotherapy. In J. H. Obegi & E. Berant (Eds.), *Attachment theory and research in clinical work with adults* (pp. 234–268). New York, NY: Guilford Press.

Mancini, A. D., & Bonanno, G. A. (2009). Predictors and parameters of resilience to loss: Toward an individual differences model. *Journal of Personality, 77*(6), 1805–1832.

Mancini, A. D., Griffin, P., & Bonanno, G. A. (2012). Recent trends in the treatment of prolonged grief. *Current Opinion in Psychiatry, 25*(1), 46–51.

Mancini, A. D., Pressman, D. L., & Bonanno, G. A. (2006). Clinical interventions with the bereaved: What clinicians and counselors can learn from the changing lives of older couples study. In D. Carr, R. M. Nesse, & C. B. Wortman (Eds.), *Spousal bereavement in late life* (pp. 255–278). New York, NY: Springer Publishing Company.

Mancini, A. D., Robinaugh, D., Shear, K., & Bonanno, G. A. (2009). Does attachment avoidance help people cope with loss? The moderating effects of relationship quality. *Journal of Clinical Psychology, 65*(10), 1127–1136.

Marganska, A., Gallagher, M., & Miranda, R. (2013). Adult attachment, emotion dysregulation, and symptoms of depression and generalized anxiety disorder. *American Journal of Orthopsychiatry, 83*(1), 131–141.

Marshall, B., & Davies, B. (2011). Bereavement in children and adults following the death of a sibling. In R. A. Neimeyer, D. L. Harris, H. R. Winokuer, & G. F. Thornton (Eds.), *Grief and bereavement in contemporary society: Bridging research and practice* (pp. 107–116). New York, NY: Routledge/Taylor & Francis Group.

Meert, K. L., Donaldson, A. E., Newth, C. J., Harrison, R., Berger, J., Zimmerman, J. et al. (2010). Complicated grief and associated risk factors among parents following a child's death in the pediatric intensive care unit. *Archives of Pediatric & Adolescent Medicine, 164*(11), 1045–1051.

Meier, A. M., Carr, D. R., Currier, J. M., & Neimeyer, R. A. Attachment anxiety and avoidance in coping with bereavement: Two studies. *Journal of Social and Clinical Psychology* (In press).

Mennin, D. S., & Fresco, D. M. (2009). Emotion regulation as an integrative framework for understanding and treating psychopathology. In A. M. Kring & D. M. Sloan (Eds.), *Emotion regulation and psychopathology: A transdiagnostic approach to etiology and treatment* (pp. 356–379). New York, NY: Guilford Press.

Mennin, D. S., & Fresco, D. M. (2014). Emotion regulation therapy. In J. J. Gross (Ed.), *Handbook of emotion regulation* (2nd ed.) (pp. 469–490). New York, NY: Guilford Press.

Mickelson, K. D., Kessler, R. C., & Shaver, P. R. (1997). Adult attachment in a nationally representative sample. *Journal of Personality and Social Psychology, 73*(5), 1092.

Mikulincer, M., & Florian, V. (1998). The relationship between adult attachment styles and emotional and cognitive reactions to stressful events. In J. A. Simpson & W. S. Rholes (Eds.), *Attachment theory and close relationships* (pp. 143–165). New York, NY: Guilford Press.

Mikulincer, M., & Orbach, I. (1995). Attachment styles and repressive defensiveness: The accessibility and architecture of affective memories. *Journal of Personality and Social Psychology, 68*(5), 917.

Mikulincer, M., & Shaver, P. R. (2007). *Attachment in adulthood: Structure, dynamics, and change.* New York, NY: Guilford Press.

Mikulincer, M., & Shaver, P. R. (2008a). Adult attachment and affect regulation. In J. Cassidy & P. R. Shaver (Eds.), *Handbook of attachment: Theory, research, and clinical applications* (2nd ed.) (pp. 503–531). New York, NY: Guilford Press.

Mikulincer, M., & Shaver, P. R. (2008b). An attachment perspective on bereavement. In J. Cassidy & P. R. Shaver (Eds.), *Handbook of bereavement research and practice: Advances in theory and intervention* (pp. 87–112). Washington, DC: American Psychological Association.

Mikulincer, M., & Shaver, P. R. (2009). An attachment and behavioral systems perspective on social support. *Journal of Social and Personal Relationships, 26*(1), 7–19.

Mikulincer, M., & Shaver, P. R. (2012). An attachment perspective on psychopathology. *World Psychiatry, 11*(1), 11–15.

Mikulincer, M., & Shaver, P. R. (2013). Attachment insecurities and disordered patterns of grief. *Complicated grief: Scientific foundations for health care professionals* (pp. 190–203). New York, NY: Routledge/Taylor & Francis Group.

Mikulincer, M., & Shaver, P. R. (2014). *Mechanisms of social connection: From brain to group.* Washington, DC: American Psychological Association.

Mikulincer, M., Shaver, P. R., Bar-On, N., & Ein-Dor, T. (2010). The pushes and pulls of close relationships: Attachment insecurities and relational ambivalence. *Journal of Personality and Social Psychology, 98*(3), 450–468.

Mikulincer, M., Shaver, P. R., & Berant, E. (2013). An attachment perspective on therapeutic processes and outcomes. *Journal of Personality, 81*(6), 606–613.

Mikulincer, M., Shaver, P. R., Cassidy, J., & Berant, E. (2009). Attachment-related defensive processes. In J. Obegi & E. Berant (Eds.), *Attachment theory and research in clinical work with adults* (pp. 293–327). New York, NY: Guilford Press.

Mikulincer, M., Shaver, P. R., & Pereg, D. (2003). Attachment theory and affect regulation: The dynamics, development, and cognitive consequences of attachment-related strategies. *Motivation and Emotion, 27*(2), 77–102.

Montgomery, A. (2013). *Neurobiology essentials for clinicians: What every therapist needs to know (Norton Series on Interpersonal Neurobiology)*. New York, NY: W. W. Norton & Company.

Moss, M. S., Moss, S. Z., & Hansson, R. O. (2001). Bereavement and old age. In M. S. Stroebe, R. O. Hansson, W. Stroebe, & H. Schut (Eds.), *Handbook of bereavement research: Consequences, coping, and care* (pp. 241–260). Washington, DC: American Psychological Association.

Muller, R. T. (2010). *Trauma and the avoidant client: Attachment-based strategies for healing*. New York, NY: W. W. Norton & Company.

Nadeau, J. (1998). *Families making sense of death*. Thousand Oaks, CA: Sage Publications.

Neimeyer, R. A. (2001). *Meaning reconstruction & the experience of loss*. Washington, DC: American Psychological Association.

Neimeyer, R. A. (2006a). Bereavement and the quest for meaning: Rewriting stories of loss and grief. *Hellenic Journal of Psychology, 3*(3), 181–188.

Neimeyer, R. A. (2006b). Complicated grief and the reconstruction of meaning: Conceptual and empirical contributions to a cognitive–constructivist model. *Clinical Psychology: Science and Practice, 13*(2), 141–145.

Neimeyer, R. A. (2009). *Constructivist psychotherapy: Distinctive features*. New York, NY: Routledge/Taylor & Francis Group.

Neimeyer, R. A. (Ed.). (2012a). Chairwork. In R.A. Neimeyer (Ed.), *Techniques of grief therapy: Creative practices for counseling the bereaved* (pp. 266–273). New York, NY: Routledge/Taylor & Francis Group.

Neimeyer, R. A. (Ed.). (2012b). Correspondence with the deceased. In R.A. Neimeyer (Ed.), *Techniques of grief therapy: Creative practices for counseling the bereaved* (pp. 259–260). New York, NY: Routledge/Taylor & Francis Group.

Neimeyer, R. A. (Ed.). (2012c). The life imprint. In R.A. Neimeyer (Ed.), *Techniques of grief therapy: Creative practices for counseling the bereaved* (pp. 274–276). New York, NY: Routledge/Taylor & Francis Group.

Neimeyer, R. A. (Ed.). (2012d). Presence, process, and procedure: A relational frame for technical proficiency in grief therapy. In R.A. Neimeyer (Ed.), *Techniques of grief therapy: Creative practices for counseling the bereaved* (pp. 3–11). New York, NY: Routledge/Taylor & Francis Group.

Neimeyer, R. A. (Ed.). (2012e). Retelling the narrative of the death. In R.A. Neimeyer (Ed.), *Techniques of grief therapy: Creative practices for counseling the bereaved* (pp. 86–94). New York, NY: Routledge/Taylor & Francis Group.

Neimeyer, R. A. (Ed.). (2012f). *Techniques of grief therapy: Creative practices for counseling the bereaved*. New York, NY: Routledge/Taylor & Francis Group.

Neimeyer, R. A. (2015). Treating complicated bereavement: The development of grief therapy. In J. M. Stillion & T. Attig (Eds.), *Death, dying, and bereavement: Contemporary perspectives, institutions, and practices* (pp. 307–320). New York, NY: Springer Publishing Company.

Neimeyer, R. A., Baldwin, S. A., & Gillies, J. (2006). Continuing bonds and reconstructing meaning: Mitigating complications in bereavement. *Death Studies, 30*(8), 715–738.

Neimeyer, R. A., Harris, D. L., Winokuer, H. R., & Thornton, G. F. (2011). *Grief and bereavement in contemporary society: Bridging research and practice*. New York, NY: Routledge/Taylor & Francis Group.

Neimeyer, R. A., & Jordan, J. R. (2001). Disenfranchisement as empathic failure: Grief therapy and the co-construction of meaning. In K. J. Doka (Ed.), *Disenfranchised grief: New directions, challenges, and strategies for practice*. Champaign, IL: Research Press.

Neimeyer, R. A., & Jordan, J. R. (2013). Historical and contemporary perspectives on assessment and intervention. In D. Meager & D. Balk (Eds.), *Handbook of thanatology* (2nd ed.) (pp. 219–237). New York, NY: Routledge/Taylor & Francis Group.

Neimeyer, R. A., Keesee, N. J., & Fortner, B. V. (2000). Loss and meaning reconstruction: Propositions and procedures. In R. Malkinson, S. S. Rubin, & E. Witztum (Eds.), *Traumatic and nontraumatic loss and bereavement: Clinical theory and practice* (pp. 197–230). Madison, WI: Psychosocial Press.

Neimeyer, R. A., Prigerson, H. G., & Davies, B. (2002). Mourning and meaning. *American Behavioral Scientist, 46*(2), 235–251.

Neimeyer, R. A., & Raskin, J. D. (2000). *Constructions of disorder: Meaning-making frameworks for psychotherapy.* Washington, DC: American Psychological Association.

Neimeyer, R. A., & Sands, D. C. (2011). Meaning reconstruction in bereavement: From principles to practice. In R. A. Neimeyer, D. L. Harris, H. R. Winokuer, & G. F. Thornton (Eds.), *Grief and bereavement in contemporary society: Bridging research and practice* (pp. 9–22). New York, NY: Routledge/Taylor & Francis Group.

Neimeyer, R. A., van Dyke, J. G., & Pennebaker, J. W. (2008). Narrative medicine: Writing through bereavement. In H. C. W. Breitbart (Ed.), *Handbook of psychiatry in palliative medicine* (pp. 454–469). New York, NY: Oxford University Press.

Nelson, E. E., & Panksepp, J. (1998). Brain substrates of infant–mother attachment: Contributions of opioids, oxytocin, and norepinephrine. *Neuroscience & Biobehavioral Reviews, 22*(3), 437–452.

Norcross, J. C. (2011). *Psychotherapy relationships that work: Evidence-based responsiveness* (2nd ed.). New York, NY: Oxford University Press.

Norcross, J. C., & Lambert, M. J. (2006). The therapy relationship. In J. C. Norcross, L. E. Beutler, & R. F. Levant (Eds.), *Evidence-based practices in mental health* (pp. 208–217). Washington, DC: American Psychological Association.

Norcross, J. C., & Lambert, M. J. (2011). Evidence-based therapy relationships. In J. C. Norcross (Ed.), *Psychotherapy relationships that work: Evidence-based responsiveness* (2nd ed.) (pp. 3–21). New York, NY: Oxford University Press.

Norcross, J. C., & Wampold, B. E. (2011a). Evidence-based therapy relationships: Research conclusions and clinical practices. *Psychotherapy, 48*(1), 98–102.

Norcross, J. C., & Wampold, B. E. (2011b). What works for whom: Tailoring psychotherapy to the person. *Journal of Clinical Psychology, 67*(2), 127–132.

Obegi, J., & Berant, E. (2010). *Attachment theory and research in clinical work with adults.* New York, NY: Guilford Press.

O'Connor, M. F. (2005). Bereavement and the brain: Invitation to a conversation between bereavement researchers and neuroscientists. *Death Studies, 29*(10), 905–922.

O'Connor, M. F. (2013). Physiological mechanisms and the neurobiology of complicated grief. In M. Stroebe, H. Schut, & J. van den Bout (Eds.), *Complicated grief: Scientific foundations for health care professionals* (pp. 204–218). New York, NY: Routledge/Taylor & Francis Group.

Ogden, P. (2009). Emotion, mindfulness, and movement: Expanding the regulatory boundaries of the window of affect tolerance. In D. Fosha, D. J. Siegel, & M. F. Solomon (Eds.), *The healing power of emotion: Affective neuroscience, development & clinical practice (Norton Series on Interpersonal Neurobiology)* (pp. 204–231). New York, NY: W. W. Norton & Company.

Ogden, P., & Fisher, J. (2015). *Sensorimotor psychotherapy: Interventions for trauma and attachment.* New York, NY: W. W. Norton & Company.

Ogden, P., Minton, K., & Pain, C. (2006). *Trauma and the body: A sensorimotor approach to psychotherapy.* New York, NY: W. W. Norton & Company.

Orange, D. M. (2010). Recognition as: Intersubjective vulnerability in the psychoanalytic dialogue. *International Journal of Psychoanalytic Self Psychology, 5*(3), 227–243.

Ott, C. H., Lueger, R. J., Kelber, S. T., & Prigerson, H. G. (2007). Spousal bereavement in older adults: Common, resilient, and chronic grief with defining characteristics. *Journal of Nervous and Mental Disease, 195*(4), 332–341.

Owens, C., Lambert, H., Lloyd, K., & Donovan, J. (2008). Tales of biographical disintegration: How parents make sense of their sons' suicides. *Sociology of Health & Illness, 30*(2), 237–254.

Panksepp, J. (2011). The neurobiology of social loss in animals: Some keys to the puzzle of psychic pain in humans. In G. MacDonald & L. A. Jensen-Campbell (Eds.), *Social pain: Neuropsychological and health implications of loss and exclusion* (pp. 11–51). Washington, DC: American Psychological Association.

Panksepp, J., & Biven, L. (2012). *The archaeology of mind: Neuroevolutionary origins of human emotion.* New York, NY: W. W. Norton & Company.

Panksepp, J., Solms, M., Schläpfer, T. E., & Coenen, V. A. (2014). Primary-process separation-distress (PANIC/GRIEF) and reward eagerness (SEEKING) processes in the ancestral genesis of depressive affect. In M. Mikulincer & P. R. Shaver (Eds.), *Mechanisms of social connection: From brain to group* (pp. 33–53). Washington, DC: American Psychological Association.

Parens, E., & Johnston, J. (2014). Neuroimaging: Beginning to appreciate its complexities. *Hastings Center Report, 44*(s2), S2–S7.

Parkes, C. M. (1964). Recent bereavement as a cause of mental illness. *British Journal of Psychiatry, 110*(465), 198–204.

Parkes, C. M. (1970). The first year of bereavement: A longitudinal study of the reaction of London widows to the death of their husbands. *Psychiatry, 33*(4), 444–467.

Parkes, C. M. (1975). Unexpected and untimely bereavement: A statistical study of young Boston widows. In B. Schoenberg, I. Gerber, A. Weiner, D. Kutscher, D. Peretz, & A. Cam (Eds.), *Bereavement: Its psychological aspects.* New York, NY: Columbia University Press.

Parkes, C. M. (1998). *Bereavement: Studies of grief in adult life* (3rd ed.). Madison, CT: International Universities Press.

Parkes, C. M. (2013). *Love and loss: The roots of grief and its complications.* New York, NY: Routledge/Taylor & Francis Group.

Parkes, C. M., & Prigerson, H. G. (2010). *Bereavement: Studies of grief in adult life* (4th ed.). New York, NY: Routledge/Taylor & Francis Group.

Pearlman, L. A., & Courtois, C. A. (2005). Clinical applications of the attachment framework: Relational treatment of complex trauma. *Journal of Traumatic Stress, 18*(5), 449–459.

Pearlman, L. A., Wortman, C. B., Feuer, C. A., Farber, C. H., & Rando, T. A. (2014). *Treating traumatic bereavement: A practitioner's guide.* New York, NY: Guilford Press.

Pennebaker, J. W., Chung, C. K., Friedman, H. S., & Silver, R. C. (2007). Expressive writing, emotional upheavals, and health. In H. S. Friedman & R. C. Silver (Eds.), *Foundations of health psychology* (pp. 263–284). New York, NY: Oxford University Press.

Pietromonaco, P., Barrett, L., & Powers, S. (2006). Adult attachment theory and affective reactivity and regulation. In D. Snyder, J. Simpson, & J. Hughes (Eds.), *Emotion regulation in couples and families: Pathways to dysfunction and health* (pp. 57–74). Washington, DC: American Psychological Association.

Porges, S. W. (2009). Reciprocal influences between body and brain in the perception of affect: A polyvagal perspective. In D. Fosha, D. Siegel, & M. Solomon (Eds.), *The healing power of emotion: Affective neuroscience, development and clinical practice.* New York, NY: W. W. Norton & Company.

Porges, S. W. (2011). *The polyvagal theory: Neurophysiological foundations of emotions, attachment, communication and self regulation.* New York, NY: W. W. Norton & Company.

Putnam, F. W., Berlin, L. J., Ziv, Y., Amaya-Jackson, L., & Greenberg, M. T. (2005). The developmental neurobiology of disrupted attachment: Lessons from animal models and child abuse research. In L. J. Berlin, Y. Ziv, L. Amaya-Jackson, & M. T. Greenberg (Eds.), *Enhancing early attachments: Theory, research, intervention, and policy* (pp. 79–99). New York, NY: Guilford Press.

Rando, T. A. (1991). Parental adjustment to the loss of a child. In D. Papadatou & C. Papadatos (Eds.), *Children and death* (pp. 233–253). New York, NY: Hemisphere Publishing Corporation.

Rando, T. A. (1993). *Treatment of complicated mourning.* Champaign, IL: Research Press.

Reed, M. D. (1998). Predicting grief symptomatology among the suddenly bereaved. *Suicide and Life-Threatening Behavior, 28*(3), 285–301.

Reiner, A. (1990). An Explanation of Behavior. *Science* 250 (4978): 303–305.

Riva, D., Njiokiktjien, C., & Bulgheroni, S. (2011). *Brain lesion localization and developmental functions: Frontal lobes, limbic system, visuocognitive system* (Vol. 25). Montrouge, France: John Libbey Eurotext.

Rizzolatti, G., Fadiga, L., Gallese, V., & Fogassi, L. (1996). Premotor cortex and the recognition of motor actions. *Cognitive Brain Research, 3*(2), 131–141.

Rogers, C. R. (1951). *Client-centered therapy.* Boston, MA: Houghton-Mifflin.

Rogers, C. R. (1957). The necessary and sufficient conditions of therapeutic personality change. *Journal of Counseling Psychology, 21,* 95–103.

Roisman, G. I. (2009). Adult attachment toward a rapprochement of methodological cultures. *Current Directions in Psychological Science, 18*(2), 122–126.

Rosen, S. (Ed.). (1991). *My voice will go with you: The teaching tales of Milton H. Erickson.* New York, NY: W. W. Norton & Company.

Rothschild, B. (2000). *The body remembers: The psychophysiology of trauma and trauma treatment.* New York, NY: W. W. Norton & Company.

Rothschild, B. (2006). *Help for the helper: The psychophysiology of compassion fatigue and vicarious trauma.* New York, NY: W. W. Norton & Company.

Rowe Jr., C. E., & MacIsaac, D. S. (1989). *Empathic attunement: The "technique" of psychoanalytic self psychology.* Lanham, MD: Jason Aronson Publishing Company.

Rubin, S. S. (1981). A Two-Track Model of Bereavement: Theory and application in research. *American Journal of Orthopsychiatry, 51*(1), 101–109.

Rubin, S. S. (1993). The death of a child is forever: The life course impact of child loss. In M. S. Stroebe, W. Stroebe, & R. O. Hansson (Eds.), *Handbook of bereavement: Theory, research, and intervention* (pp. 285–299). New York, NY: Cambridge University Press.

Rubin, S. S. (1999). The Two Track Model of Bereavement: Overview, retrospect and prospect. *Death Studies, 23*(8), 681–714.

Rubin, S. S., & Malkinson, R. (2001). Parental response to child loss across the life cycle: Clinical and research perspectives. In M. S. Stroebe, R. O. Hansson, W. Stroebe, & H. Schut (Eds.), *Handbook of bereavement research: Consequences, coping, and care* (pp. 219–240). Washington, DC: American Psychological Association.

Rubin, S. S., Malkinson, R., & Witztum, E. (2011). The Two-Track Model of Bereavement: The double helix of research and clinical practice. In R. A. Neimeyer, D. L. Harris, H. R. Winokuer, & G. F. Thornton (Eds.), *Grief and bereavement in contemporary society: Bridging research and practice* (pp. 47–56). New York, NY: Routledge/Taylor & Francis Group.

Rubin, S. S., Malkinson, R., & Witztum, E. (2012). *Working with the bereaved: Multiple lenses on loss and mourning.* New York, NY: Routledge/Taylor & Francis Group.

Rynearson, E. K. (2001). *Retelling violent death.* Philadelphia, PA: Brunner-Routledge.

Rynearson, E. K. (Ed.). (2006). *Violent death: Resilience and intervention beyond the crisis.* New York, NY: Routledge/Taylor & Francis Group.

Rynearson, E. K., & Salloum, A. (2011). Restorative retelling: Revising the narrative of violent death. In R. A. Neimeyer, D. L. Harris, H. R. Winokuer, & G. F. Thornton (Eds.), *Grief and bereavement in contemporary society: Bridging research and practice* (pp. 177–188). New York, NY: Routledge/Taylor & Francis Group.

Sands, D. C., Jordan, J. R., & Neimeyer, R. A. (2011). The meanings of suicide: A narrative approach to healing. In J.R. Jordan (Ed.), *Grief after suicide: Understanding the consequences and caring for the survivors* (pp. 249–282): New York, NY: Routledge/Taylor & Francis Group.

Sbarra, D. A., & Hazan, C. (2008). Coregulation, dysregulation, self-regulation: An integrative analysis and empirical agenda for understanding adult attachment, separation, loss, and recovery. *Personality and Social Psychology Review, 12*(2), 141–167.

Scheidt, C., Hasenburg, A., Kunze, M., Waller, E., Pfeifer, R., Zimmermann, P. et al. (2012). Are individual differences of attachment predicting bereavement outcome after perinatal loss? A prospective cohort study. *Journal of Psychosomatic Research, 73*(5), 375–382.

Schopenhauer, A. (1974). *Parerga and paralipomena: Short philosophical essays* (Vol. 2), trans. E. F. J. Payne (p. 397). New York, NY: Oxford University Press.

Schore, A. N. (2001a). Effects of a secure attachment relationship on right brain development, affect regulation, and infant mental health. *Infant Mental Health Journal, 22*(1–2), 7–66.

Schore, A. N. (2001b). The effects of early relational trauma on right brain development, affect regulation, and infant mental health. *Infant Mental Health Journal, 22*(1–2), 201–269.

Schore, A. N. (2002a). Advances in neuropsychoanalysis, attachment theory, and trauma research: Implications for self psychology. *Psychoanalytic Inquiry, 22*(3), 433–484.

Schore, A. N. (2002b). Dysregulation of the right brain: A fundamental mechanism of traumatic attachment and the psychopathogenesis of posttraumatic stress disorder. *Australian and New Zealand Journal of Psychiatry, 36*(1), 9–30.

Schore, A. N. (2002c). The neurobiology of attachment and early personality organization. *Journal of Prenatal & Perinatal Psychology & Health, 16*(3), 249–263.

Schore, A. N. (2003a). *Affect dysregulation and disorders of the self.* New York, NY: W. W. Norton & Company.

Schore, A. N. (2003b). *Affect regulation and the repair of the self.* New York, NY: W. W. Norton & Company.

Schore, A. N. (2009). Right-brain affect regulation. In D. Fosha, D. Siegel, & M. Solomon (Eds.), *The healing power of emotion: Affective neuroscience, development & clinical practice* (pp. 112–144). New York, NY: W. W. Norton & Company.

Schore, A. N. (2012). *The science of the art of psychotherapy.* New York, NY: W. W. Norton & Company.

Schore, A. N. (2013). Regulation theory and the early assessment of attachment and autistic spectrum disorders: A response to Voran's clinical case. *Journal of Infant, Child, and Adolescent Psychotherapy, 12*(3), 164–189.

Schore, J. R., & Schore, A. N. (2008). Modern attachment theory: The central role of affect regulation in development and treatment. *Clinical Social Work Journal, 36*(1), 9–20.

Schore, J. R., & Schore, A. N. (2014). Regulation theory and affect regulation psychotherapy: A clinical primer. *Smith College Studies in Social Work, 84*(2–3), 178–195.

Schut, H. A. W., Stroebe, M. S., Boelen, P. A., & Zijerveld, A. M. (2006). Continuing relationships with the deceased: Disentangling bonds and grief. *Death Studies, 30*(8), 757–766.

Shaffer, P. A., Vogel, D. L., & Wei, M. (2006). The mediating roles of anticipated risks, anticipated benefits, and attitudes on the decision to seek professional help: An attachment perspective. *Journal of Counseling Psychology, 53*(4), 442.

Shapiro, F. (2012). *Getting past your past: Take control of your life with self-help techniques from EMDR therapy.* New York, NY: Rodale Books.

Shapiro, F., & Forrest, M. S. (2004). *EMDR: The breakthrough therapy for overcoming anxiety, stress, and trauma.* New York, NY: Basic Books.

Shapiro, R. (2005). *EMDR solutions: Pathways to healing.* New York, NY: W. W. Norton & Company.

Shaver, P. R., & Fraley, C. R. (2008). Attachment, loss, and grief: Bowlby's views and current controversies. In J. Cassidy & P. R. Shaver (Eds.), *Handbook of attachment: Theory, research, and clinical applications* (2nd ed.) (pp. 48–77). New York, NY: Guilford Press.

Shaver, P. R., & Mikulincer, M. (2009). Attachment styles. In M. R. Leary & R. H. Hoyle (Eds.), *Handbook of individual differences in social behavior* (pp. 62–81). New York, NY: Guilford Press.

Shaver, P. R., & Mikulincer, M. (2010). New directions in attachment theory and research. *Journal of Social and Personal Relationships, 27*(2), 163–172.

Shaver, P. R., & Mikulincer, M. (2011). Attachment theory. In P. van Lange & A. W. Kruglanski (Eds.), *Handbook of theories of social psychology* (Vol. 2) (pp. 160–179). Thousand Oaks, CA: Sage Publications Ltd.

Shaver, P. R., & Mikulincer, M. (2014). Attachment bonds in romantic relationships. In M. Mikulincer & P. R. Shaver (Eds.), *Mechanisms of social connection: From brain to group* (pp. 273–290). Washington, DC: American Psychological Association.

Shaver, P. R., Schachner, D. A., & Mikulincer, M. (2005). Attachment style, excessive reassurance seeking, relationship processes, and depression. *Personality and Social Psychology Bulletin, 31*(3), 343–359.

Shear, K., Boelen, P. A., & Neimeyer, R. A. (2011). Treating complicated grief: Converging approaches. In R. A. Neimeyer, D. L. Harris, H. R. Winokuer, & G. F. Thornton (Eds.), *Grief and bereavement in contemporary society: Bridging research and practice* (pp. 139–162). New York, NY: Routledge/Taylor & Francis Group.

Shear, K., Frank, E., Houck, P. R., & Reynolds, C. F. 3rd (2005). Treatment of complicated grief: A randomized controlled trial. *Journal of the American Medical Association, 293*(21), 2601–2608.

Shear, K., & Shair, H. (2005). Attachment, loss, and complicated grief. *Developmental Psychobiology, 47*(3), 253–267.

Siegel, D. J. (2010). *Mindsight: The new science of personal transformation.* New York, NY: Bantam Books.

Siegel, D. J. (2012a). *The developing mind: How relationships and the brain interact to shape who we are.* New York, NY: Guilford Press.

Siegel, D. J. (2012b). *Pocket guide to interpersonal neurobiology: An integrative handbook of the mind (Norton Series on Interpersonal Neurobiology).* New York, NY: W. W. Norton & Company.

Siegel, R. D. (2009). *The mindfulness solution: Everyday practices for everyday problems.* New York, NY: Guilford Press.

Simpson, J. A., & Belsky, J. (2008). Attachment theory within a modern evolutionary framework. In J. Cassidy & P. R. Shaver (Eds.), *Handbook of attachment: Theory, research, and clinical applications.* New York, NY: Guilford Press.

Slade, A. (2007). Reflective parenting programs: Theory and development. *Psychoanalytic Inquiry, 26*(4), 640–657.

Slade, A. (2008). The implications of attachment theory and research for adult psycho-therapy: Research and clinical perspectives. In J. Cassidy & P. R. Shaver (Eds.), *Handbook of attachment: Theory, research, and clinical applications* (2nd ed.). New York, NY: Guilford Press.

Solomon, E. P., & Heide, K. M. (2005). The biology of trauma: Implications for treatment. *Journal of Interpersonal Violence, 20*, 51–60.

Solomon, J., & George, C. (1996). Defining the caregiving system: Toward a theory of caregiving. *Infant Mental Health Journal, 17*(3), 183–197.

Sroufe, A. L., & Waters, E. (1977). Attachment as an organizational construct. *Child Development, 48*, 1184–1199.

Stanton, R., & Reaburn, P. (2014). Exercise and the treatment of depression: A review of the exercise program variables. *Journal of Science and Medicine in Sport, 17*(2), 177–182.

Steele, H., & Steele, M. (2008). *Clinical applications of the adult attachment interview*. New York, NY: Guilford Press.

Stroebe, M. S. (1992). Coping with bereavement: A review of the grief work hypothesis. *Omega: Journal of Death and Dying, 26*(1), 19–42.

Stroebe, M. S., Abakoumkin, G., Stroebe, W., & Schut, H. (2012). Continuing bonds in adjustment to bereavement: Impact of abrupt versus gradual separation. *Personal Relationships, 19*(2), 255–266.

Stroebe, M. S., & Schut, H. (1999). The dual process model of coping with bereavement: Rationale and description. *Death Studies, 23*(3), 197–224.

Stroebe, M. S., & Schut, H. (2010). The dual process model of coping with bereavement: A decade on. *Omega: Journal of Death and Dying, 61*(4), 273–289.

Stroebe, M. S., Schut, H., & Finkenauer, C. (2013). Parents coping with the death of their child: From individual to interpersonal to interactive perspectives. *Family Science, 4*(1), 28–36.

Stroebe, M. S., Schut, H., & Stroebe, W. (2005). Attachment in coping with bereavement: A theoretical integration. *Review of General Psychology, 9*(1), 48–66.

Stroebe, M. S., Schut, H., & Stroebe, W. (2006). Who benefits from disclosure? Exploration of attachment style differences in the effects of expressing emotions. *Clinical Psychology Review, 26*(1), 66–85.

Stroebe, M. S., Schut, H., & Van den Bout, J. (2013). *Complicated grief: Scientific foundations for health care professionals* (1st ed.). New York, NY: Routledge/Taylor & Francis Group.

Stroebe, W., Zech, E., Stroebe, M. S., & Abakoumkin, G. (2005). Does social support help in bereavement? *Journal of Social & Clinical Psychology, 24*(7), 1030–1050.

Suzuki, S. (1973). *Zen mind, beginner's mind*. New York, NY: Weatherhill.

Swain, J. E., Dayton, C., Kim, P., Tolman, R. M., & Volling, B. L. (2014). Progress on the paternal brain: Theory, animal models, human brain research, and mental health implications. *Infant Mental Health Journal, 35*(5), 394–408.

Swain, J. E., Lorberbaum, J. P., Kose, S., & Strathearn, L. (2007). Brain basis of early parent–infant interactions: Psychology, physiology, and in vivo functional neuroimaging studies. *Journal of Child Psychology and Psychiatry, 48*(3–4), 262–287.

Szanto, K., Shear, M. K., Houck, P. R., Reynolds C. F. 3rd, Frank, E., Caroff, K., & Silowash, R. (2006). Indirect self-destructive behavior and overt suicidality in patients with complicated grief. *Journal of Clinical Psychiatry, 67*(2), 233–239.

Tang, Y.-Y., & Posner, M. I. (2013). Tools of the trade: Theory and method in mindfulness neuroscience. *Social Cognitive and Affective Neuroscience, 8*(1), 118–120.

Taylor, S. E., Pham, L. B., Rivkin, I. D., & Armor, D. A. (1998). Harnessing the imagination: Mental simulation, self-regulation, and coping. *American Psychologist, 53*(4), 429.

Tedeschi, R. G., & Calhoun, L. G. (2003). *Helping bereaved parents: A clinician's guide*. New York, NY: Brunner-Routledge.

Thoits, P. A. (2010). Stress and health: Major findings and policy implications. *Journal of Health and Social Behavior, 51*(1: Suppl.), S41–S53.

Thompson, B. E. (2012). Mindfulness training. In R. A. Neimeyer (Ed.), *Techniques of grief therapy: Creative practices for counseling the bereaved* (pp. 39–41). New York, NY: Routledge/Taylor & Francis Group.

Thompson, B. E., & Neimeyer, R. A. (2014). *Grief and the expressive arts: Practices for creating meaning*. New York, NY: Routledge/Taylor & Francis Group.

Thomson, P. (2010). Loss and disorganization from an attachment perspective. *Death Studies, 34*(10), 893–914.

Trevarthen, C. (2009). The functions of emotion in infancy. In D. Fosha, D. J. Siegel, & M. Solomon (Eds.), *The healing power of emotion: Affective neuroscience, development & clinical practice (Norton Series on Interpersonal Neurobiology)* (pp. 55–85). New York, NY: W. W. Norton & Company.

Vaillant, G. E. (1993). *The wisdom of the ego.* Cambridge, MA: Harvard University Press.

Van der Hart, O., Nijenhuis, E. R. S., & Steele, K. (2006). *The haunted self: Structural dissociation and the treatment of chronic traumatization.* New York, NY: W. W. Norton & Company.

Van der Kolk, B. (2014). *The body keeps the score: Brain, mind, and body in the healing of trauma.* New York, NY: Viking Penguin.

Vanderwerker, L. C., Jacobs, S. C., Parkes, C. M., & Prigerson, H. G. (2006). An exploration of associations between separation anxiety in childhood and complicated grief in later life. *Journal of Nervous and Mental Disease, 194*(2), 121–123.

Vanderwerker, L. C., & Prigerson, H. G. (2004). Social support and technological connectedness as protective factors in bereavement. *Journal of Loss and Trauma, 9*(1), 45–57.

Vogel, D. L., Wade, N. G., & Hackler, A. H. (2008). Emotional expression and the decision to seek therapy: The mediating roles of the anticipated benefits and risks. *Journal of Social & Clinical Psychology, 27*(3), 254–278.

Vrtička, P., Bondolfi, G., Sander, D., & Vuilleumier, P. (2012). The neural substrates of social emotion perception and regulation are modulated by adult attachment style. *Society Neuroscience, 7*(5), 473–493.

Vrtička, P., & Vuilleumier, P. (2012). Neuroscience of human social interactions and adult attachment style. *Frontiers in Human Neuroscience, 6.*

Wallin, D. J. (2007). *Attachment in psychotherapy.* New York, NY: Guilford Press.

Wallin, D. J. (2010). From the inside out: The therapist's attachment patterns as sources of insight and impasse. In M. Kerman (Ed.), *Clinical pearls of wisdom: Twenty-one leading therapists offer their key insights* (pp. 245–256). New York, NY: W. W. Norton & Company.

Wallin, D. J. (2014). We are the tools of our trade: The therapist's attachment history as a source of impasse, inspiration, and change. In A. N. Danquah & K. Berry (Eds.), *Attachment theory in adult mental health.* New York, NY: Routledge/Taylor & Francis Group.

Walsh, F., & McGoldrick, M. (Eds.). (2004). Loss and the family: A systemic perspective. *Living beyond loss: Death in the family* (2nd ed.) (pp. 3–26). New York, NY: W. W. Norton & Company.

Walter, T. (1996). A new model of grief: Bereavement and biography. *Mortality, 1*(1), 7–25.

Watson, J. C., & Greenberg, L. S. (2009). Empathic resonance: A neuroscience perspective. In J. Decety & W. Ickes (Eds.), *The social neuroscience of empathy* (pp. 125–138). Cambridge, MA: MIT Press.

Wayment, H. A., & Vierthaler, J. (2002). Attachment style and bereavement reactions. *Journal of Loss and Trauma, 7*(2), 129–149.

Wei, M., Russell, D. W., Mallinckrodt, B., & Vogel, D. L. (2007). The Experiences in Close Relationship Scale (ECR)—short form: Reliability, validity, and factor structure. *Journal of Personality Assessment, 88*(2), 187–204.

Wijngaards-de Meij, L., Stroebe, M. S., Schut, H., Stroebe, W., van den Bout, J., van der Heijden, P., & Dijkstra, I. (2005). Couples at risk following the death of their child: Predictors of grief versus depression. *Journal of Consulting and Clinical Psychology, 73*(4), 617–623.

Wijngaards-de Meij, L., Stroebe, M. S., Schut, H., Stroebe, W., van den Bout, J., van der Heijden, P., & Dijkstra, I. (2007a). Neuroticism and attachment insecurity as predictors of bereavement outcome. *Journal of Research in Personality, 41*(2), 498–505.

Wijngaards-de Meij, L., Stroebe, M. S., Schut, H., Stroebe, W., van den Bout, J., van der Heijden, P. G., & Dijkstra, I. (2007b). Patterns of attachment and parents' adjustment to the death of their child. *Personality and Social Psychology Bulletin, 33*(4), 537–548.

Winokuer, H. R., & Harris, D. L. (2012). *Principles and practices of grief counseling.* New York, NY: Springer Publishing Company.

Wood, L., Byram, V., Gosling, A. S., & Stokes, J. (2012). Continuing bonds after suicide bereavement in childhood. *Death Studies, 36*(10), 873–898.

Worden, J. W. (1983). *Grief counseling and grief therapy: A handbook for the mental health practitioner.* New York, NY: Routledge/Taylor & Francis Group (republished in 2008, Springer Publishing Company).

Zech, E., & Arnold, C. (2011). Attachment and coping with bereavement: Implications for therapeutic interventions with the insecurely attached. In R. A. Neimeyer, D. L. Harris, H. R. Winokuer, & G. F Thornton (Eds.), *Grief and bereavement in contemporary society: Bridging research and practice* (pp. 23–35). New York, NY: Routledge/Taylor & Francis Group.

Zech, E., Rimé, B., & Pennebaker, J. W. (2007). The effects of emotional disclosure during bereavement. In M. Hewstone, H. Schut, J. B. de Witt, K. Van Den Bos, & M. Stroebe (Eds.), *The scope of social psychology: Theory and applications* (pp. 277–292). New York, NY: Psychology Press.

Zech, E., Ryckebosch-Dayez, A.-S., & Delespaux, E. (2010). Improving the efficacy of intervention for bereaved individuals: Toward a process-focused psychotherapeutic perspective. *Psychologica Belgica, 50*(1–2), 103–124.

Index

Page numbers in italic refer to figures. Page numbers in bold refer to tables.